Adam Afriyie

Meritocracy, Citizenship and Education

Also available from Continuum

Philosophy of Education – Richard Pring
Theory of Education – David Turner
Education and Community – Dianne Gereluk
Key Ideas in Educational Research – David Scott
and Marlene Morrison

Meritocracy, Citizenship and Education

New Labour's Legacy

John Beck

continuum

Continuum International Publishing Group
The Tower Building   80 Maiden Lane, Suite 704
11 York Road   New York
London   NY
SE1 7NX   10038

www.continuumbooks.com

British Library Cataloguing-in-Publication Data
A catalogue record for this book is available from the British Library.

ISBN: 9781847060730 (hardcover)

Library of Congress Cataloging-in-Publication Data
Beck, John, MA.
   Meritocracy, citizenship, and education : New Labour's legacy / John Beck.
      p. cm.
   Includes bibliographical references and index.
   ISBN-13: 978-1-84706-073-0 (hardcover)
   ISBN-10: 1-84706-073-0 (hardcover)
   1. Social status—Great Britain. 2. Great Britain—Social conditions—1945-
   3. Education and state—Great Britain. 4. Labour Party (Great Britain) I. Title.

   HN400.S6B43 2008
   306.20941'09045—dc22

                            2007028766

Typeset by Free Range Book Design & Production Ltd
Printed and bound in Great Britain by Biddles Ltd, King's Lynn, Norfolk

Contents

Acknowledgements

I am particularly indebted to Michael F. D. Young, both for valuable discussions about issues addressed in this book and more specifically for his agreement to allow me to publish here, as Chapter 5, our joint paper on 'The Assault on the Professions'. I am also indebted to John Ahier, again for on-going discussions about various issues discussed here but also because the idea of writing a book about meritocracy, published to coincide with the fiftieth anniversary of Michael Young's celebrated classic, was his. I would like to express my gratitude to Nigel Kettley for allowing me to use and adapt the informative Glossary of key terms which appears at the beginning of this book, the original version of which appeared in Nigel's recently published *Educational Attainment and Society* (Kettley, 2006). I am also in Nigel's debt because he undertook, with the highest levels of professionalism, the lion's share of my teaching and examining duties, during the periods of study leave when this book was mainly written. Finally, and as always, I have learned a huge amount from my colleague Rob Moore, whose always perceptive, always original discussions on a wide range of sociological issues have been a constant source of inspiration.

The following chapters have been reproduced with the kind permission of the respective publishers:

Chapter 4. John Beck: 'Makeover or Takeover? The Strange Death of Educational Autonomy in neo liberal England', *British Journal of Sociology of Education*, 20 (2), (1999), 223–38.

Chapter 5. John Beck and Michael F. D. Young: 'The Assault on the Professions and the Restructuring of Academic and Professional Identities: A Bernsteinian Analysis', *British Journal of Sociology of Education*, 20 (2), (2005), 183–97.

Chapter 6. John Beck: '"Directed Time": Identity and Time in New Right and New Labour Policy Discourse', in R. Moore, M. Arnot, J. Beck and H. Daniels (eds) *Knowledge, Power and Educational Reform: Applying the Sociology of Basil Bernstein*, (2006), London: Routledge, pp. 181–95.

Chapter 7. Revised and extended version of John Beck: 'The School Curriculum and the National Curriculum, Conservative and New

Labour Reforms', in J. Beck and M. Earl (eds) *Key Issues in Secondary Education – 2nd Edition.* (2003), London: Continuum, pp. 14–27.

John Beck, 2008

Glossary

ASBO   Anti-Social Behaviour Order
Introduced in England and Wales in 2004, ASBOS are a part of a range of new legal sanctions in England and Wales that can be imposed without recourse to a trial before magistrates or judges; ASBOS are imposed on individuals who are deemed to have persistently displayed seriously anti-social behaviour.

ASCL   Association of School and College Leaders
The main professional association representing head teachers and school leaders of secondary schools and sixth form colleges in England and Wales.

A level   Advanced level of the General Certificate of Education
A system of examinations introduced in England and Wales in 1951 for pupils aged 17 or 18, mainly to assess their potential for university study. Typically, students sat three A level subjects over a period of two years and these subjects were assessed by written examination papers and coursework. The system has recently been replaced by AS and A2 level examinations within the overall A-level framework.

AS level   Advanced Supplementary (now Subsidiary) level
A system of examinations introduced in 1989 in an attempt to broaden the sixth form curriculum in England and Wales. These examinations carry half the value of an A (now A2) level for the purposes of university entry. New Labour introduced a revised version of the examination, the Advanced Subsidiary, as part of Curriculum 2000.

AUT   Association of University Teachers
(See NATFHE)

CEHR   Commission for Equality and Human Rights
(See CRE and EOC)

CRE   Commission for Racial Equality
           A body created following the Race Relations Act 1976 to
           oversee race relations in Britain. In 2007, the CRE was merged
           within a larger body, the Commission for Equality and Human
           Rights, which incorporated a range of previously separate
           equality watchdogs, including the Equal Opportunities
           Commission, into a single organization.

CSE   Certificate of Secondary Education
           A system of examinations introduced in 1965 in England
           and Wales, mainly for pupils in secondary modern schools
           (and later some of those in comprehensive schools) to improve
           their educational and employment prospects. The CSE was
           replaced in 1986 by the GCSE.

DES   Department of Education and Science
           Re-designation in 1964 of the former Ministry of Education.

DfE   Department for Education
           Re-designation in 1993 of the former DES.

DfEE   Department for Education and Employment
           Re-designation in 1996 of the enlarged DfE, which assumed
           responsibility for employment in addition to education.

DfES   Department for Education and Skills
           Re-designation in 2005 of the enlarged and reorganized DfEE.

EOC   Equal Opportunities Commission
           The agency responsible in the UK for dealing with sex discrim-
           ination and gender inequality issues, especially in education
           and employment. It was created following the 1975 Sex
           Discrimination Act. In 2007 the EOC was absorbed within a
           larger organization: The Commission for Equality and Human
           Rights.

FE   Further Education
           Designation for forms of non-advanced post-compulsory
           education that originated in the late nineteenth century, to
           transmit vocational skills. Redefined in the Education Reform
           Act (1988) as courses for adults at or below the equivalent
           of A level. Since the establishment of the Learning and Skills
           Council to manage all post-16 pre-university education in
           England, the term Further Education referring to provision
           in non-HE colleges, has been replaced by the Learning and
           Skills Sector which also includes work-based learning and a
           range of services by private training providers.

FEFC   Further Education Funding Council
            (See LSC)

GCE   General Certificate of Education
            School examinations in England and Wales that replaced the
            School Certificate and Higher School Certificate in 1951;
            available at Ordinary (O) and Advanced (A) level.

GCSE   General Certificate of Secondary Education
            An examination system introduced in 1986 to provide a
            single method of assessment for all pupils aged 16 (replacing
            the O level and CSE examination systems). First examined in
            1988. Typically, students who are entered sit five or more
            GCSE subjects, which are assessed by written examination
            papers and coursework.

GNVQs   General National Vocational Qualifications
            A system of assessment mainly for pupils aged 16 to 18 in full-
            time post-compulsory education, which relate to broadly
            defined vocational skills. Assessed at foundation, intermediate
            and advanced levels. The latter carry, in theory, parity of
            esteem with the A level examination system.

GTC   General Teaching Council (for England)
            The General Teaching Council for England was established
            in September 2000. The GTC is, in the words of its first
            chief executive, a body with 'responsibility for advising the
            government and other bodies on education policy' and
            which has taken on certain of the functions of a traditional
            professional association – including 'developing a code of
            professional practice with the full involvement of the
            profession' and also the regulation of professional
            misconduct.
            All qualified teachers in state schools in England and in
            Wales are obliged to become members of the GTC.

HE   Higher Education
            Advanced post-compulsory education primarily for students
            aged 18 to 21 but also for mature students. From the mid-
            1960s to the early 1990s, HE was provided mainly in univer-
            sities and polytechnics. This binary system was abolished in
            1992 and from 1993 polytechnics acquired the right to
            become universities.

HMI   Her/His Majesty's Inspectors of Schools
            (See OFSTED)

IMS   Increased Merit Selection hypothesis
'The claim that in modern societies merit becomes the key
determinant of an individual's access to education above the
basic minimum and in turn, then, of the position within the
social division of labour that he or she eventually obtains'
(Goldthorpe, 1997, p. 665).

ITT   Initial Teacher Training
The initial stage of the process of teacher training in England
and Wales. It is most commonly now certified by the award
of a PGCE (Postgraduate Certificate in Education) or an
undergraduate degree incorporating QTS (Qualified Teacher
Status), though there are also school-based training routes to
the award of QTS.

LEA(s)   Local Education Authority (Authorities)
Administrative authorities originally created by the Balfour
Education Act (1902) to provide elementary and secondary
education in defined geographical areas (originally counties
and county boroughs). LEAs acquired responsibility for the
provision of FE in 1944 and subsequently for public sector
higher education too. However, FE and HE were taken out
of the control of LEAs from 1992.

LSC   Learning and Skills Council
The government agency that replaced the FEFC in England
in 2001. It has a remit to promote participation and
attainment in FE irrespective of students' social characteristics
and backgrounds.

NAHT   National Association of Head Teachers
The main professional association representing head teachers
and school leaders in the primary school sector in England
and Wales.

NATFHE   National Association of Teachers in Further and Higher
Education
NATFHE was the largest trade union and professional associ-
ation for lecturing, managerial and research staff in FE and
HE in England, Wales and Northern Ireland. In 2006–7,
NATFHE merged with the AUT (Association of University
Teachers) to form a combined higher and further education
union UCU: The Universities and Colleges Union.

NCC   National Curriculum Council (for England)
The agency established by the 1988 Education Reform Act
to oversee the detailed planning and implementation of the

national curriculum. The NCC was replaced by SCAA in 1993.

NVQs   National Vocational Qualifications
            Qualifications intended primarily for people in work or part-time post-compulsory education, which relate to specific occupational skills.

OECD   Organisation for Economic Co-operation and Development
            An organization of thirty member countries committed to democratic government and the market economy that publishes, among other things, statistical research related to economic development, education and technical change.

OFSTED   (Ofsted) The Office for Standards in Education
            Ofsted was brought into being by the 1992 Education Act and the Schools Inspection Regulations of 1993. It replaced the school inspection functions previously performed by Her Majesty's Inspectors of Schools. As a non-ministerial department of government, Ofsted is less independent than was Her Majesty's Inspectorate. Ofsted also has responsibility for inspecting standards in Further Education and teacher training.

O level   Ordinary level of the General Certificate of Education
            An examination system introduced in 1951 for pupils aged about 15 or 16 mainly in grammar and independent (fee-paying) schools. Students in these schools usually sat seven or more O level subjects, which were formally assessed by written examination papers. Replaced in 1986 by the GCSE.

PGCE   Postgraduate Certificate in Education
            (See ITT)

PSHE   Personal, Social and Health Education
            These cross-curricular areas were officially grouped together when PSHE was designated as a non-statutory area of the English national curriculum following the 1988 Education Reform Act.

PSHEE   Personal, Social, Health and Economic Education
            PSHE was restructured by the Qualifications and Curriculum Authority's Secondary Curriculum Review in 2007, to comprise two new co-equal elements: 'Personal and social well-being'; and 'Economic well-being'.

POS   Programme(s) of Study
           Each core and foundation subject of the national curriculum
           for England has its statutorily prescribed content specified in
           a Programme of Study; there are separate Programmes of
           Study for each of the four key stages within the national
           curriculum.

QCA   Qualifications and Curriculum Authority
           This government agency was established, as two separate
           bodies respectively for England and for Wales, under the
           provisions of the 1998 Education Act, with powers to
           propose, consult upon, and prescribe revisions and amend-
           ments to the national curriculum and other government
           initiatives in the areas of curriculum and assessment in
           schools. The QCA replaced SCAA (the Schools Curriculum
           and Assessment Authority). The QCA also publishes an
           abundance of advisory and exemplar materials to assist
           schools and teachers in the implementation of the national
           curriculum.

QTS   Qualified Teacher Status
           (See ITT)

RAE   Research Assessment Exercise
           A set of procedures established in the UK in the early 1990s,
           involving competitive peer-review of research quality in higher
           educational institutions in the UK, as a basis for the allocation
           of public funding by a range of research funding councils.

SCAA   School Curriculum and Assessment Authority
           The government agency created by the 1993 Education Act
           to bring under a single authority the previously separate
           responsibilities of the National Curriculum Council and the
           School Examinations and Assessment Council. SCAA was
           replaced by the QCA in 1998.

SSAT   Specialist Schools and Academies Trust
           An agency established by government to oversee and
           promote the creation and expansion of specialist schools,
           academies, and trust schools. It was created in 2005 by
           expanding the responsibilities of the already existing
           Specialist Schools Trust to include responsibility for the
           academies programme.

SST   Specialist Schools Trust
           (See SSAT)

TDA   Teacher Development Agency
(SEE TTA)

TTA   The Teacher Training Agency for England and Wales
This was a government agency established by the 1994 Education Act with powers to advise on and in some respects prescribe standards for courses of initial teacher training, and later, for programmes of Continuing Professional Development for teachers and head teachers. It is also the funding agency for teacher training courses and related activities. In 2004, it became the TDA (Teacher Development Agency).

UCST   United Church Schools Trust
(See United Learning Trust)

UCU   Universities and Colleges Union
(See NATFHE)

UK   United Kingdom of Great Britain and Northern Ireland

ULT   United Learning Trust
A charitable body specifically created to manage a number of Academies spread across the country. ULT is a subsidiary of the not-for-profit charity United Church Schools Trust (UCST) and shares with it the objective of managing schools which 'offer students a good education based on Christian principles'.

WTO   World Trade Organization
An international organization promoting 'free trade' on a global scale.

Introduction

Metaphorical uses of the term legacy have, over the last few years, assumed an increasing prominence and rhetorical resonance. For example, the infrastructure of sports stadia, rail links etc. that remains in place after a nation has hosted the Olympic Games is now described as the legacy of the games – a usage that is increasingly employed to legitimize the spiralling costs of such spectacles. Similarly, prominent individuals, especially politicians, have become highly legacy conscious. Part of the process of image construction that now surrounds political leaders is the careful crafting of their legacy. This was conspicuously so in the case of British Prime Minister Tony Blair, not least because of his tactical error in announcing, well in advance of the event, that he would stand down as PM at some time during New Labour's third term in office. Although this had a range of negative consequences, for example heightening the endemic antagonism between the rival camps of Blairites and Brownites, it did also allow Blair's last months in office to become a period in which his legacy was conspicuously celebrated – in a variety of high profile speeches, visits, and finally a world tour.

There is, however, a more serious set of questions relating to substance rather than image: these concern the real legacy, not just of Tony Blair himself but of New Labour more generally. The main aim of this book is to offer a critical evaluation of certain key aspects of this substantive legacy. It is an assessment pervaded by a sense of loss and even betrayal. In the mid-1990s, the new leadership in its wholly understandable bid to make Labour re-electable after almost twenty years in the political wilderness embraced an approach that went much further than repudiating the disabling loony left tendencies that had split the party in the 1980s. As New Labour and under Tony Blair's leadership, it entered into a Faustian pact with the forces of neoliberalism – and has, ever since, consistently portrayed these forces as in essence unchallengeable – the only possibility on offer being to adapt to them or perish. Eric Hobsbawm's famous quip that Tony Blair was 'Thatcher in trousers' has proved prescient. Like Margaret Thatcher, Blair displayed something close to genius as a populist politician; like her he rode rough-shod over a great deal of reasonable criticism within his own party; and like her, in the end, his 'conviction politics' (in his case over the war in Iraq) led to a steep decline in his popularity both within his party and among voters. This contributed to his resignation in mid-2007 both as leader of his party and as prime minister, with Gordon Brown, the sole and unopposed candidate for both offices, succeeding him in June of that year.

The most significant of New Labour's betrayals, as far as this book is concerned, has to do with the erosion of the vitality of politics and the range of effective political choice in twenty-first century Britain and especially England. In a country with a first-past-the-post electoral system for national elections, New Labour's shift to the so-called centre ground of British politics has arguably come close to eliminating significant political choice for many citizens. This is ironic not least because New Labour was responsible, in 2002, for at long last making citizenship education a statutory requirement in state secondary schools in England and Wales, and also for introducing substantial elements of devolved political autonomy in both Scotland and (to a lesser extent) Wales. Despite such genuinely progressive moves, however, it is also New Labour's leadership that has, through a combination of an increasingly presidential mode of governing, through an unprecedented preoccupation with spin, through its emasculation of local authorities and local politics, and through its increasing subservience to business and media elites, brought Britain steadily closer to a condition of post-democracy (Crouch, 2004). Whilst overtly championing 'active citizenship', New Labour has in fact disempowered British citizens in many areas of their lives. It has eroded many aspects of social citizenship; it has weakened independent professions and marginalized trade unions; it has empowered managers and disempowered employees within workplaces; and, in its pursuit of 'homeland security', it has curtailed civil liberties to an alarming extent.

New Labour also claims to be the party of meritocracy – even if some within the leadership remain coy about actually using the 'M' word. Many of the government's most carefully crafted slogans point up its vision of creating not so much a more equal Britain, as a Britain in which the combination of talent and hard work can bring high rewards irrespective of people's different starting points in life. Thus New Labour sells itself as a party of opportunity, a party that favours enterprise, a party whose educational reforms are designed to boost chances of social mobility for talented individuals from disadvantaged backgrounds, a party that supports aspirational individuals and hard working families. How successful it has been in these endeavours is one of the questions that will be explored in this book. But there is a case for saying that though there have been some limited gains for meritocracy, New Labour has in some ways helped turn the UK into a plutocracy – a safe-haven for plutocratic refugees from other nations and a country where indigenous plutocrats are permitted to flourish while, in too many cases, avoiding paying taxes at levels at all commensurate with their income and wealth.

However this may be, the stimulus for writing a work linking together issues of meritocracy, citizenship and educational policy under New

Labour's rule, is that 2008 will be the fiftieth anniversary of the publication of the book that first introduced the *word* meritocracy into the English language – Michael Young's *The Rise of the Meritocracy* (1958). The book was a satire – intended precisely as a warning against the dangers of the headlong pursuit of meritocracy. But as Young himself came ruefully to recognize (2001), his warning was disregarded and meritocracy increasingly became the property of those bent on promoting a more meritocratic ordering of society, or indeed, of those whose saw such an ordering as part of the inbuilt logic of a post-industrial society.

Writing a book of this kind is challenging, not least insofar as it seeks to address itself to a general as well as a specialist readership. Although the analysis is rooted more strongly in sociology than in any other academic discipline, it also draws on a considerable range of other specialisms – including political philosophy, political science, philosophy of education and curriculum theory. This kind of eclecticism always runs the risk of exposing the writer to charges of superficiality (or worse). But if one aspires to deal at all holistically with certain pressing issues that now confront all of us – as British and as global citizens – then venturing across disciplinary boundaries is unavoidable. For similar reasons, I have tried to write in a style that is, as far as possible, free of specialist jargon. I have also deliberately made quite frequent reference to various newsworthy controversies highlighted in the media, and have drawn quite extensively on journalistic as well as academic commentary on these events.

The book is divided into three main parts. Parts I and III contain completely new material, while Part II consists mainly of previously published work (though Chapter 7 has been substantially updated and extended). The first two chapters of Part I focus on meritocracy, Chapter 1 presenting a brief summary of Michael Young's book and an overview of academic debates about meritocracy, while Chapter 2 examines New Labour's efforts to promote a more meritocratic ordering of society in Britain. The third chapter then changes the focus and examines issues of citizenship and citizenship education during New Labour's three terms in office. The papers collected together in Part II are focused, in the main, on governmental efforts to restructure education and the professions, particularly but not only the teaching profession and the training of teachers. In terms of their theoretical standpoint, the chapters in this section are greatly indebted to the work of the British sociologist Basil Bernstein, especially to various ideas he developed towards the end of his career, concerning the growing power of government and its various agencies over education. Bernstein also explored some of the consequences of such state control for the educational identities of students, and the professional identities of teachers and lecturers. The last chapter in this section (Chapter 7) has a somewhat different focus, being in part a general discussion of school curricula, though in the revised version presented here, it concludes with an extended analysis of some of the most important of New Labour's modernising innovations within education – notably, recent reforms of secondary schooling and the national curriculum. Part III contains a single chapter – but one concerned with issues of the greatest contemporary relevance and sensitivity: problems of cultural co-existence in the aftermath not only of 9/11 but also of the many subsequent manifestations we have seen of growing cultural antagonism both at home and abroad. It seemed appropriate to discuss these issues in a separate section because although they are in many ways inseparable from issues of citizenship (global as well as national), they have much less to do with debates about meritocracy. Also, discussion of them in relation to citizenship involves taking into consideration much broader issues than the specific policy orientations New Labour has so far developed in this area – though these are not neglected.

The various chapters in the book have been written in such a way that each can, hopefully, be read independently of the others and yet remain reasonably intelligible and coherent. The fairly extensive Glossary is designed to assist this form of reading, providing not merely a literal translation of various acronyms used but also a brief explanation of each. It is hoped that this will prove useful to readers who are less familiar with some of the details of the structure and functions of educational institutions in the UK.

Part I

MERITOCRACY, POST-DEMOCRACY AND EDUCATION

Chapter 1

DEBATING MERITOCRACY

[handwritten margin note: Selection on an oversimplistic model; assumes universal merit.]

The Rise of the Meritocracy

Fifty years ago, the distinguished British sociologist and community activist Michael Young wrote an iconic book *The Rise of the Meritocracy*, famous not least for introducing the word meritocracy into the English language. The book told the story of a fictitious society whose guiding principle was summed up by the equation IQ + Effort = Merit. What many people now forget, and some including former British Prime Minister Tony Blair seem never to have appreciated, is that Young's book was far from being a celebration of meritocracy. Quite the contrary, it was a dystopian futuristic satire, intended as a warning about the damage that single-minded pursuit of meritocratic ideas could do – both to social cohesion and to individual self-respect. It takes the form of a scholarly treatise, ostensibly written in the year 2033 by an academic specialist in historical sociology. The essay, which is addressed to the writer's fellow intellectuals, is occasioned by his growing anxiety about rising discontent among 'the lower orders', within a Britain in which meritocratic selection had become systematically institutionalized. Penned in suitably mandarin prose, the essay analyses at length the social changes that had shaped the meritocracy; its briefer conclusion then discusses the causes of growing discontent among the masses. It is written from the standpoint of a committed member of the intellectual elite, someone who might be termed a critical friend of the regime and who shares most of its assumptions. As the writer himself explains in his inimitable prose: 'I have written this essay less to honour famous men than to *warn* my fellow intelligences' (Young, 1961, p. 97).

As this quotation suggests, in constructing his fable Young's approach was heavily ironic. His pompous and pedantic narrator actually spends the greater part of his essay glorifying the achievements – in psychology, mental testing, and statecraft – that had, by the year 2033, created a Britain ruled by an aristocracy of intellect, whose ascendancy had been accepted by the majority of the population as desirable or at least inevitable. The strongly egalitarian principles that Young himself *actually* supported are repeatedly derided by his narrator – mainly as the outmoded delusions of old male socialists and certain sorts of feminists. As the storm clouds gather, the essayist complacently assesses the risk of an outbreak of serious discontent resulting from agitation on the part of these female malcontents and their supporters in 'the Populist Party'. In a passage that perfectly catches the narrator's style, he delivers his considered judgement on the likely course of future events.

> If I have succeeded in adding at all to understanding of this complex story … my purpose has been well achieved. But I am mindful that I may be expected to say a word about what is likely to happen. It can, of course, be no more than a personal opinion … Nevertheless, I hold firmly to the belief that May 2024 will be at best an 1848, on the English model at that. There will be stir enough. The universities may shake. There will be other disturbances later on, as long as the Populists survive. But on this occasion, anything more serious than a few days' strike and a week's disturbance, which it will be well within the capacity of the police (with their new weapons) to quell, I do not for one moment envisage.
>
> (Ibid., p. 188)

Famously, this sociological hubris gets it comeuppance. The book ends with a footnote:

> 1. Since the author was himself killed at Peterloo, the publishers regret that they were not able to submit to him the proofs of his manuscript for the corrections he might have wished to make before publication. The text, even this last section, has been left exactly as he wrote it. The failings of sociology are as illuminating as its successes.
>
> (Ibid., p. 190)

Michael Young died of cancer in 2002. Now, fifty years on from the book's date of publication, perhaps the most significant point to be made about its impact is that for all its wit and penetration, its basic message has gone largely unheeded. Ironically, its most lasting effect may actually have been to have helped popularize not just the word meritocracy but also the idea that a more strongly meritocratic ordering of society remains one of the most important, even inevitable goals of social and educational reform in techno-logically advanced societies. Young himself, writing only a year before his death, lamented this outcome. He went on to deplore the enthusiasm with which British Prime Minister Tony Blair, at the start of the twenty-first century, was enthusiastically promoting the vision of a more meritocratic Britain.

> I have been sadly disappointed by my 1958 book … I coined a word that has gone into general circulation, especially in the United States, and most recently found a prominent place in the speeches of Tony Blair. The book was a satire meant to be a warning (which needless to say has not been heeded) about what might happen to Britain … Much that was predicted has already come about. It is highly unlikely that the Prime Minister has read the book, but he has caught on to the word without realising the dangers of what he is advocating. It would help

if Mr. Blair would drop the word from his public vocabulary, or at least
admit to the downside ...

(Young, 2001)

The second chapter of this book will examine more closely New Labour's
efforts to construct both a modernized meritocratic discourse and a range
of policies to promote it. At this point, we will simply note that five years
after Michael Young urged Blair to consider the downsides of meritocracy,
the then prime minister was actually doing precisely the opposite. Late in
2006, and anticipating the end of his premiership in 2007, Blair took part
in an informal question-and-answer session at a Newspaper Society lunch,
where 'he allowed himself to be tempted to talk about his legacy' (Webster,
2006). Very significantly, he described 'his most far-reaching achievement'
in terms that linked together what have proved to be two of the most
important themes in New Labour's whole reforming approach: meritocracy
and modernization: 'I think the thing that has changed about the country
overall is that I think the country is basically more willing to advance
people on merit today, and ... I think we have become a far more modern
country' (Blair, quoted in Webster, 2006).

failed to achieve.

Before turning to this analysis of New Labour's achievements, however,
the remainder of this chapter will outline some of the major themes in what
has in fact been a very long-running series of scholarly debates about
meritocracy. These debates can be traced back more than 100 years – at least
as far as the seminal writings of the famous French sociologist Emile
Durkheim.

Egalitarian critiques of meritocracy

One of the places where Michael Young's warnings about the dangers of
meritocracy were conspicuously disregarded and where, instead, the
discourse of meritocracy was vigorously promoted, was in the USA in the
1960s and '70s, notably in the work of Daniel Bell, the famous theorist of
post-industrial society. The term *post*-industrial in Bell's work referred to
the growing dependence of advanced economies on expertise and techno-
logical innovation, and hence upon the quality of 'human capital'. For Bell,
it followed that: 'the post-industrial society, in its logic, is a meritocracy'
(1972, p. 30). Without selection based on educational achievement, he
argued, 'one cannot fulfil the requirements of the new social division of
labour which is a feature of that society' (Bell, 1973, p. 409). This, of course,
is a broadly functionalist argument and it is no accident that in terms of ideas
relating to meritocracy, Bell's most significant precursors were two leading
American functionalist theorists of the 1940s and '50s, Kingsley Davis
and Wilbert E. Moore, who, long before the publication of Bell's *The
Coming of Post-industrial Society* (1973), developed what came to be
known as 'the functionalist theory of stratification' (Davis and Moore,
1945). The argument they offered was in essence very similar to Bell's, but

it had two distinctive features. The first of these was the idea that occupational positions could be ranked in order of what they called 'functional importance' – positions with higher functional importance meriting higher rewards in terms of income and status. Secondly, they offered a theory of incentives. Significantly unequal levels of reward were necessary to motivate the most talented individuals to undertake the expensive and arduous training required for such positions, as well as to incentivize them to perform their roles effectively.

The pedigree of this type of this type of functionalist thinking about meritocratic allocation can, however, be traced much further back in time. Its *locus classicus* is generally accepted as being certain ideas developed by the eminent French sociologist Emile Durkheim, in his *The Division of Labour in Society*, published in Paris in 1893. One of Durkheim's main concerns was to analyse the causes of the social conflict that he saw as tearing apart the fabric of Third Republic France, and then to show how a 'scientific sociology' could identify the appropriate remedies for this 'pathological' state of affairs. As he saw it, only a very troubled kind of social solidarity could exist in newly industrializing societies so long as talented individuals were forced into accepting jobs unsuited to their abilities whilst others, on the basis of unmerited privilege, occupied superior positions. As has already been suggested, Durkheim's thinking, like that of some of his successors, was strongly influenced by functionalist assumptions. In particular, he tended to conceive of society on the model of a complex organism (analogous to a biological organism) – a system whose healthy or normal condition was a state of social harmony resulting from the appropriate functioning of each of its component parts to meet the changing needs of the whole. Non-harmonious conditions, on such a model, tend to be thought of as signs of some pathology infecting the organism. In a use of language that now strikes us as anachronistic, Durkheim referred to a perfectly meritocratic allocation of individuals to occupational positions, as a situation where the division of labour was spontaneous. By this he meant that

> … no obstacle, of whatever nature, prevents (individuals) from occupying the place in the social framework that is compatible with their faculties … labour is only divided spontaneously when society is constituted in such a way that social inequalities exactly express natural inequalities … Perfect spontaneity is then … only a consequence of … absolute equality in the external conditions of the conflict.
> (Ibid., 1964 edition, p. 377)

This was, as Durkheim saw it, the normal or healthy character of the division of labour appropriate to the modern industrial societies of his time. It is highly significant for our purposes that he went on to tie this argument quite explicitly to the notion of merit, claiming that industrial societies were steadily evolving towards this ideal state of spontaneity and also that there was a growing social sentiment supporting the idea that society should provide 'free space to all merits' and that regarded 'as unjust any inferiority that is not personally merited' (ibid., 1964 edition, p. 379).

None of these attempts to present a meritocratic ordering of society as either manifestly in accordance with the demands of social justice or as necessary concomitants of modernization, are incontestable. And indeed, such claims have been vigorously disputed for many decades. In reviewing some aspects of these critiques, it is worth initially mentioning certain well known, though rather technical, problems connected with functionalist theories as such. Perhaps the most important of these is that functionalist explanations tend to be circular and teleological. By identifying some future state of society such as its need to become more economically efficient as a kind of cause (that which brings meritocracy into existence), functionalism puts the cart before the horse. Its explanations are not properly causal. The precise mechanisms that are supposed to bring about the changes that the system is said to require are never independently specified. Rather, the social totality is endowed by functionalist theorists with an unexplained capacity to ensure that its changing needs are met.

Other more substantive criticisms of meritocratic arguments are perhaps of greater interest, and are certainly of greater practical and political consequence. Consider first the claim that, in any particular type of society, occupations can be ranked in a relatively objective hierarchy of functional importance, and secondly, the idea that sharply unequal rewards attaching to the more important of these positions are essential if talented individuals are to be appropriately incentivized to train for them and perform them effectively. Interestingly, one of the most striking things about these arguments, over the years, has been that some of the most damaging criticisms of such meritocratic claims have also been grounded in functionalist modes of thinking. For the many egalitarians who have sought to critique claims about the inevitability of meritocracy, the key attraction of functionalism has been that it can be seen as highlighting the importance of mutual interdependence among the myriad individuals who make up society. And it is precisely this inextricable interdependence of occupations within a specialized division of labour that, such egalitarians argue, makes it impossible to identify, let alone measure, the separate worth of individual contributions. Giddens and Diamond have clearly summarized the key point at stake here:

> ... scepticism about meritocracy draws on the lengthy tradition of British egalitarian social democracy, stretching back to writers such as R. H. Tawney and G. D. H. Cole, and to the radical liberalism of Leonard Hobhouse and John Hobson. As they argued, economic production has to be seen as a cooperative process, reflecting the inputs of many individuals as well as society as a whole, not as something achieved by individuals working on their own ...
>
> (2005, p. 108)

Writing in the 1920s, Hobson and a group of colleagues argued forcibly that the national income of a nation could and should be regarded as 'the result

:rative effort of the whole community', contending that 'it is not
isolate the contribution of any industry, firm or individual
:ailsford et al., 1926, p. 27). Hobson added elsewhere 'what
:s for what he does depends to a very small degree upon his own
or other personal merit, and almost wholly on the actions of
other people … ' (Hobson, 1929, p. xv). Harold Laski, who did not rely
on functionalist inspiration to the same extent as the social liberals, nevertheless wrote similarly: 'value is a social product, that is to say the result not
of individual but cooperative effort … we cannot trace the individual
contribution of any man to the sum total of production' (1927, p. 121).

These considerations, of course, bear directly on the more specific idea
introduced by Davis and Moore, that occupations can be ranked, relatively
objectively, in a hierarchy of relative functional importance. One clear
conceptual problem here is that an emphasis on function actually highlights
the point that the successful operation of any particular part of society, the
maintenance of public health for example, depends upon all the relevant
functions being performed effectively. Public health depends just as much on
the efficient working of sewerage workers, hospital laundries, waste disposal
operatives, etc. as on the work of brain surgeons or hospital managers.
Insofar as the decisive criterion is overall functional effectiveness therefore,
it is very difficult to argue on purely functionalist premises, that certain
functions are more equal than others. In effect, Davis and Moore were
obliged to concede this. When they came to try to specify those jobs that
supposedly had greater functional importance, the criterion they proposed
was the degree to which certain tasks (and those who performed them) were
clustered around and dependent upon a higher level function. An example
would be lower level health professionals supporting a consultant surgeon.
Such a criterion, however, is clearly circular and unsatisfactory for at least
two reasons. First, as argued above, in terms of interlocking specialist
functions, the efficiency of the surgeon's performance is no less dependent
on his/her subordinates than vice versa, and effective performance by all
participants is essential to operations being carried out successfully. Secondly,
Davis and Moore's proposed criterion tends, for the most part, to simply legitimate existing occupational hierarchies and differentials, doing so via specious
claims about the supposed functional indispensability of such hierarchies –
thereby assuming the very point that needs to be independently justified.

The British radical liberals and social democrats of the inter-war period
discussed these matters in ways that were both more clear-sighted and
much more critical than the ruminations of the American structural
functionalists in the 1940s and '50s. Once arguments about supposed
functional importance have been disposed of, those seeking to justify
meritocratic orderings tend to be driven back upon arguments about incentives. Such arguments, as we have seen, were indeed another key element
in Davis and Moore's theory of stratification. In the inter-war discussions
among the British social liberals and social democrats, what became central
were questions about two inter-related issues: first scarce talent, and
secondly, the incentives that might be necessary to motivate the possessors

[handwritten marginalia]: No job or function has any greater general value – Price is the arbiter; the normal rules of supply & demand apply.

for contest requirements with job specs & minimum standards well defined.

of such talents to exercise them for the common good. As Laski succinctly put it: 'we must ... pay wages in such a fashion that we attract into each socially necessary occupation a sufficiency of talent to run them adequately' (1925, p. 197). Many of the writers who acknowledged this point, however, were strongly disinclined to regard such unequal rewards as merited. For Hobson extortion, not merit, was the operative word. With considerable reluctance, Hobson came to accept that a proportion of talented individuals were, like it or not, in a position to 'extort rents of ability from society', adding caustically that these were rewards 'to which they have no moral right, but which society must pay in order to get the best fruits from such ability' (1931, p. 89). Ben Jackson, in a scholarly and highly perceptive discussion of these issues, has summarized the stance of both the left liberal and the socialist writers of this period:

Good ✓

Spot on.

> There was a general agreement ... that the defenders of the capitalist status quo greatly exaggerated the significance of financial gain as a motive in human productive activity ... Both (radical liberals and socialists) were, therefore, extremely unenthusiastic about conceding the case for incentives and supplemented their endorsement of them with the suggestion that current income inequalities were well in excess of the pay inequalities necessary to secure peak economic efficiency ... Rent of ability could, therefore, become a kind of functionless wealth, and the role of the state was to constrain these unjustified inequalities through taxation.
>
> (2003, p. 101)

Arguments of this kind lead us back more than a century, to question Durkheim's over-optimistic view that a perfect matching of social inequalities to 'natural inequalities' would be generally regarded as socially just and therefore would be productive of social harmony. For many thinkers and writers, it is clear that what such a change would mainly achieve would be to replace one arbitrary basis of social inequality with another – the outcome of a largely genetic lottery replacing the arbitrary distribution of inherited wealth or status. Of the two alternatives, meritocracy might indeed be significantly more efficient than nepotism and inherited privilege but it is far from self-evidently fair. Steven Lukes' comments on Durkheim in this regard remain highly pertinent:

> ... Durkheim ... did not consider a number of crucial difficulties latent in his ideal picture of social equality (let alone a number of formidable obstacles to realising it). How are individual aptitudes to be identified, how can 'natural' talents be distinguished from their socialised forms? ... How, in any case, could 'social inequalities' express 'natural inequalities'? Why assume a pure meritocracy would engender social solidarity? To these and other such questions Durkheim gave no answer; and, unfortunately, he never subsequently returned to them.
>
> (Lukes, 1973/1975 edition, p. 177)

Neoliberal and methodological critiques of meritocracy

Many people may be surprised to learn that one of the most vigorous and coherent arguments against meritocracy ever formulated, comes from a writer who is widely regarded as the high priest of free-market neoliberalism and of Thatcherism – Friedrich von Hayek. Perhaps the most impressive aspect of Hayek's argument is his unremitting candour: he explained more clearly and honestly than any other neoliberal theorist precisely why rigorous adherence to free-market liberalism was incompatible with espousing, or pursuing, meritocracy. Hayek's starting point is that it is fundamentally mistaken to view society 'anthropomorphically' – as being like a person with characteristics such as needs which, in his view, could only properly be attributed to individuals (or perhaps to certain sorts of organization that have established for themselves a clear set of purposes). In a sense therefore, Hayek subscribed to Margaret Thatcher's mantra that there is no such thing as society, only individuals (and their families).

In a brilliant discussion of meritocracy, John Goldthorpe gets to the heart of just why it was that Hayek was so critical of meritocracy:

> Hayek … insists that it is meaningless to speak of economic activities as possessing 'value to society'; goods and services can have value only to individuals, or organizations, and will tend, moreover, to have very different values for different recipients (Hayek, 1976, p. 75). Achievement cannot therefore be calibrated as being more or less meritorious in the sense of contributing to a greater or lesser degree to fulfilling societal needs. If judgements of merit are made, and do in fact determine rewards, then this can only be on the basis of ultimately political decisions and enforcement. Hayek, one could say, would certainly regard it as no accident that Young's meritocracy was of a highly authoritarian character … it is a further point in Hayek's case against meritocracy that while it must be an illiberal form of society, it is also likely, despite its ideology, still to be an inefficient one …
>
> For Hayek … maximum efficiency is achieved, or rather approximated, not by seeking to meet societal needs but simply by giving individuals maximum freedom to choose and pursue their own economic activities and goals in response to market signals. Whatever inequalities then emerge can be seen as the concomitant or expression of efficiency and, more importantly, of freedom.
>
> (Goldthorpe, 1997, pp. 670–1)

A further and in a certain sense scandalous consequence of Hayek's position, which he nevertheless did not flinch from facing, is that, as Peter Saunders has pithily put it, sometimes in a free-market society 'morally reprehensible people can get lucky and those who are more deserving will get nowhere: Hayek says that is the price you pay for a free society' (Saunders, 2003).

In the essay from which the quotation above is taken, Goldthorpe discusses a further major 'problem of meritocracy' – the difficulty, indeed impossibility, of defining the concept in a sufficiently consistent and objective way as to permit sociologists to measure whether particular societies are becoming more (or less) meritocratic. This, he argues, is particularly true of the many attempts that have been made to measure the links between individuals' origins, their education, and their occupational destinations – as a means of confirming (or disconfirming) what Jonsson (1992) has termed 'the Increased Merit Selection (IMS) hypothesis' i.e. 'the claim that in modern societies merit becomes the key determinant of an individual's access to education above the basic minimum and in turn, then, of the position within the social division of labour that he or she eventually obtains' (Goldthorpe, op. cit., p. 665). Goldthorpe's review of a selection of the most significant relevant empirical studies available to him highlighted a complex set of uncertainties and ambivalences:

> Unless the indexing of merit exclusively by education is accepted – and there seems to be no cogent reason why it should be – formidable problems of interpretation arise. Apparent evidence of increasing merito-cratic selection can alternatively be construed as evidence of creden-tialism, which serves to maintain existing inequalities of opportunity and condition alike ...
>
> (Ibid., p. 669)

Goldthorpe's overall conclusion is at once highly illuminating but also deeply discouraging to those who still aspire to produce firm evidence about progress towards or decline from a meritocratic allocation of individuals to appropriate places in either higher education or the occupational sphere.

> These difficulties (of definition and measurement) stem ultimately from the fact that within societies ... that possess a market economy and a pluralist polity the concept of merit, even if widely invoked and applied, is not one that can be specified in any consistent manner, but has rather to be defined in large part situationally and in ways that necessarily involve subjective judgements.
>
> (Ibid., p. 670)

Conclusion

This brief resumé of some of the key issues addressed in this long-running set of academic debates should serve to highlight the likelihood that the concept of meritocracy (and related issues of measurement) seem destined to remain perennially contested matters. This, however, appears to have had remarkably little effect on politicians, particularly those of the centre Left or centre Right, in whose discourse and policies, meritocratic ideas remain persistently prominent, even when, as in the case of New Labour, they are often now expressed in a new linguistic idiom. I shall consider these matters further in the next chapter.

Chapter 2

NEW LABOUR, NEW MERITOCRACY

New Labour's overarching ideological and policy framework

In discussing New Labour's approach to promoting a more meritocratic society, it is worth noticing first of all, that several leading Party figures and advisors have explicitly repudiated meritocracy, at least in its pure form. Anthony Giddens, for example, has argued that 'pure' meritocracy is both impractical and incoherent. It is impractical because the high levels of downward social mobility it entails would create unacceptable social dislocation, as well as despair or disaffection among the individuals directly affected. It is incoherent because it is self-contradictory. It would be impossible under such a model to completely prevent elites from passing on a range of economic and educational advantages to their children, thereby undermining the key meritocratic principle of giving equal mobility chances to the most innately talented individuals in each successive generation (Giddens, 1998; Giddens and Diamond, 2005). Some leading New Labour politicians are similarly on record as disavowing old-style meritocracy. Ardent Blairite Alan Milburn, for example, has argued that 'a narrow meritocracy isn't the answer', adding: 'as Anthony Crosland wrote, "only a few exceptional individuals hauled out of their class by society's talent scouts can ever climb upwards"' (Milburn, 2004).

None of this, however, means that New Labour really repudiates the vision of a more meritocratic Britain. Far from it. A great deal of effort in recent years has been devoted precisely to the task of developing a range of more nuanced and appealing ways of presenting this vision, as well as to devising policies to promote it. Until recently at any rate, some New Labour apologists have remained quite happy to call a spade a spade. For example, in *Where now for New Labour?* (2002), Anthony Giddens posed the question 'What sort of society should Britain become?' and his response was unequivocal:

> The answer ... is clear and Labour should have no qualms about articulating it. We should want a society that is more egalitarian than it is today, but which is meritocratic ... a meritocratic approach to inequality is inevitable ... a meritocratic order, or one that goes some way towards it, should be valued for its own sake. Fluidity is morally as well as economically desirable, since talented individuals have the chance to live up to their potential.[1]

(2002, pp. 38–9)

Others, however, have been more chary of the M word. In the last few years, a coterie of New Labour politicians and spin-doctors has been busily crafting a new and ostensibly more inclusive language that, whilst avoiding all mention of the word meritocracy, nevertheless preserves the meritocratic vision intact. Alan Milburn, for example, in a speech in 2004 outlining priorities for Labour's third term in office, deployed virtually every key term in this new lexicon.

> If the aspirations that most hard-working families have for themselves ... are thwarted, then responsibility, innovation and enterprise are all undermined ... This is why social mobility matters. When it is present it provides a fair set of easily understood rules – social incentives – that earn rights through responsibilities, and earn advancement through effort ... When it is absent ... poverty of aspiration then kicks in ... Fairness in life-chances is what we should seek ... By liberating the potential of each individual *as* an individual. By enabling people, regardless of wealth or status, to take greater control over their lives ... Where the State seeks to equalise opportunities throughout life and citizens take them ... Traditional income redistribution deals only with symptoms not causes. Today, a different approach is required, opening the door to greater independence, self-reliance, and aspiration for more people ... Our goal should be social justice ... a fair society where nobody is left behind, but all can bridge the gulf between what they are and what they have the potential to become. A country that is open to the innate talents of people according to their worth not birth. This is a Labour end. Achieving it requires New Labour means ... The New Labour model is about levelling up not levelling down.
>
> (Milburn, 2004)

The discursive strategy here is too obvious to dwell on. Explicit talk of meritocracy is replaced by the carefully crafted newspeak of 'hard-working families', 'aspirational' and self-reliant employees, 'empowered' individuals, a society open to talent, and so on.[2] The key terms encapsulating this new vision are 'opportunity', 'social mobility' and 'life chances'. What all this actually means, of course, is chances for some – ostensibly those with the talent who make the effort – to rise in the social scale within a society that remains highly unequal but claims to offer opportunity to all.

The heart of the policy is thus redistribution of opportunity to become unequal, rather than seeking to bring about a significantly more equal redistribution of income and wealth. In another influential slogan (borrowed from the Clinton years in the USA), the guiding idea is that 'it is better to give people a hand up rather than a handout'. Old approaches to welfare are criticized as inducing welfare dependency. Another crucial element in the policy repertoire therefore, is that individuals are to be 'responsibilised' (Rose, 1999b) so that everyone understands that they have a duty to enter the labour market (whose floor in the UK has, after all, been set at an ethically acceptable level by the introduction of the minimum wage). Individuals have a further responsibility: to become lifelong investors in themselves – with the primary aim of maintaining or enhancing their employability. This, in turn, involves projects of re-skilling as well as psychological reorientation – so that individuals acquire what Giddens has revealingly called 'the cognitive and emotional *compe-tence*' to become risk-takers and be more effective in capitalizing on the investment opportunities offered to them, whether by the state or the market (Giddens, 1998, p. 125, my italics). As Perkins et al. have pointed out, 'lack of access to knowledge and loss or absence of skills are the new social risks of the knowledge based economy' and it is, in this approach, up to individuals, appropriately supported by agencies of the state, to 'enhance their economic competitiveness' (Perkins et al., 2004, p. 3). The key vehicle for these policies is 'the social investment state' (see for example: Dobrowolsky, 2002; Giddens, 1998; Midgley and Sherraden, 2000; Perkins et al., 2004). Public spending to enable individuals to become more capable and employable is legitimized (with a wary eye on neoliberal critics) as an essential form of public investment – very different from the 'tax and spend' and 'something for nothing' policies said to be characteristic of discredited old Labour approaches. Two further key terms in the repertoire therefore, are 'enablement' and 'empowerment'. As early as the run-up to the 1997 election, New Labour was already declaring that at the heart of its new approach was the creation of 'a dynamic knowledge-based economy founded on individual empow-erment and opportunity, where governments enable, not command, and the power of the market is harnessed by the public interest' (Dobrowolsky, 2003, p. 4, cited in Perkins et al., 2004).

Widening educational opportunity

In the light of this, it should be clear that Tony Blair's famous mantra on taking office in 1997, that his government's priorities would be 'education, education and education', was not lightly chosen. If social and economic opportunity were to be effectively enhanced, then, in the minds of key New Labour thinkers, the reform of educational institutions clearly constituted the 'road royal' to achieving this goal. The essentials of New Labour's education reform agenda are familiar enough (and various aspects of them will be discussed in more detail in Part II of this book, particularly in Chapter 7). In brief, they have involved first, 'research-led' efforts to identify what makes some schools more effective than others, followed by the devel-opment of school improvement initiatives aimed at making every school an effective school.[3] Second, the imposition of the standards agenda – involving the use of ever-rising attainment targets and the development within schools of a culture of 'performativity' (Ball, 2001). A third key element has involved decisively breaking with the so-called 'one size fits all' policy of compre-hensive schooling, in favour of a more differentiated system of secondary schools designed to offer both wider choice and enhanced opportunity – especially, it is claimed, to the most disadvantaged. This has been promoted, most obviously, through the expansion of specialist schools, and the creation of faith schools, academies and most recently trust schools. This policy of diversification in secondary education has been further legitimized as reinvigorating 'civil society' – by promoting greater parental and also community involvement in schooling, and by increasing participation in the provision of schooling by a range of non-state providers: notably, religious groups, business organizations and wealthy individuals (see Chapter 7 for a fuller discussion).

The inter-connectedness of these different agendas is well caught in the following comments by Michael Barber back in the days when he headed-up the 'Prime Minster's Delivery Unit' in 10 Downing Street:

> We are intentionally breaking the mould in our relationships with the voluntary and religious sectors, by, for example, providing for the first time, state funding for Muslim, Sikh and Seventh Day Adventist schools … The central challenge is to build social coalitions in the drive for higher standards and radical reform. It is clear in Hong Kong and elsewhere that the business and religious sectors are strong allies. This is true in the USA too … Each a different combination, each fit for purpose.
>
> (Barber, 2003)

Even the independent (private fee-paying) schools have not been left untouched by policies intended to widen opportunity. In 2006, indirect government pressure was exerted via the Charities Commission, for England's independent schools to justify their charitable status by making greater contributions to 'the public good'. This led a small number of the best endowed schools in the sector to 'voluntarily' introduce, from 2007, some element of a new 'needs blind' admission system, with entry, or at least a proportion of the entry, dependent on individual performance in competitive entrance examinations, and with generous bursaries provided for successful candidates from poorer homes.

The appeal of these education reforms should not be underestimated. They can be plausibly represented as at one and the same time addressing concerns about unreformed 'bog-standard' comprehensive schools, whilst avoiding the problems that undermined confidence in the old tripartite system of grammar and secondary modern schools in the 1950s and '60s. By promoting access to a diversity of types of secondary school within what remains, at least formally, a non-selective framework, the new approach avoids the demonstrable unfairness of premature academic selection at eleven plus. It can also be portrayed as achieving greater parity of esteem between the diverse types of schools now available than was ever possible in the days of the old tripartite system when a minority of children passed for the grammar school and most of the rest failed the eleven plus and were consigned to a secondary modern. Moreover, it is argued that parents can, to a much greater extent than was possible in the past, now exercise signif-

what does success look like?

icant choice in the type of secondary school they prefer for their children. In the light of this, it is perhaps not as surprising as it might seem, that in 2007 the leader of the British Conservative Party, David Cameron and his shadow education spokesman David Willetts, moved to distance their party from its traditionally unswerving support of grammar schools, whilst strongly endorsing academies and trust schools.

Although educational reform has been salient, it is, however, far from being the only sphere in which strenuous efforts to enhance opportunity have been pursued. Social investment in children and young people outside full-time education has also been prioritized. There is not space here to examine the relevant policies in depth, but it is worth highlighting the point that, in common with the focus on schooling, the great majority of the initiatives in question are strongly future oriented – as perhaps befits a government whose watchword is modernization. Indeed, the Canadian sociologists Jenson and Saint-Martin are guilty of only a little overstatement when they say of social investment approaches generally that 'the sentiment that children are one hundred per cent of the future prevails' (2003, p. 92).

In sum, we may say that overall in these respects, there has been under New Labour, a combination of increased expenditure involving both universal policies for every child, as well as an array of targeted initiatives focused on children from the most highly disadvantaged backgrounds. We have seen, for example, funding via parental vouchers for universal pre-school education – which can be accessed, as parents choose, from private or community providers or in nursery classes in some state schools. Another universal policy (at least in intent) has been the introduction of the Child Trust Fund, which is aimed at encouraging individual saving for the future from an early age. Among the most important targeted initiatives have been Sure Start, and a range of measures to reduce child poverty – in part by encouraging more single parents into paid employment and also by elimi-nating some aspects of the poverty trap. This has been accomplished via such policies as Child Tax Credit, Working Families Tax Credit and other reforms to the Child Benefit system. The importance of such policies within and beyond education, and the contribution they have made to significantly reducing child poverty, should not be underestimated.

However, whilst it is important to acknowledge these real advances, it is no less important to note that the claims made by New Labour about its successes in widening opportunity have been far from modest. Almost exactly ten years after his famous 'education, education, education' speech of November 1996, Tony Blair delivered another address which was seen by not a few commentators as 'Blair (moving) to entrench educational reforms as a substantial feature of his legacy' (White, 2006). Significantly, the prime minister began by reiterating his faith in educational reform as the key to widening social opportunity and building a just society: 'I knew then that changing educational opportunity was the surest way to changing lives, to social justice. I am as certain of that today as I was 10 years ago when I said it.' (Blair, 2006a) He went on to contrast New Labour's faith in centralized prescription during its first term, with the subsequent shift to embracing diversity – both individual and institutional. The speech goes on to celebrate not only the diversification of educational providers (it was, after all, delivered at the Annual Conference of the Specialist Schools and Academies Trust) but also to make far-reaching claims about the potential for raising the attainment of 'each and every child' through the development of 'personalised learning':

> ... what is obvious is that 'different' is what each and every child is ... The key to education today is to personalise learning, to recognise different children have different abilities and in different subjects ... only through the pursuit of excellence can equity be achieved; only through schools being free to personalise learning, can a child really be given the opportunity suitable for them.
>
> (Ibid.)

Blair went on to adroitly link this emphasis on personalisation[4] to school diversification, by contrasting the sameness of 'bog-standard' comprehensives with the 'new system of secondary education we have been creating': 'what was once monochrome is now a spectrum offering a range of freedoms and pathways' (ibid.). At the end of the speech, however, Blair was at pains to spell out that there was a quid pro quo for these enhanced opportunities that were now being so skilfully tailored to individual differences and aptitudes. This was that it is now the individual's responsibility to make the most of these new opportunities. Stressing that on-going meritocratic reform is vital – because if people 'fail to get an opportunity, they have no choice' – Blair added the following very revealing rider: 'If people fail to *take* their opportunities, *that is their choice*' (ibid., my italics).

Many of the policy initiatives discussed in this section are, of course, in themselves both welcome and significant. Taking steps to widen educational and social opportunity, particularly for the most disadvantaged, is clearly to be applauded;[5] so too is more sensitive matching of teaching and learning to individuals' distinctive gifts and interests. But what has at the same time to be kept in mind is that this array of policies is both embedded in and helps legitimize what is repeatedly portrayed as a brave new world of greatly enhanced opportunity and improved life chances. On closer inspection, however, this vision proves to be a mirage. The fundamentals of Britain under New Labour turn out to have involved significantly widening inequalities – of wealth and income, and of power and influence, especially as between the new elites at the top and those at the bottom, but also between the 'middle-mass' (Crouch, 2004) of relatively lower paid white collar employees and those who increasingly shape and manage their destinies.

Reaching for the stars

New Labour's meritocracy that chooses not to speak its name has two core legitimating principles. The first, already discussed, is that of seeking to

realistic meritocracy

enhance educational and social opportunity (albeit within the limits of what is realistic in an economy that must be functionalized to compete effectively in a globalized world). The second principle is that higher levels of reward must flow to hard-working individuals of talent and enterprise. This is assumed to be both an increasingly accurate description of current social arrangements as well as an aspiration to progress further in this direction. In a certain sense it can be argued that even though the rhetoric has changed, this second principle operates to sustain the Thatcherite doctrine that the prosperity and well-being of the nation depends, more than anything else, on an elite of individual wealth creators and on those who occupy key leadership positions. Such assumptions thus seek to make sacrosanct what is actually a very particular and contestable doctrine of individual merit: that the key individuals who are the wealth creators or who lead the most effective organizations unquestionably deserve 'to keep more of what they earn' (to use yet another slogan from the Thatcher years). Such individual 'excellence' must be encouraged and more highly rewarded in all spheres.

State must recognise value of each individual as equal

Certain major organizational reforms that have swept all before them, at least in Anglo-Saxon countries in the last three decades, have had a major role in cementing these meritocratic doctrines in place. The growth of the hierarchically managed organizational structures that increasingly provide the framework of most people's working lives appears to have generated a new common sense that involves growing acceptance (however reluctant on the part of some employees) that there are now no real alternatives but to 'obediently … climb the career ladders established by the business elites' (Crouch, 2000, p. 42). Within the corporate sphere, the most significant of these changes were ushered in by the financial deregulation and other reforms associated with the 'Big Bang' of October 1986, which opened up national institutions like the stock market and investment banking in Britain to overseas and especially American ownership and influence. Inter alia, these changes powerfully consolidated, right across the corporate sector, the power and prerogatives of the chief executive – the single individual (nearly always a man) who carries prime responsibility for delivering 'shareholder value' and who can be held to account if he fails to do so. More generally, and across much of the public as well as the private sectors, the apparently unstoppable march of *managerialization* has been no less potent in consolidating this one-eyed vision of effective organizational leadership. Here, two key developments were particularly important. The first was the New Right's doctrinal insistence on 'management's right to manage' – and the very great empowerment of senior managers that went with it. Second was the increasing responsibilization (Rose, 1999a) of senior management – for efficiently delivering services and for managing their organizations 'within budget'. As commentators such as John Clarke and Janet Newman as well as Nikolas Rose have pointed out, a related neoliberal strategy – the introduction of 'government at a distance' (ibid., pp. 49–50) – further increased both the responsibilities and the vulnerability of senior managers, especially within the public sector. Governing at a distance involved attempts by politicians 'to depoliticise decision-making' by representing many aspects of it as

'a matter of operational management' (Clarke and Newman, 1997, p. 14
(An important consequence of this has been that various political miscalcu-
lations are now commonly represented, or more accurately misrepresented,
as 'management failures' – though this no longer always carries conviction
either with increasingly sceptical voters or with the consumers of the relevant
services.)

It is little exaggeration to say that 'the chief executive model' of institutional
leadership is now close to becoming hegemonic across the public as well as
the private sector – and at a remarkable variety of scales. In education, for
example, it is not only vice-chancellors of universities but primary school head
teachers whose posts have been reconstructed along these lines. The belief
that the performance of educational institutions, and of departments within
them, at every scale, depends more on the leadership quality of a key
individual than on anything else, seems to increasingly negate any possibility
of serious consideration being given to any alternatives. There has been in
recent years, for example, almost no serious policy discussion about how
more democratic and collegiate forms of governance of educational institutions might be promoted. And as far as schools are concerned, the formation
and funding of the National College of School Leadership based at the
University of Nottingham, has further consolidated what threatens to now
also become a research-led consensus about the one best approach to
effective school organization and to raising standards.[6]

It is worth also noting in this connection that the increasingly influential
discourse of 'transformational leadership' has played a major supporting role
both in promoting and legitimizing such developments. Janet Newman, for
example, has noted how, under New Labour,

> The discourse of transformational leadership ... assumed an authori-
> tative status because of its twin association with the US ... and within
> the business world. These associations invoke images of individual
> dynamism, risk taking and entrepreneurship that have strong associa-
> tions with Labour's espoused values, fitting well with its social as well
> as economic goals.
>
> (2005, p. 720)

Cath Lambert in a recent article exploring the complexities of the gendering
of New Labour's use of this discourse within education, cites an exemplary
distillation of the key ideas, in a speech by David Miliband, during his brief
sojourn as Minister for School Standards:

> We need more not less flexibility in schools, and that means getting
> leadership right ... Call it transformational leadership ... To succeed to
> their full potential, teachers need to work in a school that is creative,
> enabling and flexible. And the biggest influence is the head ... Every
> teacher is a leader in the classroom. Every head must be the leader of
> these leaders.
>
> (Miliband, 2002, p. 6)

. 157) goes on to observe how this discourse has been closely
ghtened flexibility opened up by new policies of ' "earned
ıead teachers of schools, made manifest through structural
: localised financial and staffing decisions (Her Majesty's
02)'. And she further explains how these discourses and the
ake on school leaders do more than merely legitimize new
rial empowerment. They increase the real strategic impor-
tance of heads in winning consent, or at least acquiescence, in the implementation of the new policy agendas:

> These ... demands ... emphasise how ... in effectively securing the
> commitment of educational professionals to New Labour's vision,
> leadership remains a central apparatus through which representatives of
> central government attempt to win consent for reform. It is head teachers
> who are depended upon to implement reform by gaining consent or
> compliance from teachers. Such a task locates heads in a structural
> position of power in terms of the impact their leadership may have on
> the professional identities of their staff.

> (Ibid., p. 158)

We may note in conclusion here, that despite the genuineness of the aspira-
tions to enhance efficiency that motivated these various modernizing reforms
of management, what has been brought into being can, quite plausibly, be
seen as the creation of new constellations of vested interests – ones that are
increasingly embodied in self-perpetuating and costly bureaucratic and
managerial hierarchies – and perhaps even in some cases, in effect replacing
one version of 'producer capture' with another.[7]

Developments in higher education

In higher education in the England and Wales, there are other issues to be
addressed in addition to those of the income and power differentials between
senior management and other sections of the workforce. Here, a particular
form in which meritocracy has been institutionalized, at least within research
orientated universities, is now seen by some as producing increasingly malign
effects. The proximate culprit, in Britain at any rate, is the Research
Assessment Exercise (RAE), which allocates sharply differential levels of
research funding to universities on the basis of competitive peer-reviewed
rankings of 'research quality', buttressed by indices of 'levels of esteem',
capacity to attract externally funded research, and the like. But the RAE has
arguably only intensified what is a longer established shift within the most
prestigious universities in the UK (and in many other countries) towards an
ever-growing preoccupation with 'research excellence' – driven on strongly
by ambitions to achieve or sustain world class status. However, some of the
downsides of these tendencies are beginning to ring alarm bells – even in those
institutions that derive greatest advantage from them. In a magisterial and

remarkably candid analysis, the vice-chancellor of Cambridge University in her 2006 Annual Address to the Regent House (Cambridge's parliament of dons) highlighted the negative effects of the growing preoccupation with research for the quality of teaching offered to undergraduates.

> The fact is that rankings, prestige and investments are strongly weighted towards our research endeavours. This ... makes it ever harder for research-intensive universities to give serious attention to the education of undergraduates. The standing of individual academics, in their disciplines and universities, depends more and more on research accomplishments and less and less on their contributions as teachers. Investment from the public and private sectors reflects and reinforces this asymmetry ... The real problem, I believe, is not lack of talent or interest but that teaching makes diminishing professional and economic sense in the eyes of a growing number of academics ... Research is accorded higher status – by the rankings and by academics themselves. At universities, particularly those with big research programmes, institutional arrangements and culture are not fully aligned with the importance we say we attach to teaching. In short, the *activity* of teaching is threatened.
>
> (Richard, 2006a)

Putting these issues onto the agenda of public discussion in this way is clearly valuable and timely – and is in accordance with how this particular vice-chancellor sees her role: 'my responsibility ... is to ensure that things are being talked about and thought about' (see MacLeod, 2006). However, finding effective remedies is far more difficult. And Richard's speech, so strong on its analysis of the problems, had very little specific to say in this regard. This should occasion little surprise. The pressures in the opposite direction are systemic and becoming ever more strongly entrenched – and meritocratic ideology is one of their most potent sources of legitimization.[8] There is increasing competition to attract those who are regarded as 'star' researchers. And to do this, it is persuasively argued, any individual institution has no choice but to compete in a global marketplace and pay the going rate.

However, as Alison Richard's comments imply, the impact is by no means limited to the brightest stars in the academic firmament. There is a pervasive trickle down effect which not only widens internal differentials between highly rated researchers and those who devote more of their time to teaching and assessment and administration, but also widens differentials between academic institutions, particularly in terms of their status and ability to attract the most gifted (or at any rate highly qualified) staff and students. A major consequence has been that in the last three decades, and at an accelerating rate, there has been a proliferation of new tenured professorial and other senior research posts, in the main awarded to those with strong track records in research and/or with a proven capacity to win resources from external funding bodies. The counterpart of this trend has been to intensify the workloads and reduce the status and rewards of those whose main concern is with 'lower level' teaching, assessment and 'routine' administration – all in fact, of course, indispensable functions of British universities considered as a national system. It has also led, in many of the old research-oriented universities, to a growing US-style reliance on doctoral students taking an increasing role (at remarkably low rates of pay) in the teaching of undergraduates.[9] A further pernicious effect is that ambitious academics are strongly incentivized to delegate lower level tasks to others, e.g. by using external research funding to 'buy themselves out' of such duties. In these ways, a growing proportion of these less glamorous but vitally important functions of universities are shed to hourly paid, often female, and increasingly 'flexibilized' staff. For all these reasons, and as Richard's admonitions so clearly indicate, the oft-repeated claim that teaching quality in higher education institutions is directly related to their involvement in research appears increasingly threadbare.

Another consequence of this increasing widening of differentials between different groups of academics is that it results in a growing asymmetry of power, not only in relation to newly empowered senior managers but also as between different levels of senior and junior academic staff. It is increasingly the case that academic boards, research committees, and the proliferating number of sub-committees that are now such a feature of university life, are dominated by professorial and other senior staff, who normally sit on such bodies in an ex officio capacity. The proportion of elected representatives therefore shrinks and their influence diminishes even more. The forums in which ordinary academic and research staff can feel they have any voice are increasingly marginalized and the powers of such bodies are highly circumscribed. A further consequence is that managerial and academic leadership groups may easily come to develop a common interest in encouraging the growth of even more highly stratified institutional structures, for example by further increasing the proportion of appointments made at senior levels. Of course, one of the ironies here is that such changes can very plausibly be represented as not only clearly meritocratic but as furthering the overall interests of the institution or of departments within it. However, collegiality, and a sense of collective responsibility for sustaining real quality across the full range of services that universities provide, is at risk of being increasingly undermined. A further consequence, is that especially in many of the old universities in the UK, developments such as these, by inflating the salary bill (including funding the 'on costs' of final salary pensions for an increasing proportion of highly paid and long-lived academic staff), have very considerably increased the overall cost of higher education – not only to taxpayers (who in Britain still provide the lion's share of higher education costs) but also to students and/or their parents and families, now paying increased levels of tuition fees in addition to maintenance costs. It is not unreasonable to conclude that these ultimate funders and consumers of higher education are increasingly entitled to ask hard questions about value for money. Whether they will do so in significant numbers remains to be seen.

As has been indicated already, it is difficult if not impossible for single institutions, in higher education or elsewhere, to row against the current

– particularly when that current is so powerful. Such problems are compounded by the fact that those in public sector organizations who are highly rewarded relative to their more junior colleagues can all too easily point to many clearly less talented individuals and groups in other spheres, whose rewards are considerably and in some cases inordinately greater than their own. The veneration of research stars, trophy professors and the like in higher education has its even more visible counterpart in the cult of celebrity in the media, in sport, among business leaders, and also increasingly in politics. In many of these instances, and even in cases where the individuals concerned are unquestionably talented within their own fields, the exorbitant levels of rewards that flow to them are in no sense proportional to the degree to which their talent is superior to that of others. Rather, these rewards, more than anything else, reflect the growth of the global marketplace for certain kinds of products and the enormous earnings potential that this marketplace creates for the fortunate few.

A quasi-meritocracy

Modern Britain is a quasi-meritocracy increasingly dominated by market forces and (in the public sector) by quasi-markets – and the reward structures that go with them. The allocation of individuals to leading positions, and the flow of increasingly unequal levels of reward to those at the top is based on a broad, though highly imperfect, application of meritocratic principles. Those in leading positions have typically achieved them at least partly on the basis of the level (and sometimes the content) of their educational achievements, and most do also demonstrate the ability to discharge their functions with at least reasonable effectiveness. There is little outright nepotism. Michael Young himself described the first Blair cabinet of 1997 as in these senses 'largely filled ... with members of the meritocracy' (2001).

Also, it needs to be acknowledged that New Labour's efforts to widen opportunity by lifting a proportion of the poorest in society out of poverty have met with at least some success. (It is more difficult to be sure about the effects of educational reforms, not least because attempts to measure changing rates of educational and occupational mobility are fraught with problems.) At the same time, however, the rewards flowing to the most highly rewarded elite groups have increased very considerably indeed, and income differentials within organizations and fields of work have also widened significantly. As Stewart Lansley has summed up the situation:

New Labour has embarked on an ambitious programme to tackle poverty. Despite some success in this, in 2004, Britain still had a level of relative poverty that was higher than in the late 1970s and higher than in most developed countries – only Ireland, Greece, Italy and the United States had higher rates. What progress has been achieved is the result of redistribution from middle rather than rich Britain. While those on lower incomes have got richer, so have the rich themselves and at a faster rate than the poor. Hence the rising wealth and income gap between the very top and the very bottom.

(2006, p. 221)

Data for the year 2005–6 produced by the UK Office for National Statistics showed that not only had differentials in real incomes widened further, with the poorest quintile actually losing ground in real terms while the richest quintile gained by 1.5 per cent, but also that the five year trend in reducing child poverty had been reversed, with 200,000 more children living in relative poverty in 2005–6 as compared with 2004–5 (see Elliott, 2007).

Overall then, it seems fair to say that roughly speaking, contemporary elites in Britain are in some measure meritocratic – though some are much more genuinely meritocratic than others, and some are far more highly rewarded than others. Yet it is highly questionable whether these widening differentials, whether between elite groups in different fields, or between elites and other workers within particular fields, are really justifiable – even in meritocratic terms. It is even more doubtful if most of them serve the public good. Will Hutton, back in the year when New Labour first took office, was already drawing attention to the perverse effects of what Frank and Cook (1996) call 'winner takes all' markets.

At the top are emerging ... winner-takes-all markets. Top performers in professions as disparate as law and football, hospital surgery and investment banking are earning ever higher salaries in relation to the average. More and more high quality people are flocking to these sectors, however poor their prospects of reaching the summit, because the indifferent odds are more than compensated for by the exceptional rewards. Meanwhile there is a parallel fall-away in the quality of recruits in engineering, the Civil Service and teaching. But the economic returns to the wider society from these areas are as great as, or greater, than those with winner-takes-all markets.
Here again we see the malign impact of an over-reliance on the contract model to generate efficiency, and what happens when individualism is accentuated and the trust ethic becomes degraded.

(Hutton, 1997, p. 34)

Yet, as numerous commentators have pointed out, New Labour's response, across a period of more than ten years, has in the main been to treat these widening economic and power differentials with, at best, insouciance, whilst at worst, some prominent New Labour figures have actively encouraged such developments and even personally benefited from them. In Stewart Lansley's words, 'the political consensus persists that the growing wealth gap does not matter' (op. cit., p. 221), while Anthony Giddens similarly acknowledges that: 'New Labour since 1997 has focused firmly on the poor. The reasoning is that the priority should be to concentrate on the most disadvantaged, rather than worry about the overall levels of income inequality. *The rich were to be largely left alone* ... ' (Giddens and Diamond, 2005, p. 103, my italics).

Finally, there can be little doubt that the promotion of meritocratic ideology – whether expressed in the language of meritocracy or through the new euphemisms of aspiration, opportunity and life-chances – has played a significant role in fostering a social climate in which those at the top seem to feel increasingly entitled to the rewards and privileges they enjoy. Some can even, apparently, feel resentful that their true worth is still not sufficiently recognized – what Lansley dubs the 'because I'm worth it' syndrome (op. cit., Ch. 4). In this regard, Will Hutton has pointed out that 'In an individualist society there is less shame in denying the role others have played in your success and insisting on the unalloyed importance of your own efforts' (op. cit., pp. 34–5). More recently, *Guardian* economics editor Larry Elliott has similarly commented:

> There seems no reason why this trend should end; salaries at the top, exemplified by the £27 million (in one year) paid to Bob Diamond of Barclays Capital, have been going up and up. Wages at the bottom have been kept in check by government pay restraint, low-cost producers overseas and an inflow of cheap workers. Globalisation is used by those at the top to explain both why they should be paid more (talent is mobile in the modern world) and why their workers should be paid less (the disciplines of the borderless world).
>
> (Elliott, 2007)

Michael Young himself made the same point even more trenchantly:

> If meritocrats believe, as more and more of them are encouraged to do, that their advancement comes from their own merits, they can feel they deserve whatever they can get ... So assured has the elite become that there is almost no block on the rewards they arrogate to themselves. The old restraints of the business world have been lifted, and as (my) book also predicted, all manner of new ways for people to feather their own nests have been invented and exploited. Salaries and fees have shot up. Generous share option schemes have proliferated. Top bonuses and golden handshakes have multiplied.
>
> (op. cit., 2001)

Despite these signs of excess and widening inequality, it seems highly probable that meritocracy, both as a concept and as a slogan, will continue to have strong appeal to politicians of the centre. This is in part because it can be seen as, and if need be presented as, 'a necessary myth'. Many such politicians are not unaware of how far the existing structure of overall inequality and equality of opportunity in fact departs from a state of perfect meritocracy. But a key part of the attraction of preserving the meritocratic myth is that it enshrines a more palatable and appealing vision than, say, Friedrich Hayek's all too honest recognition of the way free markets may actually allocate rewards (Hayek, 1976). As Peter Saunders has pointed out, Hayek's acknowledgement that free markets commonly distribute rewards on the basis of sheer chance, so that equally deserving people may profit or not, and also that markets frequently reward individuals whose moral qualities are less than appealing, is deeply unattractive politically. It is no basis for constructing a viable legitimizing rhetoric to underpin modernizing political programmes in a society of ameliorative neoliberalism.

> The liberal position is offensive when it says I don't care why you've got your money, I don't care whether you deserved it, and I'm not going to make an effort to rectify what, as Hayek himself says, appears to be a gross injustice. The fact that really hard-working people don't get rewarded, and that this situation is not worth rectifying, is offensive to popular sentiment.
>
> (Saunders, 2003)

However, even as potent and pervasive a myth as this cannot carry all before it, not even in the favourable economic circumstances New Labour enjoyed during its first ten years in office. Where the real character of inequality departs too glaringly from the prevailing meritocratic justifications, it may become expedient to call for at least some degree of realignment. In this regard, it is noteworthy that even 'Professor Lord Giddens, high priest of the Third Way' (Peel, 2006) has, in some of his most recent writings, become highly critical of instances of the conspicuous accumulations of riches that are manifestly unmerited.

> The accumulation of wealth is excessive and unjust where it arises not from hard work and risk-taking enterprise but from 'brute luck' factors such as rising returns to property and land. Inheritance (of wealth or property) itself is a form of brute luck inequality, enabling citizens to share in the social product while violating the principle of reciprocity ... The case for liberty does not therefore defeat the case for taxation of wealth transfers. The present inheritance tax regime of the UK still offers loopholes for the affluent, and is inequitable in its impact on the modestly well off. The government should look again at capital transfer tax extending beyond simply inheritance, and including all lifetime gifts.
>
> (Giddens and Diamond, 2005, p. 117)

But while such criticisms are pertinent and timely, they do little to dent the hegemony of the underlying meritocratic vision. Indeed, they may actually help legitimize it by sustaining the belief that such excesses are remediable pathologies of meritocracy rather than being, as Michael Young so clearly saw, intrinsic to it.

Conclusion

Despite the accumulating evidence of such conspicuous excess, there are few signs that mainstream politicians or leading civil servants have any serious intention of abandoning the pursuit of quasi-meritocracy, or of significantly challenging the still widening gap in wealth and income across society as a whole.[10] In a world where celebrity is uncritically worshipped, and where people are told that globalization makes ever-rising inequalities at the top inevitable,[11] there seems little prospect of reviving serious public and political debate focused on arguments of principle relating to the justification of different degrees and kinds of inequality of rewards. Political parties that increasingly gravitate to the centre ground, and which are themselves increasingly beholden to wealthy donors (or lenders), have strong interests in not disturbing a situation in which the rich continue to be largely left alone and where the burgeoning elites, including those in and around politics, continue to thrive.

As far as opportunity is concerned, there is little reason to believe that the significant but still limited improvements so far delivered for the worst off children, or (the often unsustainable) attempts to increase the effectiveness of failing schools, or the expansion of the academies and trust schools programmes, will counterbalance the even more strongly enhanced opportunities for more advantaged children that may well flow from the expansion of educational choice agendas. Whilst marked inequalities of condition persist and in some areas conspicuously widen, the chances of enhancing educational opportunity for the less advantaged (or even some sections of the middle class), remain severely limited (see Esping-Andersen, 2005). In A. H. Halsey's prophetic words, it continues to be the case, partly as a result of credentialism and other obstacles to social mobility, that 'as the working-class clears one hurdle, so another is set in their path, leaving the service class ("higher" middle class)[12] always one flight ahead' (Halsey, Heath and Ridge, 1980, p. 218).

It is worth noting finally here that, as this book went to press, Anthony Giddens wrote a piece in *The Guardian* newspaper in which he went further than ever before in unequivocally accepting that enhancing social mobility will only ever be possible in modern Britain if social inequality itself is reduced.

> Reducing inequality and creating greater chances of mobility are not alternatives, but are interdependent. Education often reflects wider inequalities rather than muting them. We have to work to reduce inequalities at source if we want to establish a fairer society ... Meeting the targets Labour has set – reducing child poverty by half by 2010, and abolishing it by 2020 – would have a profound impact on social mobility. Since child poverty is a relative measure, lowering it means reducing inequality overall. Experts agree that the programmes the government has in place will not allow it to get near the 2010 target. Gordon Brown should be looking at new policies,

and further investment, in order to fulfil the commitment he has made.

(Giddens, 2007)

But even here, there was no mention of the M word.

Chapter 3

NEW LABOUR'S CITIZENSHIP AGENDA

Introduction

The previous chapter briefly drew attention to the ways in which New Labour's spin doctors increasingly sidelined the language of meritocracy and crafted a new discourse to replace it: a discourse of individual aspiration, of people as investors in themselves, of opportunity, of individual responsibility, and so on. Such linguistic inventiveness has not, of course, been confined to discussions of meritocracy. Rather, as Ruth Levitas has noted, 'the peculiar language of New Labour has been a matter of journalistic comment at least since 1996, and there have also been more systematic studies of the new political discourse such as ... Levitas 1998 and ... Fairclough 2000' (Levitas, 2004 p. 2). One of many issues highlighted by such commentators has been the rapidity with which terms judged no longer fit for purpose are abandoned and replaced by new improved versions. This can apply as much to overarching descriptors such as 'the Third Way'[1] and 'the stakeholder society' as to more general-purpose terms like step change, best practice, fit for purpose, and the like. New Labour's citizenship and citizenship-education discourse is similarly characterized by a profusion of shifting and sometimes apparently contradictory terminology – for example, enthusiasm for multiculturalism and 'cosmopolitan citizenship' alongside exhortations to revivify 'shared English values' and foster 'modern patriotism'.[2]

The gyrations of this linguistic carousel can easily create the impression of a febrile obsession with presentation that conceals an underlying lack of consistency of purpose. Yet, for all the appearance of flux, as well as the existence of some real contradictions within the government's agenda, it is important to appreciate that there are in fact very important continuities in New Labour's approach to both to citizenship in general and also to the formation of citizens. These continuities, moreover, have often united the otherwise contending camps of Blairites and Brownites, as well turning out to have a good deal in common with certain Conservative approaches to citizenship that were influential in the mid-1980s. The key influences that produced this underlying coherence of approach can be explained by employing certain ideas developed by the British sociologist Basil Bernstein (see especially 2000, Ch. 4). This aspect of Bernstein's work focused on intensified efforts on the part of central state agencies in Britain since the late 1970s, to shape new kinds of 'official' identities – both adult citizen identities and *educational* identities. He argued that the 're-centred state', as he called it, was doing this in an attempt to adjust identities to changed political and economic circumstances, within the framework of the strongly neoliberal policy orientations adopted by successive Conservative and New Labour governments (ibid. pp. 66-8). Bernstein identified two contrasting forms of 'centred' identity:[3] 'retrospective' and 'prospective'. Here we shall discuss only the latter. Prospective identities, as the name implies, are primarily *future* oriented – seeking to reshape individuals as particular sorts of producers, consumers and citizens. Bernstein emphasized, however, that prospective identities can never be *purely* future-orientated. They are actually always shaped by '*recontextualising selected features of the past* to stabilise the future through engaging with contemporary change' (ibid. p. 68, my italics). This project of identity formation therefore involved a double task: reconfiguring the past as well as projecting a vision of the future that fitted this 'imaginary' past. Bernstein's brief sketch of the pedagogic identity that New Labour was seeking to project is worth quoting here in full:

> We can consider Blair's New Labour's entry into the official pedagogic arena as launching a new prospective identity; an identity drawing on resources of a different past (from either Old Labour or 'Thatcherism'). An amalgam of notions of community (really communities) and local responsibilities, to motivate and restore belonging in the cultural sphere, and a new participatory responsibility in the economic sphere. Thus the underlying collective of New Labour appears to be a recontextualising of the concept of the organic society.
>
> (ibid., p. 68)

Forming New Labour citizens

To illustrate the strong elements of continuity in New Labour's vision of its ideal citizenry, I shall briefly examine a number of statements by leading party figures, taken from across the decade 1996–2006. In each case, the statements carry the particular inflection of whatever overarching ideas were currently in vogue – community, stakeholding, respect, the Third Way, modern patriotism, and so on. But, as will become increasingly apparent, they also reveal the existence of a developing and coherent citizenship agenda.

- Several commentators have drawn attention to ways in which *communitarian* ideas, mediated mainly through the work (and in some respects the person) of American sociologist Amitai Etzioni (see 1993) fed into New Labour's citizenship discourse in the years immediately preceding the election victory of 1997 (e.g. Rose, 1999b; Delanty, 2003). Delanty, indeed, labels the dominant approach of the period precisely as 'governmental communitarianism' (ibid. p. 87). These emphases are clearly evident in Tony

Blair's 'Stakeholder Society' speech, originally delivered in Southwark Cathedral in 1996:

> ... people are more than separate economic actors competing in the market place of life. They are citizens of a community. We are social beings nurtured in families and communities and human only because we develop the moral power of personal responsibility for ourselves and each other ... Successful communities are about what people give as much as what they take, and any attempt to rebuild community for the modern age must assert that personal and social responsibility are not optional extras ... We owe duty to more than the self.
>
> (Blair, 1996, pp. 299–300)

- Although the government's respect agenda has been foregrounded mainly in the last three years, it is significant that it began to figure in the leadership's citizenship discourse a good deal earlier. Thus, in a carefully placed 'special article' in *The Observer* late in 2002, the vocabulary of respect is deployed (as it has been more recently) partly in generalized ways but also with a more direct reference to then impending reforms of criminal justice – a theme that was central to the Queen's Speech at the opening of parliament that same year.

> Respect is a simple notion. We know instinctively what it means. Respect for others ... Respect for neighbours; respect for the community that means caring about others. Respect for property which means not tolerating mindless vandalism, theft and graffiti. And self respect that means giving as well as taking.
> Respect is at the heart of a belief in society. It is what makes us a community, not merely a group of isolated individuals. It makes real a new contract between the citizen and the state, a contract that says that with rights and opportunities come responsibilities and obligations.
> We are putting behind us the narrow, selfish individualism of the late 1980s, but also the 1945 'big state' that wrongly believed it could solve every social problem. We are building an enabling state founded on the liberation of individual potential ... a modern civic society ... won't emerge simply through better laws ... we also need to revise the spirit of community and social cohesion.
>
> (Blair, 2002a)

- By 2004, welfare reform was beginning to be highlighted as a key element in setting out the leadership's third term vision. This was linked, in many speeches and articles of the period, to another new agenda – that of widening opportunity and raising rates of social mobility. In Blair's 2004 'welfare reform speech', (which sought to map out these third term priorities ahead of the writing of the election manifesto), a conception of citizenship is articulated in which the individual citizen is portrayed primarily as an aspirational user and chooser of flexibly delivered public services:

> Together, we and the British people have achieved much in the past few years ... But there are still too many denied opportunity. Too many hard-working families[4] in difficulty or distress ... Until Britain is a land of opportunity, we cannot rest.
> We have made real progress ... but ... for almost 30 years, social mobility has stayed relatively constant. I want to see social mobility, as it did in the decades after the war, rising once again as a dominant feature of British life. Now, the third term vision has to be to alter fundamentally the contract between the citizen and state at the heart of that 20th century settlement ... We need to move from mass production in what the state does. At the centre of the service or the structure has to be the individual. They have both the right and responsibility to take the opportunities offered and to shape the outcome. The role of government becomes to empower, not dictate. The nature of provision – public, private, voluntary sector – becomes less important than the delivery of the service the user wants.
> All this requires an inversion of the state/citizen relationship, with the citizen not at the bottom of the pyramid taking what is handed down; but at the top of it with power in their hands to get the service they want.
>
> (Blair, 2004)

- The theme of national identity was never very far away in the policy and citizenship discourse around the turn of the century – but it has received significantly greater prominence more recently, with Gordon Brown strongly supported by former Home Secretary David Blunkett, taking a leading role in highlighting the theme of British/English identity – and doing so, moreover, in ways that are linked directly to the figure of the active consumer-citizen depicted above. Thus Gordon Brown early in 2006, in an article symptomatically entitled 'We have renewed Britain, now we must champion it', wrote:

> With its focus on an enabling rather than centralising government, the British ideal of liberty gains new strength for this century as the empowerment of each individual, and the idea of responsibility comes alive in new forms of active civic engagement. Out go old assumptions of individuals passively receiving services; think instead of the responsible parent, the informed patient, the active citizen ... who – with an extension

of choice and voice, individual and collective – are taking control and driving change forward.

(Brown, 2006)

- Significantly, this aspirational British citizen is depicted as also increasingly active in community-centred voluntary endeavour. In a passage directly linking the consumer citizen with the contributing citizen, (and suggesting that such citizens can be collective as well as individual), Brown writes:

    This renewal of Britain springs from a welcome new culture of rising aspirations, is shaped by a reinvigorated sense of community and is being led by courageous local reformers – from environmentally responsible companies to path-breaking charities, and committed councillors.

    (Ibid.)

- This emphasis on civic renewal was not in fact a new development. In an interview with *Daily Telegraph* writers Charles Moore and George Jones, as early as February 2000, Brown, in his capacity of chancellor of the exchequer, was already talking up his plans to foster a 'new civic patriotism' in Britain:

    I want to propose a new financial foundation for civic renewal – a modern financial foundation for charitable, voluntary and community action … Active citizenship, call it little platoons, community work or the giving age. There is a spirit in our country where people do want to do more and I want to encourage it …

    (Moore and Jones, 2000, p. 4)

Communitarian 'active' citizenship

Rhetorical appeals to and celebrations of active citizenship recur throughout these and many other programmatic statements by those who have played a prominent role in shaping New Labour's citizenship agenda. Yet, as the above analysis already begins to suggest, the activism that these ostensibly active citizens are allowed turns out to be remarkably circumscribed. This is the case not only in terms of some of the effects of Labour's broader policy mix – which has radically disempowered certain major groups of citizens whilst simultaneously empowering and enriching others (a point which will be developed below) – it is also borne out when one turns to examine specific characterizations of the active citizen offered by a range of leading party figures.

An interesting case in point is the following account by David Blunkett, former secretary of state for education and then home secretary, of how his own approach to politics was influenced by the civic republican tradition.

> The 'civic republican' tradition of democratic thought has always been an important influence for me ... The tradition offers us a substantive account of the importance of community, in which duty and civic virtues play a strong and formative role. As such it is a tradition of thinking which rejects unfettered individualism and criticises the elevation of individual entitlements above the common values needed to sustain worthwhile and purposeful lives.
>
> (Blunkett, 2001a, p. 190)

These reflections do lucidly summarize one important strand within civic republicanism – one that focuses on community and is critical of radical neoliberal notions of the 'unencumbered self'. And this emphasis, of course, also conveniently allows New Labour's approach to citizenship to be portrayed as the antithesis of 'uncaring' Thatcherite economic individualism. What receives significantly less emphasis in Blunkett's account, however, are those elements of civic republicanism which are repeatedly highlighted by, for example, Sir Bernard Crick's writings on democracy and citizenship. More than once, Crick has found it necessary to insist that the centrally defining characteristic of civic republicanism is its emphasis on extensive and active political participation, and participation in high consequence as well as peripheral and local aspects of decision-making. Very significantly for our purposes, Crick has explicitly drawn attention to the fact that 'some leading politicians ... try to bridge the contradiction between the convenience of liberal democratic theory for the conduct of government and the more disruptive, unpredictable civic republican theory; they try to reduce, whether sincerely or cynically, citizenship to 'volunteering' (Crick, 2002, p. 19). Elsewhere, Crick has elaborated this stance and linked it more directly to education.

> I am an Aristotelian. I believe, with him, that preparation for political life in its broadest sense is part of education, and that freedom depends on widespread participation, not just good leadership. Some politicians are fond of praising volunteering amongst the young. But not all volunteering involves active citizenship. Some volunteers are just cannon fodder, and are never given the chance to influence the activity.
>
> (Crick and Green, 2002, p. 18)

More recently, both David Blunkett and Gordon Brown have been vigorously engaged in promoting a vision of active citizenship that is at once modern in the sense of buttressing New Labour's policies of individualism and choice, whilst also claiming to be 'rooted'. That is to say, the characteristics of the good citizen are portrayed as being rooted in an inheritance of what are represented as shared British traditions – particularly traditions of concern for community and of active involvement in voluntary endeavour within civil society. Blunkett, writing in March 2005, heaped lavish praise on various speeches and television programmes in which Gordon Brown had 'put forward a clear view of British values, stemming from both our history and our beliefs as a people', adding, in phraseology redolent of Stanley Baldwin,

> He made clear that an open, adapting society needs to be rooted, and Britain's roots are in the most solid foundation of all: a passion for liberty anchored in a sense of duty and commitment to tolerance. I share his view of a golden thread twining through our history of common endeavour in villages, towns and cities – of men and women united as neighbours and citizens by needs and common purposes, by a sense of duty and fair play. I believe Britishness is defined not on ethnic and exclusive grounds but through shared values, our history of tolerance, openness and internationalism and our commitment to democracy, and liberty, to civic duty and the public space. These values ... tell a national story open to all citizens ... It provides a shared framework for national and local identities ... My contribution to this debate has been an emphasis on the development of shared citizenship ... That is why I introduced citizenship and democracy into the school curriculum in England and Wales.
>
> (Blunkett, 2005)

Gordon Brown himself has, as we have seen, been promoting this kind of vision of the British active citizen since at least the beginning of the new century, often fondly citing his own origins in the type of community in which, since the nineteenth century, 'people had a view of society which started from the family and went outwards to the school, church and the local community, and then outwards again to the nation and the state' (op. cit., 2006). Indeed, Brown has had the temerity to offer an expanded version of this conception as a response to the radically critical analysis of democratic deficit and voter disenchantment in modern Britain vigorously set out by the Power Commission in 2006.[5]

> Having talked to young people shaping youth services, parents who run schools and under-five services, and social entrepreneurs transforming their communities, I am convinced that quietly and unannounced, Britain is seeing the rise of a new kind of citizen, involved in their neigh-bourhoods and now demanding the right to set the agenda ... This renewal of Britain ... is a 21st century expression of the enduring ideas that Britain gave the world – a commitment to liberty, a strong sense of civic duty, a belief in fairness ... This vision is light years away from the anti-state libertarianism beloved of some Tories – the bleak Tory definitions of liberty as self-interested individualism and social responsibility as a form of paternalism ... Britain is advancing liberty not as self-interested individualism but as empowerment.
>
> (Brown, op. cit., 2006)

It is fascinating to observe how closely this attempt to situate New Labour as the authentic voice of a rooted British tradition of active citizenship and community involvement, in contradistinction to selfish Conservative economic individualism, quite uncannily echoes speeches made by Sir Douglas Hurd when he was foreign secretary in Margaret Thatcher's second administration. The difference is, of course, that Hurd was claiming these self-same virtues for what he sought to portray as an authentically rooted British Conservatism.

> As we (the Conservative government) expand the scope for voluntary acts of citizenship, the left is still stuck with the bureaucratic definition of citizenship as something to which we are compelled by the state ... Underpinning our social policy are the traditions – the diffusion of power, civic obligation, and voluntary service – which are central to Conservative philosophy and rooted in British (particularly English) history ... So the shift of government policy is to shift power outwards, away from the corporatist battalions to the small platoons. Thus parents will get a bigger say in education; council tenants will get more control over the management of their estates ... What is new is the rediscovery that schemes based on this tradition are often more flexible and more effective than the bureaucratic plans drawn up on the Fabian principle.
>
> (Hurd, 1988)

Such discursive convergence speaks volumes. It suggests that we are in the presence of a serviceable and durable rhetoric which represents its favoured version of active citizenship – one that is basically neoliberal citizenship tempered by a social conscience – as more authentically rooted and British than, for example, those stronger forms of social democratic citizenship which more closely follow the European model. This then makes it possible to represent forms of citizenship which confer stronger social entitlements as being in some measure foreign to our traditions – despite their having been fought for and established by Britons (especially the British labour movement) over many decades. Moreover, the version of activism that is being promoted is, as we have seen, one that is prepared to encourage weak forms of local democracy complemented by volunteering, whilst systematically eroding citizens' powers of self-determination as well as democratic accountability in many other spheres. Under successive Tory and New Labour administrations since 1979, what has arguably been most salient in the sphere of citizenship reform has been the use of the powers of 'the small but strong state' (Gamble, 1983) to erode and in some respects dismantle 'Marshallian' social citizenship[6] and also to radically disempower those sources of organized democratic influence, such as local government, the trade unions and the professions, which once had some capacity to seriously challenge the dominant neoliberal model and to act as a counterbalance to the dominance of the centralized state. The highly selective moralism[7] that has accompanied this shift to more conditional and attenuated forms of citizenship, employs a species of neo-communitarian rhetoric which, among other things, seeks to paper over the growing divisions in British society by appeals to supposed common origins and historically rooted values. However, as Gerard Delanty has argued,

> Governmental communitarianism is often a superficial politics of legitimacy. The appeal to community can be easily compatible with many different political positions, ranging from the right to the left. It is almost invariably another word for citizenship, but an aspect of citizenship that stresses less the entitled citizen than the dutiful citizen. (Delanty, op. cit., p. 90)

Citizenship in post-democratic Britain

An impressive range of political scientists, as well as a number of journalists and some politicians, have discerned in modern Britain evidence of a serious and growing democratic deficit, whose counterpart is increasing domination by closely interlinked elites. Various striking metaphors have been offered as images of these trends. Thus, Colin Crouch speaks of a parabola of waxing and then waning democratic influence, contending that Britain is now moving steadily away from the highpoint of more 'maximal' institutionalisation of effective democracy: 'politics and government are increasingly slipping back into the control of privileged elites in the manner characteristic of pre-democratic times; and ... one major consequence of this process is the growing impotence of egalitarian causes' (2004, p. 6). David Marquand, similarly, has spoken of 'a downward curve ... at the start of the twenty-first century, there are no signs that the institutions, values and practices of the public domain are about to end the long retreat that began in the 1970s' (2004a, p. 126). Hywel Williams, in a trenchant polemic, goes even further: 'Britain's power elites illustrate the extent to which modern democracies – when it comes to the practicality of power – are governed by an iron law of oligarchy' (2006, p. 12). And finally, as we have seen, the Power Commission (2006) and its chair, Dame Helena Kennedy, also see British citizens as having been 'evicted from decision-making' in a world in which 'politics and government are increasingly in the hands of privileged elites' (see Note 5).

Manifestly, it is not possible to summarize here, let alone evaluate, the arguments and evidence marshalled by these writers to support their claims that Britain is moving towards what Colin Crouch has termed post-democracy (Crouch, 2004). Two points, however, are of decisive importance. The first is that there was nothing inevitable about this remarkable shift of power to elite groups and to central government and its agencies, along with the regimes of privatization, quasi-marketization, managerialization, target-setting and audit culture that accompanied it. This point is vital because many within government and the new elites are prone to represent such change precisely as if there was and is no alternative. In particular, they repeatedly portray successive concessions to neoliberalism as unavoidable if the nation's economy, education system, and welfare services are to be modernized in the ways required to maintain national competitiveness in a globalizing world. Against such claims, writers like Marquand have drawn attention to the relatively autonomous part played by politics and by key politicians in using Britain's monarchical state to deliberately impose change in these directions. Under Thatcher 'the core executive at the heart of the state set itself, quite deliberately, to force the public services and the professionals who staffed them into a market mould' (Marquand, 2004b, p. 59, and see also Chapter 5 of this volume for a more extensive discussion of the disempowerment of the professions). What is even worse, Marquand contends, is that since the Thatcher years, New Labour has 'pushed marketization and privatisation forward at least as zealously ... narrowing the frontiers of the public domain in the process' (2004a, p. 118).

The second key point that needs to be emphasized concerns the way economic and political events are narrated. Colin Hay has highlighted the significance of this issue, against both populist representations that 'there is no alternative' and, in relation to much more sophisticated theories of the supposed 'tendential' characteristics of post-Fordist capitalism, like those of Cerny (1997) and Jessop (2002). Hay, for example, draws attention to an important strand in Jessop's own argument – that 'responses are not made to crises *per se* but to their often politically motivated construction *as* crises' (Hay, 2004, p. 44). Moreover, both Hay and Marquand have independently argued that a key outcome of New Labour's endorsing rather than challenging such narrations has been the entrenchment of a new common sense both among political elites and more widely – something the Tories could never have accomplished on their own (Hay, 1999). As Marquand remarks,

> Neo-liberal political economy has become part of the mental furniture of the political elite – in part, of course, because it runs with the grain of the world's capital markets and echoes the assumptions of the institutions of global economic governance; in part because many, if not most, of the institutions and practices which used to protect the public domain from market incursions, were destroyed in the Thatcher and Major years. Like their predecessors, Blair and his ministers have internalised the axioms of the capitalist renaissance of our time: privatisation, de-regulation, free trade, low taxation, budgetary orthodoxy. These define the limits within which their domestic policies are framed. When they say they are new, they mean that ... the new global economic order is an iron cage, to which all governments and all societies must adapt; and that the hyper-individualistic Anglo-American version of capitalism offers the only route to adaptation.
>
> (Marquand, 2004a, p. 118)

Insofar as the above analysis is persuasive, the implications for what might be termed 'really active citizenship'[8] appear discouraging. Marquand has drawn particular attention here to the populist character of both Thatcherite Conservatism and Blairite New Labour, observing that 'Populist centralism

has no place for the civic ideal of open debate and public engagement ...
Citizenship is hollowed out. The people are passive, not active – consumers
of public policy, not participants in shaping it' (Ibid., p. 128).

In similar vein, Colin Crouch sees the lower ranks of contemporary
white-collar workers in Britain, who form part of what he calls 'the middle
mass', as passive and as to a very considerable extent, relating to politics
in the ways post-democracy demands. He outlines New Labour's attempts
to assimilate them to a condition in which they are supposed to have

> ... no discontents except with the quality of the public services ...
> They are encouraged to seek no means of social improvement other
> than for themselves and their children obediently to climb the career
> ladders established by business elites. From this follows the obsessive
> concern of contemporary politics with education.
>
> (Crouch, 2000, p. 42)

Promoting respect or corroding character?

There is probably no single area where the contradictions in which New
Labour has enmeshed itself are more evident, or go deeper, than in relation
to its respect agenda.[9] There is not space here to examine this agenda in
depth. But it is clear that it encompasses at one level, reiterated moralistic
exhortation, and at another, hard-nosed policies targeted particularly at
recalcitrant 'disrespectful' individuals whose anti-social behaviour is increasingly being dealt with by the imposition of ASBOs (Anti-Social Behaviour
Orders) and similar technologies of community surveillance. As far as the
tough end of this spectrum is concerned, it is, of course, important that
critics of these aspects of the respect agenda should neither minimize the real
disruption caused by persistent anti-social behaviour (especially in some of
the nation's most disadvantaged inner cities and housing estates), nor
romanticize those involved in it, for example by depicting them as crypto-
class-warriors (or race-warriors) in revolt against new forms of state authoritarianism. But, accepting these caveats, criticism is nevertheless called for.

One key element of the respect rhetoric is its shifting of the demand for
greater social responsibility onto individuals, especially though by no means
only, onto those receiving welfare benefits. Thus, in Tony Blair's 2002 'My
vision for Britain' speech cited above, there is to be found, first, a characteristically false historical polarization (see Chapter 6 of this book for other
examples) that counterposes the 'new emphasis on individual responsibility'
to the 'permissiveness' allegedly fostered by of an earlier generation of
liberal social democrats, who are held responsible for the corrosion of
individual responsibility.

> Social democrats in Britain and the US who held a liberal view of the
> 'permissive society' divorced fairness from personal responsibility. They
> believed that the state had an unconditional obligation to provide

welfare and security. The logic was that the individual owed nothing in return. By the early 1970s this language of rights was corroding civic duty and undermining the fight-back against crime and social decay.

(Blair, 2002a)

Later in the same speech, the essence of what is to be New Labour's 'social contract with the disadvantaged' is spelled out. It is, with breathtaking oversimplification, offered as an exchange of equivalents: individual responsibility for individual opportunity:

> *Our commitment to equalising opportunity* has ... meant a concerted effort to support and sustain poorer families under pressure. The life chances of children are hugely influenced by their earliest experiences, which is why access to post-natal support, parenting classes and early years provision are so important *in a fair society.*
> *With these new opportunities come (sic) responsibility.* The street crime initiative, for example, has been one of the most successful partnerships between government and the police in living memory. But the truth is people don't feel more secure ... So this autumn we will focus on tackling these problems ... We are pursuing radical reform of the Criminal Justice System, tackling anti-social behaviour and restoring social cohesion to fragmented communities ... But a modern civic society, underpinned by reformed public services and an active welfare state won't emerge simply through better laws, though enforcement of obligations, sanctions and more police ... *We also need to revive the spirit of community and social cohesion* ...

(Ibid., my italics)

The key rhetorical move here is, of course, to position New Labour as radically different from both Old Labour and neoliberal Conservatism because it alone has now re-connected fairness with individual responsibility, in a pact for social cohesion that all reasonable citizens, including the least advantaged, have a clear obligation to support. Just how unequal this supposed exchange of equivalents (responsibility for opportunity) really remains has, hopefully, been sufficiently highlighted in the previous chapter – and we will not discuss it further here.

At the centre of the effort to 'revive the spirit of community and social cohesion' has, of course, been New Labour's rediscovery of civil society as the sphere for active citizen involvement. Civil society is the pre-eminent domain in which people are now being encouraged to become 'social entrepreneurs',[10] to involve themselves in regenerating their own run-down communities, are exhorted to generate trust by building social capital (Putnam, 1995, 2003), and to engage in acts of philanthropy. This 'renewal of civil society' is, as we have seen, also portrayed by leading New Labour figures, as involving a return to authentically British traditions of 'bottom-up' participatory democracy. Yet, as the various critiques reviewed in the previous section so clearly show, this so-called renewal of civil society is more accurately seen as New Labour setting out to reinvent civil society in its own image. This modernized version, however, is emphatically not the old civil society of genuinely autonomous and powerful voluntary organizations, including trade unions and independent professions, involved as much in political contestation as in cooperation with government agendas. Instead, the new civil society is above all a managed sphere – within which, it is fondly imagined, civility, a sense of community, values of personal responsibility, and mutual respect can all be revived. Here then, is the sphere where the harm done by both Sixties permissiveness and Thatcherite selfish individualism – the corroding of character and the avoidance of personal responsibility – can, supposedly, begin to be reversed.

The hollowness of this conception becomes strikingly evident once we take into account the fact that the majority of citizens, women almost as much as men, spend most of their time in the workplace rather than in civil society. And it is in the disjuncture between workplace realities and the imaginary community of civil society, that the essential hollowness of government claims about building trust and respect becomes so evident. There is no need to elaborate on the key arguments here. Some will be discussed in more detail in subsequent chapters. But the required reading in this area of respect and trust, is a series of studies by the distinguished American sociologist Richard Sennett and his co-workers, including *The Corrosion of Character* (1998), *Respect* (2003 and 2005) and *The Culture of the New Capitalism* (2006a) – as well as Onora O'Neill's *A Question of Trust* (2002). Two points are essential. The first is that, as Sennett sees it, corporate bureaucracies in both the private and public sectors (though to differing degrees), have increasingly given up on any idea that they owe long-term responsibilities let alone obligations to their employees. The rationale (or alibi) is that in a globalizing world, restructuring and flexibilization are unavoidable. Only lean organizations with flat management hierarchies that outsource much of their work, and take on and shed labour as market circumstances dictate, can remain competitive in a world of global competition. But for middle-range workers in particular, Sennett argues, this creates a world of permanent insecurity, uncertainty, and short-termism. Moreover, in this brave new organizational world, it is increasingly difficult for employees to sustain any coherent belief in their work as a meaningful career, or of the workplace as an arena where commitment to the organization commands any respect, or of work as a sphere in which experience is valued.

The second and paradoxical key point, however, is that it is precisely within such radically transformed work contexts that there has emerged a pervasive mystificatory discourse that highlights the importance of everybody working together in teams, of everyone taking responsibility for quality, and of coordination by team leaders who are enablers rather than authority figures. In pursuit of such team building, organizations devote substantial budgets to training programmes and away days, for staff at all levels. These constitute the new initiation and commitment-building rituals of the supposedly post-Fordist workplace. However, drawing on their extensive interviews with various groups of workers in the USA and Britain over the last twenty years or so, Sennett and his colleagues reveal a radically different reality. At its core are working relationships characterized by pseudo-mutuality, the essence of which is falsity.[11] Pseudo-mutuality involves systematic obfuscation of the true character of interpersonal relationships, especially power relationships. It puts people in a double-bind situation in which they cannot voice what they really feel because those with power repeatedly tell them that they feel something different. People are told they are valued, that a firm's most precious asset is its people. But they are told this by organizations that are all too evidently manipulating and exploiting them, and that are prepared to lose people at a moment's notice (whether as a result of restructuring, takeover, changes in market conditions, or whatever).

Sennett discusses the emergence in such workplaces of the team leader – a figure who typically denies that he/she is the boss or that how well the team performs is their responsibility, as leader. Instead, team leaders characteristically disavow responsibility and hide their power behind a 'new-speak' of inclusiveness: 'all members of the team are in this together'; 'we need to pull together as a group', and so on. Another aspect of the situation is that the brief life expectancy of many of these teams, (before their members are dispersed and reconstituted into new teams to tackle whatever happens to be the next task), requires workers to develop what Sennett calls 'an instant ability to work well with a shifting cast of characters' (1998, p. 110) and to maintain a prudent distance from deep or longer-term loyalties to other workers. These things also lead employees to hide behind what Gideon Kunda calls 'masks of cooperation' and to engage in 'deep acting': '"How interesting ... What I hear you saying is ... How could we do this better?"' (ibid., p. 112, and Kunda, 1992). In many organizations, practices of this kind are hegemonized by an overarching 'culture of cooperation' typically mediated by falsely 'egalitarian symbols' (Graham, in Sennett, 1998, p. 112). On this analysis then, the sphere of employment has, for increasing numbers of citizens, become a domain of increasingly inauthentic relationships, where rhetorics of respect and cooperation thinly conceal situations that actually involve intensified work demands, new 'soft' forms of coercion (suggesting someone is not a team player), and covert forms of manipulation.

The contradiction in which New Labour is caught is all too obvious. New Labour is itself one of the main instigators and promoters of these changes. Indeed, during his sojourn in Britain in 2006, Sennett actually labelled these kinds of changes as 'the new labour syndrome: bureaucratic reform for its own sake' (2006b). Pointing out that the flexible firm and the 'short, flat organization' have, under New Labour, increasingly become models both for the organization of public institutions and the delivery of welfare services (2006a p. 185), Sennett goes on to attack the shallowness and inadequacy of the policies that have, in Britain, the USA and elsewhere, shifted responsibility for welfare provision away from public employees towards community organizations and voluntary provision within civil society. He points out that

Volunteering is a poor remedy for binding strangers together, or dealing with social complexities. It lacks what might be called an architecture of sympathy – that is, a progressive movement up from identifying with individuals one knows to individuals one doesn't know ... Saying this is not to denigrate volunteers, but rather to criticise the idealisation of these "friends" when something other than friendship is required ... In the same measure that welfare reformers have celebrated the local volunteers, they have attacked public service workers – and indeed the very ethos of public service. *For the last quarter of a century, the honour of public service has been slighted.*

(2006a p. 200, my italics)

New Labour is then, mired in contradiction. Its preachy rhetoric tells people that its policies are restoring respect – and that the recalcitrant few will be brought into the fold by a combination of being given the social skills they lack, the introduction of parenting classes and the like, and, if all else fails, by zero tolerance, ASBOS and summary justice. On the other hand, the basic thrust of New Labour's core modernizing agenda, in the economy and the workplace, is actually promoting a set of practices that deeply and systemically undermine real respect and real valuing of individuals. As Sennett has so persuasively argued, this – the sphere of 'the personal consequences of work' (1998) – is where the real 'corrosion of character' is occurring. What New Labour has helped bring into existence is a world in which it is actually increasingly difficult for individuals to find meaning or purposes in their working lives. It is, for example, a sphere in which growing numbers of employees find it hard to fashion a coherent narrative of their working lives in which old-fashioned virtues like honesty, effort, loyalty and commitment count for something. Instead, they find themselves increasingly condemned to live in a world of fragmented meaning, of ever-shifting institutional goals and purposes, of superficial and segmental relationships with co-workers, of distrustful relationships with their superiors, and, as a final mark of such disrespect, managerial and political discourses that misrepresent these new realities as their opposites: as empowerment, autonomy, consultation, teamwork.

Some implications for citizenship education

Perhaps education can help resolve some of these tensions? After all, one of New Labour's undeniable achievements is, after decades of indecision by successive governments (see Beck, 2003a, pp. 158–60), to have introduced citizenship education as a statutorily required element of the national curriculum in England.[12] This has certainly opened up a potential space in which really active citizenship or at least some renewal of wider interest and involvement in politics might be encouraged. And there are other positive signs. In the first place, mainstream politicians themselves find it ever harder not to recognize that the political class is held in depressingly low esteem by the public at large. Many of them also acknowledge the evidence of growing disenchantment with mainstream politics, especially among younger groups of voters, which is reflected, for example, in depressingly low turnouts in elections. It was, indeed, evidence of this kind, and growing concern about such apathy and alienation, that led many though not all members of the Labour cabinet in the late 1990s to support the introduction of statutory citizenship education. A further indicator that offers at least some grounds for optimism is the clear evidence that despite this widespread disen-chantment with official politics, very many British citizens of all ages do care intensely about specific political issues. Furthermore, large numbers of individuals continue to be actively involved, sometimes passionately, in a huge range of single-issue causes – and some of the best citizenship education work done in schools is linked to student involvement in activities of these kinds.

Yet it remains hard to be optimistic about the prospects of citizenship education significantly changing attitudes and behaviour in the direction of greater democratic involvement, or even of doing very much to raise levels of political literacy. In the space available, it will only be possible to indicate a few of the most important reasons why this may prove to be the case. One key problem is succinctly highlighted by Davies, Gorard and McGuinn in a recent paper about citizenship education and 'character education':[13]

> Both citizenship education and character education ... emerge from a perception of crisis (and make use of that perception in order to gain curricular footholds), have supporters who employ highly ambitious rhetoric and enjoy high status support, *while experi-encing low status in practice* ...
>
> (2005, p. 342, my italics)

The problem of the low status of such areas within the wider curriculum, a marginality which also includes PSHE (personal, social and health education), is well documented. To take just one example, Whitty, Aggleton and Rowe (2002) have discussed the problems of effectively implementing the teaching of what were known as cross-curricular themes (one of which was citizenship) within the English national curriculum during the 1990s. Their research indicated that neither separate PSHE lessons nor a 'perme-ation' approach of teaching citizenship through other areas of the curriculum enabled pupils to make effective connections between their everyday experience and formal curriculum knowledge. A key stumbling block to students achieving any significant holistic political understanding, let alone an understanding that was linked meaningfully to their everyday lives, was the overall structuring of the secondary school curriculum as a set of high status academic subjects, each taught by specialist teachers who were primarily committed to raising standards in their own subject area.

Basil Bernstein calls such a curriculum a 'collection code' (see for example, Bernstein, 2000, pp. 10–11) – a form of curricular organization now powerfully reinforced by the national curriculum, especially in the case of academically successful pupils. Whitty et al. (op. cit.) also suggested that lack of clear definition of what PSHE is supposed to be exacerbated the problems of it being regarded as a serious subject. Subsequent reforms of the national curriculum, as well as the publication of high stakes school performance data in the years since this research was conducted, seem likely to have further reinforced in the minds of many students and parents the belief that the curriculum remains divided into 'important subjects' and those more 'peripheral' areas like citizenship, that seem condemned, not least because of the government's own policy emphases, to be seen as 'not serious subjects'.

Of course it is important to acknowledge here that the introduction of citizenship as a foundation subject has allowed some schools and teachers to develop impressively challenging approaches to citizenship education – approaches that encourage students to think seriously about issues of social justice and injustice, equip them to question received opinion, and to develop these capacities in relation to a range of issues from the local to the global level. Moreover, a range of high quality teaching and learning material is available from the QCA and many citizenship education organizations. Very recently, the publication of the 'Ajegbo Report' (Qualifications and Curriculum Authority, 2007d) and the revisions to the citizenship programmes of study as part of the QCA's Secondary Curriculum Review, have provided further stimulus to enhancing good practice in this area (see the final sections of Chapters 7 and 8 in this book for more detailed discussion of these matters). Critical approaches to citizenship like these, however, run the risk of becoming marginalized insofar as they are located in a kind of no man's land between two significantly more potent influences. On the one side, as described above, there are the pressures that, especially for academically successful students, create close identifications with particular specialist subjects as the prime source of their educational identities. For them, curricular activities that are not grounded in a single important discipline, that are non-examined, that are often taught by non-specialists, and that have no apparent instrumental pay-off, can easily be perceived as of marginal importance even in those cases where they may be seen as interesting. On the other hand, for the growing number of students whose identities are being increasingly shaped by the wide range of vocational curricula that have mushroomed in many state secondary schools and colleges since the 1993 Dearing Report, critical approaches to citizenship education may not be developed, partly (and ironically) because they may be seen as too academic for such students, and on the other hand (again) because they have little apparent instrumental value. Furthermore, as will be argued in the final section of Chapter 7 of this book, certain very recent developments in 'education for economic well-being' and 'enterprise education' seem to almost completely ignore citizenship and citizenship education.

Such considerations, of course, might seem to suggest that although in many schools citizenship education may be unlikely to foster critical political awareness or really active citizenship, it may, for these very same reasons, prove no more effective in promoting governmental communitarianism (Delanty, op. cit.). Such a conclusion, however, could prove to be mistaken – not least because in this regard, the role of the hidden curriculum may be of decisive significance. Precisely because the overt curriculum of citizenship education may have limited impact, the role of extra-curricular influences may prove correspondingly stronger. The relevant hidden-curricular influences here include the following: the whole apparatus of subject hierarchies; pressures in schools to maximise examination success; tacit knowledge about the relative status of different universities and the kinds of activities (such as internships and the right kind of gap years) that count in obtaining access to higher status institutions (see Power et al., 2003; Reay et al., 2005); and finally, the growing effort to form young people into 'entrepreneurial citizens' who are encouraged to regard investment in their own education as both an opportunity and a responsibility (see Ahier et al., 2003, and Chapter 7 in this volume).

Beyond all this, and of possibly even greater significance, may be the pervasive instrumentalism embodied in the management culture of many secondary schools and colleges. Bernstein highlighted here the tension between a formal curriculum of mainly academic subjects (whose hidden curriculum is, in part, the value of knowledge for its own sake), and various forms of instrumentalism arising from quasi-marketization and managerialization now pervasive in education.

> The management structure has become the device for creating an entrepreneurial competitive culture. The latter is responsible for criteria informing senior administrative appointments and the engaging or hiring of specialised staff to promote the effectiveness of this culture. Thus there is a dislocation between the culture of pedagogic discourse and the management culture. The culture of the pedagogic discourse … is *retrospective*, based on a past narrative of the dominance and significance of disciplines, whereas that of the management structure is *prospective*, pointing to the new entrepreneurialism and its instrumentalities … The emphasis on the performance of students and the steps taken to increase and maintain performance for the survival of the institution is likely to facilitate a state-promoted instrumentality. The intrinsic value of knowledge may well be eroded even though the collection code of the curriculum appears to support such a value.
>
> (Bernstein, 2000, p. 61)

It is of course true that we have as yet very little knowledge of the ways in which such influences *are* shaping students' identities and outlooks, let alone about the extent to which different approaches to citizenship education may either reinforce or work against such tendencies. But the combination of state-promoted and institutionally embedded instrumentalities that now structures most young people's educational experience, seems calculated to promote just those more highly individualistic, aspirational, and entrepreneurial conceptions of the self that are the core of the identity of New Labour's new model citizen.

And depressingly, these are no the only influences that threaten to limit the development of critical approaches to citizenship education. There is a very real possibility that many schools will choose to structure their citizenship work around relatively uncritical and de-politicized forms of community involvement and volunteering. Here, and despite Bernard Crick's own championing of critical democratic activism (see above), the dominant legacy of the Crick Report (Advisory Group on Citizenship, 1998) and perhaps even more of the current citizenship programmes of study,[14] could in many cases be to encourage these more anodyne approaches. For example, although paragraph 2.5 of the Crick Report began relatively uncontroversially: 'We firmly believe that volunteering and community involvement are necessary conditions of civil society and democracy. Preparation for these, at the very least, should be an explicit part of education … ' it continued, however, in an apparently more prescriptive vein that some have read as directly endorsing government policy: 'This is especially important at a time when government is attempting a shift of emphasis between, on the one hand, state welfare provision and responsibility, and, on the other, community and individual responsibility.' (Advisory Group on Citizenship, 1998, p. 10)

Sociologists Gamarnikow and Green contend that such statements could easily encourage forms of education that underwrite a specific political policy thrust in which

> Marshall's social citizenship as a site for welfare *rights* disappears, and its place is now occupied by duties of volunteering and community development. The Crick Report constructs the Third Way citizen whose individual and civic responsibility enables the Third Way state to provide opportunities rather than services …
>
> (2000, p. 106)

Even if this judgement could be construed as somewhat unfair to Crick himself, it clearly illustrates how difficult it may be to develop forms of citizenship education that are genuinely impartial, or that enable students to become critically aware of some of the most significant political and ideological forces now shaping their lives and their futures. Community involvement and community service can so easily be seen as politically innocent – and very often they are. But a basically apolitical approach to citizenship education, or even an approach which merely emphasizes information (in the style of old-fashioned civics), arguably runs the risk of implicitly endorsing just those kinds of educational agendas which deceptively claim to have transcended ideology or to have gone beyond left and right (Fukuyama, 1992; Giddens, 1994). As Ahier et al. have commented

> ... it seems more than plausible ... that (some) schools will have ... a
> natural affinity with those approaches ... which subtly reinforce
> circumscribed forms of localised 'active' citizenship while fighting
> shy of more fundamental and more controversial political debates
> focused on ... competing views of ... citizenship and citizenship rights
> ... In such a context, the absence (in Britain) of a strong *language* and
> consciousness of citizenship may further reinforce such convenient
> myopia.
>
> (Ahier, Beck and Moore, 2003, p. 170, my italics)

It is to this issue of language that I wish finally to turn. Ahier et al., in
common with many other commentators such as Turner (1990),
emphasize that historically, the British have not really thought of
themselves as citizens and that, partly as cause and partly as effect, there
is no extensive shared language of citizenship in terms of which people
readily conceptualize their relationship to the state, society and the wider
world. New Labour has clearly sought to change this situation at least in
some respects, both through the kinds of political interventions discussed
above and through its promotion of citizenship education. However, a
growing number of commentators have contended that far from
enhancing the linguistic and communicative resources conducive to really
active citizenship and democratic engagement, the overall effect of
government policies in the last three decades, has been in various ways
to degrade and distort the ways in which political issues are presented and
discussed.

* The most widely remarked phenomenon here is the way in which
  the discourse of market-managerialism has insidiously and perva-
  sively displaced simpler, more direct, and less distorting ways of
  speaking and thinking. In relation to the public services and the
  work of professionals for example, Marquand has pointed out that
  'the language of service and citizenship was subtly transformed into
  a language of buyers and sellers ... funding cuts became efficiency
  gains ... and departmental chairmen became line managers' (2004b
  p. 59). Ross McKibbin claims that this language, which was first
  devised in business schools then taken over by government, 'now
  infests all our institutions' – adding the significant rider that
  although this 'language might be laughable[15] ... it is now shared
  by all who command ... and is one way they wield power' (2005,
  p. 6).
* The connection between discourse and power is highlighted by
  Richard Pring – particularly in relation to the ways this new
  language has permeated education itself and not merely its organizational forms:

> More fundamentally, language changes our understanding of
> that which is to be controlled. It shifts the moral framework of

liberal education to a business framework of vocational training. But education (properly understood) is not that sort of thing. It is about the formation of persons ... However ... one cannot avoid the moral language through which the exploration of one's humanity is conducted – which makes the language of business, ideal for social control, an impoverished one for education ...

(Pring, 1995, p. 180)

- Colin Crouch has drawn attention to ways in which the increasing domination of corporate elites and the profit motive, across both the private and the public domains, has significantly damaged the quality of political discussion and presentation within the news media.

    The power of ... the media industry is ... involved directly in reductions of choice and the debasement of political language and communication which are important components of the poor health of democracy ... The press and, increasingly, radio and television are part of the commercial sector of society – rather than, say, the charitable or education sectors, as they might well have been. This means that news broadcasts and all other polit-ically relevant communications need to be modelled on a certain form of the idea of a marketable product. The attention of the reader, listener or viewer has to be grabbed quickly if one media firm is to take custom from another. This prioritizes extreme simplification and sensationalization, which in turn degrade the quality of political discussion and reduce the competence of citizens ... Political actors themselves are then forced into the same mode if they are to retain some control over how they formulate their own utterances ... The headline was the father of the soundbite.

    (Crouch, 2004, pp. 46–7)

- Finally, there are more directly linguistic modes of over-simplifi-cation and distortion of meaning that are associated the language of market-managerialism and the wider neoliberal discourse in which it is embedded. This is nowhere more evident and more ironic than when this allegedly neutral language is employed in calls for greater 'transparency' and 'accountability' (see McKibbin, op. cit.). At a more sophisticated level of linguistic analysis, sociolinguist Ruqaiya Hasan uses the term 'glibspeak' to refer to certain instances of what sociolinguists call 'resemantization', where 'a word and its meaning are ... divorced from each other so that a new meaning can be attached to the word'. Glibspeak, however, involves a further strategy, 'namely, *subverting meaning*' (Hasan, 2006, pp. 214–5). It is not possible here to recapitulate Hasan's complex argument, but she illustrates the idea by reference to the term 'the *liberalization* of trade'. She points out that the positive valency of normal uses of liberalization carries over to this very different economic usage. It not only creates a feel good impression but also functions to disguise the fact that these particular kinds of liberalization are controversial, because, by certain criteria, they embody the very opposite of the widening of freedoms that liberalization normally implies. As Madely puts it: 'The WTO's "free-trade" philosophy effectively *reduces the freedom of governments* to buy locally produced materials or to use local labour' (Madely, 2000, cited in Hasan op. cit., my italics).

Taken together, this evidence of the narrowing and distortion of the linguistic means of thinking seriously and communicating effectively about political issues, points to a further obstacle, though hopefully not a wholly insuperable one, to developing the kinds of citizenship education we as a society need if education is to play any significant part in slowing the decline towards post-democracy. But, to reiterate, the auguries are not good.

Part II

'MODERNIZING' EDUCATION AND THE PROFESSIONS

Chapter 4

MAKEOVER OR TAKEOVER? THE STRANGE DEATH OF EDUCATIONAL AUTONOMY IN NEOLIBERAL ENGLAND

1997: A Merry Christmas from the Teacher Training Agency

No self-respecting quango would be complete without its corporate Christmas card. The 1997 seasonal offering from the Teacher Training Agency was a particularly revealing example of the genre. On the front was the teacher recruitment poster which the Agency had been running for several months in national newspapers and in cinemas throughout the land, carrying the slogan 'No-one forgets a good teacher' – but here surrounded by a border of stylized snowflakes. Above this were six images of enthusiastic teachers – all wholly absorbed in their teaching and all clearly deriving great satisfaction from it.[1] On the back, the card carried the TTA's logo – seasonally transformed into a Christmas pudding topped by a sprig of holly. Inside, the card was blank save for the signatures of Clive Booth the TTA's newly appointed chairman and of Anthea Millett its chief executive. The semiotic of this text is intriguing. Right down to the seasonally adjusted logo, it was as wholly 'on message', as the teachers it depicted were 'on task'. The Christmas cheer on offer was the thoroughly secular vision of national economic salvation achieved through raising educational standards by following government prescriptions. More significantly, the deep structure of its message was indicative of weakened boundaries: on the one side government, its policy priorities and the educational agencies inherited from the previous Conservative administration, all now increasingly oriented to a unified set of purposes and targets, and on the other, teachers, schools, and teacher training institutions all increasingly subordinated to the dictates of these agencies. Against this background, the TTA's Christmas card could be read as epitomizing Tony Blair's election campaign declaration that New Labour's key priority would be 'education, education, and education'. But, as some recipients of this message may have felt, once education has become so thoroughly subordinated to such instrumental purposes and agencies, what may be left of education itself? Read in this light, the card may portend not merely a fashionable makeover of education in a modernized New Labour image but rather, a far more significant and insidious process of takeover in which any significantly independent set of educational values may be increasingly at risk.

Educational autonomy and neoliberal modes of educational governance

It is, of course, now a commonplace that the autonomy of educational institutions in the UK – from the highest status universities right through to the
smallest primary schools – has, over the last quarter century or so, been very
significantly weakened as a result of the radical restructuring initiated in the
Thatcher years and continued by subsequent Conservative governments.
Many commentators have employed vivid military metaphors to describe
what happened. Thus Perry Anderson, writing in 1990, spoke of a climate
of growing 'government hostility and intimidation – a campaign of harassment
described (in private) by a Ministerial spokesman with brutal candour as "a
kulturkampf against British universities"' (Anderson, 1990, p. 42). Spokesmen
of the New Right themselves have depicted the onslaught in similar terms.
Oliver Letwin, for example, described the New Right attack on various
groups of organized professionals as follows: 'In each case, what was being
"taken on" was an establishment which was thought to constitute a "cosy
cartel", a source of complacency, a centre of defeatism, an obstacle to vigour
...' (Letwin, 1992, p. 41).

Such analyses have focused primarily at the level of changing modalities of
institutional control – resulting from various combinations of marketization
and central government dirigisme. They have, for example, drawn attention
to the paradox that Thatcherism combined two philosophically contradictory agendas, those of neoliberalism and neo-conservatism, in a manner
that was, nevertheless, extremely potent in undercutting effective resistance
from those seeking to defend professional autonomy – whether on the basis
of appeals to academic freedom within higher education, or in terms of the
rights of teachers' organizations to be consulted about curriculum reform, or
with reference to the pedagogic autonomy of individual classroom teachers
(see, for example, Jones, 1989; Whitty, 1990). Similar processes relating to
the changing governance of education and other public sector institutions
have, of course, been identified in many other countries (see, for example,
Dale, 1997; Avis, 1996b) – notably, strategies framed within what Whitty has
called 'that broader project to create the free economy and the strong state'
(Whitty, 1997, p. 302).

The British sociologist Basil Bernstein has, in some of his recent writings,
provided an account of these changes that, while overlapping the institutional
analyses already discussed, contains a significantly different focus. This
difference of orientation derives primarily from the fact that Bernstein's
chief intellectual preoccupation has always been with the analysis of the structures and processes that lie at the very heart of education – with pedagogy
itself and the structuring of pedagogic institutions and discourses. As Paul
Atkinson has recently noted, one of Bernstein's perennial complaints about
the sociology of education over the last forty years has been that, in the main,
it has tended to treat education primarily as 'a site for the discussion of race,
class and gender', regarding pedagogy itself merely as a relay – 'a transparent
or neutral "ether" carrying messages without having any substance of its
own' (Atkinson, 1997, pp. 117–18). Bernstein himself, however, has consis-

tently sought to render this ether (or at least its hidden structure) visible and intelligible.[2] It can be argued that policy sociology has, somewhat similarly, focused upon educational change as, in the main, the effect of wider political and economic events.

A concern with boundaries pervades Bernstein's writing. Strong boundaries create and sustain strong insulations: their implicit rule is 'things must be kept apart'. For this reason, strong boundaries carry the potential to create clear-cut categories and unambiguous identities; furthermore they provide insulations within which both autonomy and certain kinds of privacy can be established and sustained. Strong boundaries also commonly demarcate the domain of the sacred and separate it decisively from the mundane. In pre-modern societies, the sacred was, of course, primarily the province of religion. But Bernstein, drawing his inspiration from Durkheim,[3] applies the term more broadly. For him, the category of the sacred in modern societies (early modern as well as late modern) relates primarily to knowledge – and it picks out two socially conferred characteristics of certain kinds of knowledge:

a) from one point of view, it refers to knowledge and orders of meaning that are transcendental and esoteric; this centres on the pursuit of knowledge for intrinsic, non-instrumental purposes, such knowledge thereby being accorded a higher legitimacy and authority than that tied to mundane and instrumental practices;
b) from another point of view, the realm of the sacred is the place where the possibility of otherness cannot be completely hidden – it is the domain where it is possible to glimpse the fact that all orderings of knowledge are in some measure provisional, where the secret of uncertainty is disclosed.

The sacred, as Bernstein employs the term, is thus a paradoxical territory: it is the place of authoritative codings of knowledge but also the place where the ultimate insecurity of much of what is taken as established can be recognized. Because of this, societies typically seek to limit access to these dangerous insights about the provisional nature of even the most apparently secure cultural orderings and of the social orderings that depend upon them. Societies do this primarily by seeking to ensure that only those who have been 'legitimately pedagogized' are given access to these ultimate mysteries (Bernstein, 1996, p. 45). The socialization of appropriate guardians has traditionally involved long and arduous apprenticeship in which, as Bernstein put it many years ago, stable identities and loyalties are fostered, and the ultimate mystery – 'the potential for creating new realities' – is revealed 'very late in the educational life' (Bernstein, 1971, p. 57).

In some of his most recent work Bernstein suggested that contemporary late-capitalist societies may be witnessing a fundamental rupture in the structuring of the relationships governing educational transmissions – a rupture which decisively (and in new ways) subordinates academic communities and priorities to purposes determined elsewhere – notably through the operation of neoliberal modes of governmentality. As Bernstein sees it, these changes go to the very heart of the processes of knowledge creation and transmission: they threaten to fundamentally reconstruct the relationship between knowledge and the knower, creating an unprecedented situation in which 'knowledge, after nearly a thousand years, is divorced from inwardness and literally dehumanized' (Bernstein, 1996, p. 87).

The divorce of knowledge from the knower?

At first sight this warning may seem excessive: a thousand years of continuity of humane learning now receiving its quietus? Does the situation really justify such a dramatic verdict? It is probably too soon to judge. However this may be, Bernstein's recent work does at least make a major contribution to enabling us to better understand the nature and the seriousness of the threat. The apocalyptic pronouncement quoted above comes as the conclusion to a short paper which discusses the structuring of pedagogic discourse within the medieval university. The structure in question involved a dualism which both separated, but also linked into a unity, the Trivium (grammar, logic and rhetoric) and the Quadrivium (arithmetic, astronomy, geometry and music) – and decreed that the one should precede the other. This, says Bernstein, created 'a specialization of two discourses to two different time periods, the first progression and sequencing of official knowledge' (ibid., p. 83). The central point of Bernstein's complex (and, as he accepts, tentative) argument is his claim that this structuring had its roots in the peculiar form of selfhood – a form created by Christianity and which the Christian religion required in those who converted to it. He argues that the distinctive characteristic of such conversion was that while it did not require any change of nationality, culture or even outward practice, it did require 'a revolution of inwardness, a turning to recognition of Christ'. He perceptively adds:

> Note here that Christianity takes a point outside the culture and practice of those to be converted as the basis for conversion and then colonizes from within. Christianity drives a gap between inner self and outer practice. It creates a gap which becomes the site for new awareness ... Thus the dislocation of inner and outer, to open up a new existential self, is intrinsic to Christianity ...
>
> (Ibid., p. 84)

This fundamental dislocation of the self, the necessity to securely form the inner Christian self as the basis for reappropriating the outer realm of particular mundane cultures and experience, became, he suggests the structuring principle behind the organization of official educational knowledge through the Trivium and the Quadrivium. The inner self was formed first, through the study of the Trivium, with its selective and Christianized appropriation of Greek thought (philosophy in particular) before students were allowed to engage with the outer world – essentially of science. And, crucially, *'the construction of the inner was the guarantee for the construction of the outer'* (ibid., p. 86, my italics). Of course, this attempt to make Greek thought safe was not ultimately successful – and over a long period of more than five hundred years 'there was a progressive replacement of the religious foundation of official knowledge by a humanizing secular principle' (ibid.). But what is decisive in this analysis for our purposes is that throughout this long period, a university education still centred in the formation of a humane relationship of the self to knowledge. Knowledge and the knower were at some essential level integrated. Moreover, as Bernstein insightfully points out, this extended to the formation of the liberal professions – the term liberal picking out the important truth that the conception of a profession involved not simply a utilitarian business of acquiring technical skills but rather the shaping of humane practitioners, capable, for example, of independent and informed ethical judgement and possessing a wider vision of the place of their expertise within the realm of a broader intellectual culture. What was central and enduring in all of this was that educational institutions, at their best, creatively reproduced a relationship between knowledge and the self which was generative of a certain form of integrity: individual moral integrity but also a sense of collective responsibility for professional practice and standards. This is expressed in the idea of a profession as a vocation – in which, to use Althusser's language (Althusser, 1971), human subjects were 'interpellated' by voices representing both a tradition of ethical responsibility and also traditions of scholarship – creating identities centred not merely in expertise – let alone solely in occupational self-interest – but in dedication to worth-while knowledge and to the intellectual life for its own sake.[4]

What we are now experiencing, warns Bernstein, is a situation where, in an unprecedentedly radical way, knowledge is being 'separated from inwardness, from commitments, from personal dedication, from the deep structures of the self' (ibid., p. 87). The new neoliberal technologies of institutional control and accountability are identified as the key mechanisms which now increasingly subordinate education to the economic imperatives of the latest phase of globalized, post-industrial capitalism. These technologies have the capacity not only to impose the new dominant principles of market relevance but also to ensure that these principles extend into every corner of every sector of education – from the organization of research in universities to the nursery school classroom. This is achieved through a formidable combination of indirect market controls (competition for funding, clients, research contracts, etc.) and direct controls (highly prescriptive government criteria, inspection regimes, appraisal regimes, as well as – and crucially – a restructuring of the formation of the new profes-sionals who will service the needs of these re-formed institutions).[5]

Within individual educational institutions, the most conspicuous manifes-tation of these developments is probably the phenomenon which Newman and Clarke call 'managerialization' and other writers dub 'the new managerialism' (see Newman and Clarke, 1994; Esland, 1996, pp. 33–7) – with powers to impose new agendas (or at least priorities) for research and teaching, more exploitative conditions of service for employees, less contractual security, etc. But pivotal as these managerial functionaries are, the new managers themselves are thoroughly subordinated to the imperatives of the structures within which all must now operate.

Such institutional re-formation requires a remaking (if possible) of the person – i.e. of the human subjects at the centre of these changes. And it is here that Bernstein is at his most penetrating. The essentials of his analysis are as follows:

a) The new institutional priorities are centred in market responsiveness. (In fact, this often includes a requirement for rapid response to changing demands imposed by governmental agencies; for example, in the field of teacher training this involves responsiveness to the latest directives from the QCA, TTA and OFSTED.)

b) These imperatives work to create a climate of short-termism – which requires a disposition to pursue whatever opportunities are offered next. In such a world, strong attachments to identities centred in notions of the intrinsic value and integrity of academic disciplines (let alone humane culture) can evidently come to signify rigidity, obsolescence and a range of other dysfunctional if not pathological characteristics.

c) Within teacher training and teaching in schools, Bernstein argues that professional re-formation is becoming centred in the idea of *'trainability'*: the capacity – ideally internalized as a need – 'to profit from continuous pedagogic re-formations' designed to equip the individual to cope effectively with the accelerating pace of externally imposed changes (op. cit., pp. 72–3). At one level, these training requirements are strongly competency-based and highly specific – formulated as lists of closely prescribed behaviours which competent practitioners must display, and in relation to which their professional progress is assessed.[6] These competencies are, of course, specified by the agencies of the Official Recontextualizing Field – and are now being designed to extend across the whole of the professional life of teachers.[7]

d) At another level, however, there is a symptomatic *emptiness* in this notion of the endlessly re-trainable employee. The flexible, marketable self has no centre - no attachments to intrinsic value, no sense of the sacred. It is, rather – and by definition – oriented to a perpetually 'pedagogized future' (ibid., p. 73) in which *others* determine its destiny and purpose. Bernstein suggests that this central hollowness is likely to be filled by attachment to extrinsic, consumerist signifiers of worth and value: positional authority and its material perquisites.[8]

e) Such changes – affecting a wide range of areas including much of higher education, the organization of academic research (e.g. the

Research Assessment Exercise, the role of the TTA and OFSTED in defining priorities for educational research), the market-led pressures towards modularization and semesterization, the training of teachers and other semi-professions, etc. – are in aggregate, Bernstein suggests, of fundamental significance:

> ... there is a new concept of knowledge and of its relation to those who create and use it. This new concept is a truly secular concept. Knowledge should flow like money to wherever it can create advantage and profit. Indeed knowledge is not like money, it *is* money. Knowledge is divorced from persons, their commitments, their personal dedications. These become impediments, restrictions on the flow of knowledge, and introduce deformations in the workings of the symbolic market ... Once knowledge is separated from inwardness ... then people may be moved about, substituted for each other and excluded from the market ...
>
> (Ibid., p. 87)

New Labour: relativizing value whilst rationalizing control?

Let us now return to our starting point. What may New Labour portend in relation to the issues we have been discussing? Perhaps most significantly, it has seemed to some observers that at the very heart of the new administration, there is that same essential hollowness which Bernstein has diagnosed at the core of recent educational changes. In both areas, it appears, the outer has become the inner. The government, and more particularly its modernizing inner core leadership, has seemed to be in danger of losing its soul. If the production of the plastic, endlessly re-formable teacher is the goal of the new educational managers, then the political equivalent is an MP whose antennae are permanently attuned to focus-group feedback, who remains at all times on message, who understands the importance of flexibly endorsing the latest policy pronouncement. Thatcherism, whatever else it may have been and whatever practical compromises it may have made, was accurately seen as centred in 'conviction politics'. New Labour in office – and particularly the dominant fraction of the leadership – has seemed to many commentators to lack any consistent commitment to the major issues that were once at the centre of the Labour Party's concerns: notably, equality and social justice. The preoccupation with spin and presentation, the ferocious party discipline that insists that not only backbench MPs but also ministers remain at all times on message, can be seen as symptoms not of confident and unified purpose but rather as devices to avoid being caught out. The dominant buzz-words – new and modernizing – have been seen as similarly revealing. It is not that there is any lack of new policies: there is, indeed, a breathless pursuit of new initiatives. But the core identity signified by new and modernize – terms which, symptomatically, are virtually content-free – appears as empty of significant value

commitment as the Millennium Dome promises to be. The chief preoccupation has seemed to be with superficial re-branding exercises (see the
Sunday Telegraph, 1997; Wintour, 1997) combined with a reactive readiness
to formulate policy via 'focus group feedback and to appease vocal lobbies
representing the sectional interests of the privileged and the powerful' (see
Hattersley, 1998a).[9]

Such criticisms are pertinent and seem in many ways justified. Yet a more
interesting and, in the longer run, far more significant set of questions has
to do with how such developments might be adequately explained. One
important fact here is that many of the tendencies which critics in the UK
have seen as characterizing New Labour have been evident, and have been
carried even further, by other erstwhile socialist (or at least social
democratic) parties elsewhere – conspicuously so, for example, in New
Zealand, Australia and Canada (see, for example, Avis, 1996b, p. 105).
In a recent paper 'Marketization, the State and the Re-Formation of the
Teaching Profession', Geoff Whitty has briefly examined a range of
explanatory accounts bearing on these phenomena. First, he considers
accounts grounded in postmodernism (op. cit., 1997, pp. 299–300),
discussing not only optimistic postmodernist analyses which emphasize the
capacity of markets to open up greater choice and diversity and thereby
offer liberation from what some regard as 'the oppressive uniformity of
much modernist thinking' (ibid., p. 300), but also more pessimistic assess-
ments such as that offered by Kenway, which stress the manipulative
powers of transnational corporations to 'shape and reshape our individual
and collective identities as we plug in ... to their cultural and economic
communications networks' (Kenway, 1993, quoted in Whitty, ibid.).
Whitty himself, however, is more impressed by the essentially modernist
character of that hybrid combination of marketization and strong state
dirigisme which now, in so many countries, seems to dominate the restructuring of public sector institutions. Commenting, for example, on claims
that competency-based teacher training encourages restricted rather than
extended notions of professionality (Hoyle, 1974) and that it displaces the
once dominant liberal humanist discourse of educational theory with one
of technical rationality (Jones and Moore, 1993), Whitty points out:
'Neither (of these claims), though, involves the abandonment of notions
of rationality associated with the Enlightenment project, which might be
expected if these changes represented the abandonment of the dominant
assumptions of modernity' (ibid., p. 304).

This comment takes us closer to the heart of the explanation we are
seeking. The new modalities of control do indeed seem to involve an intensification of certain forms of rationality – essentially new modes of technical
rationality which are peculiarly suited to what Whitty suggests may be the
key imperative: that of reshaping the state and its remaining public sector
institutions to be better adapted to the underlying project of restoring conditions favourable to capitalist accumulation in a neo-Fordist (as distinct from
post-Fordist) globalized economy (ibid., p. 300–1). This includes powerful
pressures to:

- contain public expenditure and public borrowing within limits acceptable to global financial markets; (this applies with particular force to unproductive forms of welfare spending including education);[10]
- promote or at least not impede the values of enterprise culture (especially in terms of principled inequality in the distribution of income and wealth, flexibilized labour markets, and 'management's right to manage');
- develop effective mechanisms of legitimation appropriate to neo-Fordist economies with a higher proportion of relatively affluent citizens.

Nikolas Rose has probably identified more clearly than any other commentator precisely what was so significantly novel about the modalities of control which neoliberalism introduced.

> Neoliberalism managed to reactivate the sceptical vigilance of classical liberalism and link it up with a series of techniques – none of them in itself particularly new or remarkable – which could render them operable – techniques such as monetarization, marketization, enhancement of the powers of the consumer, financial accountability and audit … It is this capacity to create operable technical forms for exercising perpetual scrutiny over the authority of authority that make the formulae invented by neoliberalism so versatile for all those other programmes and strategies that sought to govern in an advanced liberal way.
>
> (Rose, 1993, pp. 294–5)

Moreover, it was the capacity to link these diverse techniques to form a functionally effective ensemble of operational controls – an ensemble exceptionally resistant to effective contestation – which makes it plausible to claim, as Rose does, that we are dealing here with a new mode of governmentality. The changes do indeed constitute a 'durable transformation in the rationalities and technologies of government' (ibid., p. 295). The essential features seem to be the following:

a) The yoking together of marketization and central dirigisme. This does not seem to be either an accidental or a temporary feature. Many of the institutions over which, and within which, the new forms of control and scrutiny are exercised remain (at least within existing possibilities of effective legitimation) public sector institutions. Radical privatization is not yet on the agenda. Such institutions can operate, in the main, only through quasi-market mechanisms and conditions – for example, the funding and access rules which pressurize schools to compete for pupils.

b) This janus-faced character of contemporary modes of governmentality thus requires that two distinct kinds of control be exercised in tandem:

> i) quasi-market mechanisms (competition, localized entrepreneurial initiatives, delivery of value-for-money via competitive tendering, etc.), and
>
> ii) direct controls in terms of imposed targets, outputs, efficiency gains, performance criteria, etc. – as well as mechanisms to monitor performance, reward efficiency and penalize failure (audit, inspection, selective funding mechanisms, appraisal, performance-related pay, etc.).
>
> (In the UK, the combination during the 1980s of neoliberal and neoconservative elements within the New Right may well have reinforced this dualism – but the dualism itself seems to be intrinsic.)
>
> c) A 'distantiated' relationship between the centre of decision making (which remains an arena of overtly political contestation and accountability) and a hierarchy of ostensibly non-political institutions (where quasi-autonomous and politically neutral managers are required to demonstrate efficiency and responsiveness to consumers' wishes – all within a framework of cash limits, externally imposed performance targets, etc.). Intermediate levels of significant political debate, decision-making and accountability are correspondingly diminished.[11] In their place, and constituting a functionally necessary part of the whole ensemble, is the machinery of the quango state through which policy is not merely implemented and monitored but also, increasingly, defined. (The powers and constitutional position of quangos protect them, at least to some degree, from both effective parliamentary scrutiny as well as from criticism from below.)

In one sense this is thoroughly familiar. And various of the attractions to government of these developments are all too evident. The new modes of distantiation, for example, provide the basis of new rationales for governments to claim credit for successes whilst attributing failure to technical problems, managerial inadequacy, and other non-political factors outside their control.[12] What is worth highlighting in the context of our present discussion, however, is the way in which these new institutional forms embody technical/calculative rationality operating at all levels of the structure in a top down manner. A powerful means–ends logic in the service of institutional efficiency is the requisite mode of operation. Consequently, the new managerialism is much more than fashionable management jargon. It signifies a systemic operational requirement both for new kinds of expertise and for functionally necessary managerial autonomy. The most pertinent forms of expertise relate to effective financial audit and regulation, quality control, and the motivation of the workforce. Moreover, managerial autonomy, in the form of a relatively unimpeded right to manage, is similarly intrinsic. Within the overall structure of institutional relationships, predictability of performance and outcomes is essential to success. A further effect of the hybrid overall structure of control (the combination of centralized dirigisme and market forces) is that the need for rapid institutional response is at a premium – in some respects even more so than in the case of enterprises operating in a completely free-market context. Central government quangos can, for example, require their subordinate institutions to respond to initiatives of major importance within extremely limited time frames. This tends to mean that any remaining vestiges of internal institutional democracy are squeezed out of the system as managers hasten to formulate (or even improvise) strategic responses in very short order.

A further relevant characteristic of these new modalities of control is their paradoxical compatibility with certain tendencies which are beginning to emerge as a central element of New Labour's overall agenda and which, whilst not inspired by postmodernism, are capable of being understood within a postmodernist account of contemporary social change. Although the contours of the much discussed Third Way are still only partly discernible, one significant element does seem to be a turning away from 'statist' (Old Labour) forms of common provision in favour of a proliferation of institutional diversity and choice. A good example of this is the succession of initiatives, each characteristically small-scale and low key, which taken together promise to significantly further diversify the variety of types of school that parents – or at least some parents – can choose for their children. For example, in January 1998, David Blunkett approved grant-maintained status for two previously independent Muslim primary schools; two Jewish schools also successfully applied for grant maintained status (Lepkowska, 1998). In a related development, a proposed pattern of school reorganization in Bradford seems likely to create one Islamic and two Anglican secondary schools in a city which currently has no state secondary schools with a religious affiliation, as well as increasing the number of Anglican primary schools (Hugill, 1998). The establishment of specialist schools is another significant form of differentiation. Here one concern voiced by some critics has been with the possibility of creeping selection – on top of the formal permission given to these schools to select 10 per cent of their intakes by aptitude (Mortimore, 1998). As Tony Edwards has warned: 'specialization is hard to separate from selection, certainly in conditions where schools compete for pupils ... Selection by interest also tends to produce socially-segregated intakes' (Edwards, quoted in Hattersley, 1998b).

The keenness to involve the business community in various forms of school partnership is another aspect of the enthusiasm for diversity. This is evident both in the funding arrangements for the specialist schools initiative, where government grants must be matched by equivalent business sponsorship amounting to £100,000 in each case – and also in the attempts to involve the private sector in the Education Action Zones initiative. Private sector participation has also been a feature of the selection process of the first cohort of Advanced Skills Teachers who took up their appointments in September 1998 (with a two-year salary boost of around £5,000 per annum). The manner in which this initiative was introduced highlights a further aspect of the government's approach to diversification. Only designated technology colleges (including CTCs) and certain other specialist schools were permitted to bid for inclusion in the first phase of the AST scheme. It is probably no accident – given the perceived potential of the AST scheme to become a Trojan Horse for the wider introduction of performance-related pay – that certain of these institutions are constitutionally in a position to bypass various kinds of trade union recognition and negotiation, and to employ their staff under more flexible contracts of employment. In such ways, schools that are non-mainstream provide a diversity of sites where new practices may be introduced, initially on a pilot basis, then extended. The Manpower Services Commission in the 1980s showed the way (see Moore, 1987; Hickox and Moore, 1995). Moreover, the School Standards and Framework Act 1998 now provides a national framework within which this push towards diversification can be further promoted. Under the Act, the position of the churches has been secured and in some respects strengthened; grant maintained schools have been, in their essentials, preserved as foundation schools, while, revealingly, LEA schools are redesignated community schools (the de facto accent being on the local rather than the national community). Although the abolition of the Assisted Places Scheme has been reinforced by clauses in the Act which prevent LEAs from reintroducing backdoor assisted places, any criticism of the principle of private schooling is completely off the agenda of mainstream party politics. Also, the proposals relating to parental ballots, which (in theory) permit the abolition of grammar schools, seem in practice more likely to preserve them.

One can, as yet, only speculate about the overall effects of such creeping diversification in education and elsewhere. But it is easy to see its compatibility with a loosely postmodernist way of thinking which treats the sphere of value as being, in the main, beyond rational and objective evaluation, and as therefore a realm of relatively unconstrained individual choice and, even more pertinently, of consumer sovereignty. In such circumstances, it is likely to become progressively more difficult to build political support for positions which stress collective societal responsibilities organized around principles of social justice and progress back towards greater egalitarianism. Whitty has perceptively highlighted the extent to which the institutions of civil society have already become marketized – so that instead of being a sphere where conceptions of social citizenship can be developed in new ways, the institutions of civil society may become increasingly fragmented whilst the institutions of welfare are simultaneously partially privatized (Whitty, 1997, op. cit., pp. 299–301; see also Beck, 1998, Chapter 5). In this context, it is vital to recollect that the Enlightenment project was not only about the advance of scientific and technical reason. It was also a grand narrative of moral progress and collective human betterment. Perhaps the most insidious effect of neoliberal modes of governmentality is their capacity to embody calculative reason in institutional forms which systematically undermine the force of moral reason and collective welfare, and instead promote individualistic and institutional competitiveness and self-interest. This is the main reason why Bernstein's apocalyptic warning is so compelling. The forces which threaten to detach knowledge from the knower are enshrined in an ensemble of institutional forms that have become so entrenched and so potent that effective contestation is becoming increasingly difficult.

Such a conclusion may seem overly pessimistic. However, it worth considering the following points:

a) First, a number of commentators have drawn attention to the emergence during the late 1980s and 90s of a new consensus uniting modernizers of both Left and Right around a strongly instrumentalist agenda of educational reform – particularly within post-16 education and higher education. James Avis, for example, cites the following claims made in the Robertson Report – a document published (symptomatically) by the Higher Education Quality Council:

> The pursuit of student choice and flexibility commands widespread support in principle. It conveniently unites radicals of the Right (markets, freedom of choice) and of the Left (democratic participation, student empowerment) against conservatives of the Right (elite participation and the preservation of standards) and of the Left (sovereignty of the academic, supremacy of the unified course ...
> (HEQC, 1994, p. 119)

> There appears to be a common agenda across the political spectrum to introduce greater flexibility and student choice, to encourage markets within higher education and to expand access. This is likely to embrace student loans, a personal commitment to learning *and an acceptance that professional academic sovereignty should not remain a barrier to the achievement of these objectives.*
> (Ibid., p. 334, my italics – quoted in Avis, 1996b, p. 114)

This constitution of academic authority as little more than an anachronistic impediment to what forward looking people regard as self-evidently progressive and democratizing developments is highly revealing. Defenders of a scholarly relation to knowledge tend to be positioned by such polarizing discourses as elitists or romantics or both – and in any case, as groups whose views can be overridden with impunity.

b) Secondly, at the level of values and beliefs, various influences are at work which may, inadvertently, further undermine egalitarian collectivism and social citizenship. Certain strongly relativistic stances within some postmodern writing are, somewhat paradoxically, of significance in this regard. Take, for example, the currently pervasive and influential discourses of voice.[13] Although the aims of these discourses are indeed genuinely emancipatory, nevertheless, the epistemological relativism which informs them could prove disabling to those who wish to continue to argue the case for a greater degree of objectivity attaching (intrinsically) to moral discourse (see Moore and

Muller, 1999; and Luntley, 1995, especially Chapters 8, 9 and 10).

c) Thirdly, the new neoliberal modalities of control are already evolving their own built-in structures of legitimation and motivation – which are becoming persuasive to an alarming though perhaps unsurprising extent. For example, if Bernstein is right in perceiving a fundamental threat to identities grounded in an intrinsic relationship to knowledge, then other signifiers of valued identity may become increasingly attractive (see Beck, 1998, pp. 122–5). Here, the glamour as well as the material rewards that collaboration with the private sector can bring may exert an insidious appeal. The obverse of this coin is that, as careers within education and especially teaching come to be mainly structured through managed progression within a hierarchy of competency levels, career advancement is likely to require at least an outward accommodation to the system. In a world where a key danger is precisely that the outer has become the inner, the risk is all too evident that such tactical adaptation may, over time, slide imperceptibly into redefinition of the self.

d) Fourthly, the ostensible depoliticization effected by the new modalities of control contains its own threats and sanctions. Collective forms of resistance on the part of employees, for example, can with increasing plausibility be represented as outmoded, as evidence of inflexibility, and as impairing institutional efficiency. Those who engage in such activities, or who are active members of trade unions (or even of the wrong kind of professional association), risk being branded as disloyal, unconstructive, uncommitted – and, worst of all, as political. Such resistance can also often be represented as directed against the individual institution (school, college, hospital) and its clients – and thus as constituting politically motivated interference with the well-being of innocent parties. Conversely, management can represent itself as neutral, while its enhanced powers of patronage can be used to reward those who either acquiesce or, better still, enthusiastically embrace the new role definitions and opportunities which are proffered.

e) Finally, and beneath it all, there is what some have seen as the self-interested conspiracy of silence among the relatively affluent majority of voters in many of the world's most advanced economies. As J. K. Galbraith has argued, this may operate to set strict limits to the extent to which seriously redistributive or egalitarian policies can hope to command significant electoral support in these societies:

> The attitudes … are present in all the fortunate lands … Perhaps it is time to bring them out into the open … In the modern economy let us say simply that the rich do not want to pay for the poor; that unemployment is necessary and good; that recession can be tolerated, certainly by the many who do not suffer as compared with the smaller number who do …
>
> (Galbraith, 1996)

Conclusion

Such considerations do not mean that the new modalities of control are hegemonic. Nor is the political debate closed. As commentators like Will Hutton have reminded us – albeit in terms increasingly qualified by pessimism – New Labour is by no means a unitary entity (see, for example, Hutton, 1997, pp. 105–10; 1998a and 1998b). Nevertheless, on the evidence so far, it seems increasingly clear that any Third Way which commends itself to those who are proving to be most influential in shaping the party's agenda is rather unlikely to be equidistant between Thatcherism and those versions of social democracy which take egalitarian aims and social citizenship seriously.

Ultimately, the central issue this paper has discussed concerns two contending bases of authority. One is a modernized (and partially marketized) form of technical-bureaucratic authority which tends to reduce politically contentious matters to what are represented as technical questions of managerial competence, which tends to operate in the service of private profit and corporate interests, and which governs partially privatized state services in ways which are increasingly congruent with these interests – in both the short and the longer term. The other is grounded in humanely educated and ethically committed understanding and judgement, and was, for a long period institutionalized, albeit very imperfectly, in certain of the learned professions and within higher education. Two salient values (and conditions of existence) were associated with this academic/professional form of occupational control (Johnson, 1972): one was a capacity for independence of judgement (especially independence from government and commercial interests) and the other was a certain kind of dignity accorded to certain professions (itself grounded not only in undesirable patterns of deference but also in respect for humane learning). Although this could and did degenerate into arrogance, elitism and what the New Right so tellingly dubbed 'producer self-interest', nevertheless at its best (and value judgements are inescapable here), professional/academic authority constituted a vital basis of authoritative, socially respected and at least partially independent judgement. Although traditional modes of professional organization may no longer be feasible or appropriate under conditions of globalization and neo-Fordist production, there is at present an evident absence of institutional arrangements which can lend authority and influence to reasoned, ethically serious, independent thinking, judgement and practice.

Chapter 5

THE ASSAULT ON THE PROFESSIONS AND THE RESTRUCTURING OF ACADEMIC AND PROFESSIONAL IDENTITIES: A BERNSTEINIAN ANALYSIS

John Beck and Michael F. D. Young

Introduction

In recent decades, professions and professionals have faced unprece-dented challenges: to their autonomy, to the validity of any ethical view of their calling, to their relatively privileged status and economic position, and to the legitimacy of their claims to expertise based on exclusive possession of specialized knowledge. Such challenges have gone far beyond mere criticism: professional practice is being more or less radically restructured, sometimes by direct government intervention, sometimes as a result of the more indirect but no less potent effects of marketization. All this has had profound consequences for professionals, particularly with regard to their relationship to knowledge, to clients, and to the organizational structures within which most of them now work. Similar challenges and changes have been experienced by many who teach and research in universities. There too, the imposition of an audit culture (Power, 1994; Strathern, 2000), requirements to meet externally imposed performance criteria, demands to demonstrate the relevance of their work in relation to new institutional mission statements, and the like, are generating a mixture of anomie and alienation – at least for some of those caught up in these changes. Both within the universities and in many of the professions, a generation of practitioners has experienced what is, to some, a sense of crisis and of loss. Cherished identities and commitments have been undermined and for some, this has been experi-enced as an assault on their professionalism (Freidson, 2001, Ch. 8).

Perhaps no one saw more clearly what was most central to this sense of crisis than the British sociologist Basil Bernstein. As he put it, 'Of fundamental importance, there is a new concept of knowledge and its relation to those who create and use it ... Knowledge, after nearly a thousand years, is divorced from inwardness and literally dehumanised ... what is at stake is the very concept of education itself.' (2000, p. 86)

Bernstein, with his penetrating sociological imagination, perceived more clearly than most that what was pivotal to these changes was a restructuring not merely of the external conditions of academic and professional practice but even more fundamentally of the core elements of academic and professional identity. For generations, such identities had centred, he suggested, in a particular kind of humane relationship to knowledge – a relationship which was centred in what he termed 'inwardness' and 'inner dedication'. And it was this that was now most profoundly threatened by the rising tide of marketization, external regulation, and audit culture.

In order, however, to take appropriate account of the possible effects of both marketization and external regulation on academic and professional fields previously protected from them, the professional/knowledge relationship needs reconceptualizing. In this chapter, we draw on the work of Basil Bernstein to provide an analytical framework which we hope will prove to be more illuminating and less partisan than either the pseudo-egalitarian rhetoric of many educational modernizers or the siren voices of postmodernists whose relativist epistemologies implicitly undermine the very idea that professional authority could be grounded in well-founded claims to expert knowledge. Bernstein's work is particularly suitable for this task of reconceptualization because, as a follower of Durkheim, one of his most enduring concerns was to illuminate a range of relationships between the 'inner' and the 'outer' – and in particular how orderings of knowledge and forms of pedagogic transmission had consequences for identity and identity change. It is true, of course, that Bernstein himself did not systematically analyse professions or the distinctive character of professional knowledge. But, especially in his later work, his interest in (as well as concern about) the increasing dominance of marketization and state regulation of both knowledge production and pedagogic transmissions led him to develop the outlines of an analytical framework which has much to offer for the analysis of change within the professions as well as within the universities and other institutions of formal education.

Knowledge relations, 'inwardness' and 'inner dedication'

Much of Bernstein's work focuses on knowledge relations – and this is true in a double sense. First, his theorization of pedagogic transmissions and (at least implicitly of knowledge more generally) directs attention in an almost structuralist manner, to the way in which the definition and identity of different domains of knowledge depends not so much on the character of their internal contents as on the structuring of relations between the domains – most importantly on the strength or weakness of their boundaries, especially the strength of the dominant form of classification. In this respect his approach differs fundamentally from that of certain philosophers of education such as Paul Hirst who focused, at least in his earlier work, on what he took to be the fundamental internal, logical differences, which differentiated distinct forms of knowledge from one another (Hirst, 1974).[1] The second sense in which Bernstein is preoccupied with knowledge relations is that he is interested in 'relations *to* knowledge' – on the part of both knowledge practitioners and those undergoing socialization into differently structured knowledge domains. In particular, he repeatedly returned to the consequences for the identity of both practitioners and learners, of different knowledge structures.

One issue of enduring interest for Bernstein is the conditions which promote the formation of identities centred in inwardness and which give rise to inner dedication – characteristics which are central to traditional conceptions of both the scholar and the professional. Leaving aside for the moment the issue of how idealized such conceptions may or may not be, it is useful to focus first on Bernstein's account of the formation of such identities. They are, for him, primarily associated with the type of knowledge structure he calls 'singulars'. Singulars are most clearly exemplified by the traditional 'pure' academic disciplines. As we have already noted, Bernstein is non-committal about the epistemological standing of different disciplines and he defines singulars as socially constructed knowledge structures '... whose creators have appropriated a space to give themselves a unique name, a specialised discrete discourse with its own intellectual field of text, practices, rules of entry, examinations and licences to practise.' (2000, p. 52)

Despite the language of 'field theory' employed here, Bernstein's main interest, unlike Bourdieu's, is not in the analysis of positional struggles within and between such fields, but more in their implications for identity formation. The key characteristic of singulars in this respect is their strongly bounded character, which creates the possibility of a purity of identity which 'partakes of the sacred' (in Durkheim's sense of radical otherness in contrast to the mundane world). Singulars, he contends, generate strong inner commitments centred in the perceived intrinsic value of their specific knowledge domains. Central to their formation, Bernstein argues, is 'socialisation into subject loyalty: for it is the subject which becomes the linchpin of identity' (1971, p. 56). In another passage, written much later but expressing essentially the same view, he states that 'the sacred face (of singulars) sets them apart, legitimises their otherness and creates dedicated identities with no reference other than their calling' (2000, p. 54).

Such formulations might seem to suggest that Bernstein naively accepts at face value the self-images of academics and professionals as ascetic practitioners driven by nothing other than the pursuit of knowledge for its own sake, or by an ethic of disinterested service to those who depend upon their expert ministrations. This is far from being the case however. Bernstein's more inclusive and realistic view is summed up in his metaphor of a singular being like a coin with two faces – one of which is indeed the 'sacred' face of inner dedication. The other, however, reveals the 'profane' dimension of singulars and the intellectual fields in which they are rooted – a dimension concerned with mundane issues of economic existence and power struggles. What is perhaps most significant about this metaphor is Bernstein's insistence that although 'only one face (of this coin) can be seen at any one time' (ibid., p. 54), both are real. The point is reinforced by Bernstein's choice of the term 'narcissistic' to characterize 'the autonomous and self-sealing' sacred identities that singulars develop (ibid., pp. 54–5). Despite this salutary realism, however, what needs equal emphasis is that the sacred face of inner dedication is not illusory: both faces are real – and to underestimate the significance of either is to risk misunderstanding the reality of the whole.

As we have pointed out, in most of his work, Bernstein stresses that in his view, such highly specialized identities and the sense of inner dedication to which they give rise are a consequence of a particular structuring of knowledge relations:

> The form taken by educational practices – that is, their degree of speci-ficity, the extent to which practices are specialized to categories – depends entirely upon the relation between these categories ... The specialty of each category is created, maintained and reproduced only if the relations between the categories of which a given category is a member are preserved. What is to be preserved? ... 'the *insulation between the categories*'.
>
> (1990a, p. 23, original italics)

Reading Bernstein, however, can be a little like reading Marx. The more abstract theoretical statements can appear uncompromising but when more specific historical matters are under consideration, the apparent rigidity of the formal framework seems to be softened. There is, for example, at least one instance in which Bernstein offers a more historicist account of the sources of inwardness. It will not be possible to recapitulate this complex and controversial discussion at all adequately here (see Bernstein, 1995 and see also Wexler, 1995). But in his paper 'Thoughts on the Trivium and Quadrivium', Bernstein developed but also revised Durkheim's argument about the dualistic curriculum associated with the University of Paris in early medieval times. This involved a pedagogic sequencing in which the Trivium (logic, grammar and rhetoric) focusing on 'the word', preceded the Quadrivium (arithmetic, geometry, astronomy and music) which focused on 'the world' (Durkheim, 1977). What Durkheim highlights as the striking abstractness of this curriculum may, Bernstein proposes, have in part resulted from certain distinctive charac-teristics of the Christian religion: 'only Christianity is intrinsically and necessarily abstract as a consequence of the dislocation between inner and outer, and the form of its resolution: the new mediation between God and human' (1990b, p. 149). Christianity is a religion of ambiguity in which faith is not assured but has to be won and re-won, creating a need for 'theology, and then more theology', with the consequence that 'in Christianity the word as relation takes precedence over the act as doing' (in the world). On the basis of this argument (which is presented here in drastically simplified form), Bernstein offers a revisionist version of Durkheim's own explanation of 'how the classification (and sequencing) of the Trivium and Quadrivium came about' (ibid., p. 151):

> I shall propose that the Trivium ... is concerned to constitute a particular form of consciousness ... to regulate a distinct modality of the self. To constitute that modality in the Word, yes, but the Word ... of the Christian God ... The Trivium comes first, because the construction of the inner, the valid inner, the true inner, is a necessary precondition that the understanding of the world be valid, will also be true ... will also be legitimate in terms of the discourse of Christianity. The sacredness of the world is guaranteed or should be guaranteed by the appropriate construction of the inner, the truly Christian self. (Ibid., 2000, p. 83)

For us, what is particularly noteworthy here is that this is an historicist rather than a structuralist form of explanation: the particular form of inwardness involved and the relations between the inner and outer within the pedagogic discourse under discussion, as well as the structure and sequencing of that discourse, are all derived from particular historical characteristics of Christianity. Even more pertinent for our purposes is that Bernstein concludes his analysis with a striking if cryptic claim – that it is precisely in this pedagogic sequencing, in which inwardness and commitment shaped the terms of practical engagement in the outer world, that '*we can find the origins of the professions*' (ibid., p. 85, our italics). Tantalizingly, he does not elaborate on this terse observation. But its meaning seems clear enough: professional commitment and its accompanying sense of inner dedication has at least one of its origins in a particular period of history, rather than being simply a consequence of the structuring of the professional knowledge base.

However, when we turn to consider what Bernstein has to say about the knowledge structures that underpin professional knowledge, we find that he normally categorizes them not as singulars but as 'regions'. At first sight, this presents something of a paradox, since regions are defined as involving a recontextualization of a collection of singulars with the consequence that there 'necessarily is a weakening of the classification' of the component discourses which the region recontextualises for its own purposes. Moreover, while singulars face inwards, regions face outwards to various fields of practice in the everyday world. This would seem to suggest that the identities associated with regions might be more diffuse, even in the case of 'the "classical" university regions such as engineering, medicine, architecture' (ibid., p. 55). Bernstein does not himself discuss the mode of formation of identities historically associated with these classical regions and their links to the established professions; instead, he goes on to examine the phenomenon of regionalization which we shall discuss further below.

But taking the hints offered above, we may perhaps legitimately infer that the strong forms of inner dedication associated with certain of the established professions might legitimately be seen as deriving from the historically particular character of the linkage between the organizational form of such professions and their knowledge base. Of crucial importance here would be the following:

- that established professions historically achieved an exceptional measure of collective collegiate autonomy over their conditions of professional training, certification of professional competence, and conditions of work and practice (Johnson, 1972; Freidson, 2001;
- that such professions themselves largely defined the boundaries of their own knowledge base, which in most cases was eventually institutionalized in the form of a curriculum taught by a 'professional school' based within institutions of higher education (Freidson, 2001 Ch. 4) and which therefore partook of the liberal educational ethos associated with such a location;
- that as a condition of maintaining trust on the part of both their clients and the state, such professions were constrained to develop and implement a code of ethics through which individual professionals could be held to account by the profession itself;
- that professional training typically involved more than the imparting of specialist expertise; it also involved intensive socialization into the values of a professional community and its standards of professional integrity, judgement, and loyalty – in other words, the creation of a professional habitus.

Such conditions operated not only to insulate such professions from the profane pressures of unrestricted free market competition; they also insulated professional knowledge and values, at least to some degree, from external interference and contamination. This particular form of autonomy and the insulations that protected it were, therefore, key to the development of forms of inner dedication to ends and values which transcended (at least in some respects and to some extent) mundane considerations of profit, the demands of powerful clients, etc. Similarly, a sense of genuine ethical responsibility can only arise, among such service-providers, where it is the practitioners themselves who are responsible for the quality of the service offered.[2] Finally, in terms of the professional knowledge base, such conditions created exceptionally strong external boundaries around each corpus of professional knowledge, even if the internal classification was necessarily weaker.

In conclusion here, we should perhaps once again stress that we are not blind to the abuses which such privileged conditions of occupational existence periodically made possible: it was, after all, Talcott Parsons who once described the American Medical Association as a predatory conspiracy against society. On the other hand we do wish to insist that the idea of inner dedication is more than a self-serving myth.

Regionalization

We suggested earlier that Bernstein offers not only an illuminating account of the conditions which gave rise to the forms of inwardness we have been discussing so far, but that his work also provides an original set of conceptual tools for analysing the forms and consequences of the dramatic and (for some) traumatic impact of marketization and state regulation. It is in his discussion of what he calls, respectively, 'regionalization' and 'generic' pedagogic modes (or what we shall for convenience label 'genericism') that he most directly addresses these issues. Both regionalization and genericism, he suggests, have far-reaching consequences for identity and identity change.

Regionalization of knowledge is clearly not new – but as a dominant principle for the structuring of higher educational curricula it has assumed a qualitatively new significance in recent decades and may well, Bernstein speculates 'become the modal form from the late twentieth century onwards' (2000, p. 55). Regionalization is partly driven by demand-led calculations on the part of higher education managers concerned to maximize take up of courses in their institutions. Singulars themselves are not unaffected by such pressures. Not only does modularization, for example, fragment the unity of singulars – simultaneously eroding the intellectual authority of subject specialists to control the content, sequencing and pacing of knowledge in their own fields, it also facilitates the proliferation of new regions, especially in lower status HE institutions like the new universities in the UK. Although changes of this kind may in certain respects empower students and broaden access, these are not their only effects. Higher education managers are increasingly constrained to restructure courses to meet the perceived demands of students, employers and government. What is of greatest importance is that regions become increasingly dependent on the requirements of the external fields of practice to which they are linked and, that, especially in the case of contemporary regions like business studies, tourism, or journalism, commercial considerations are likely to become increasingly dominant not only in shaping the content but also in determining the pace and directions of change. The implications for the central issue of identity are far reaching, pointing, according to Bernstein, towards a requirement for what might be termed an increasing flexibilization of the self:

> Identities … are what they are, and what they will become, as a consequence of the *projection* of … knowledge as a practice in some context. … The future of the context will regulate identity and the volatility of the context will control the nature of the regionalization and thus the projected identity. (Ibid., p. 55)

Overall therefore, regionalization insofar as it becomes modal, promotes a progressive loss of academic autonomy and authority across higher education, albeit unequally as between higher and lower status institutions and different subject areas. The terms on which singulars contribute to regions are increasingly shaped by external forces; singulars themselves are increasingly fragmented; insulations between higher education and business become weaker; 'good' managers of higher education institutions become those with the skills to successfully market their educational 'product', attract 'customers', respond to the needs of employers, and so on.

Regrettably though understandably, Bernstein's analysis of regionalization remains partial and incomplete. For example, the concept of regionalization itself is left undeveloped and we get very little detailed sense of the different 'integrating frameworks' within which groups of singulars have been brought together. And from the point of view of our major concern in this paper, differences between new and 'classical' regions, and their implications for the future of the professions and professionalism, are touched upon only briefly. Bernstein does imply however, that within the various classical regions, the word and the world were held in mutually beneficial tension with each other; at the same time he saw on-going regionalization as shifting this delicate balance strongly in favour of the world. This trend, moreover, he saw as closely associated with the emergence of another kind of knowledge structure – genericism – in which connections between the world or practice and the word (and therefore to singulars) can be lost altogether. It is to this issue that we now turn.

The emergence of 'genericism'

Bernstein notes that from the 1980s when regionalization was beginning to take hold in universities, a distinctively new kind of knowledge structure, genericism, also emerged. Unlike singulars and regions, generic modes had their origins at pre-university level. Their features included the following:

- they arose outside of and independently of the formal curriculum;
- they were directed primarily (and initially) to extra-educational experiences;
- they originally appeared in further education not universities;
- they were linked explicitly to the perceived demands of employers and to their assertion that future employees would need to become more flexible;
- they assumed that becoming more flexible was a demand that was common to a wide range of occupations, tasks and jobs.

Since Bernstein first published this account (Bernstein 1996, Ch. 3) the proliferation of generic modes in both higher education and professional training justifies the use of the term genericism (by analogy with regionalization) to label what is now an on-going phenomenon of considerable potency and significance. Elements of genericism have multiplied and been extended far beyond their origins in youth training schemes and prevocational education. Attempts to introduce generic skills can even be found in doctoral programmes. Typically, they are characterized by such terms as key skills, core skills, thinking skills, problem solving and teamwork. They are assumed to apply to all subjects, all regions, all fields of practice and all levels. References to generic modes can be found in virtually every recent education White Paper in the UK, most noticeably in association with such ideas as life-long learning as well as the increasing tendency for government publications to refer to learning and skills rather than education.[3]

As Bernstein puts it, the new emphasis on genericism arises from a view that we are in a world in which 'life experiences cannot be based on stable expectations of the future and one's location in it' (2000, p. 59). Wider claims for genericism typically also link it to the spectre of globalization depicted as an irreversible reality to which national economies and education systems, including universities must adapt or perish. Thus in a lecture delivered at the University of Greenwich at the start of the new millennium, David Blunkett, then education and employment secretary for England, could confidently assert that:

> Universities need to adapt rapidly to the top-down influences of globalisation and the new technologies, as well as to the bottom-up imperatives of serving the local labour market, innovating with local companies and providing professional development courses that stimulate economic and intellectual growth. (Blunkett, 2000)

With characteristic penetration, Bernstein goes straight to the key pedagogic implication. At the heart of generic modes, he suggests, is 'a new concept of "work" and "life" which might be called *short-termism*'. He continues:

> Under these circumstances it is considered that a vital new ability must be developed: 'trainability', the ability to profit from continuous pedagogic re-formations and so cope with the new requirements of 'work' and 'life'. These ... will be based on the acquisition of generic modes ...
>
>   (2000, p. 59)

The concept of trainability clearly has considerable similarity to the more widely used term 'learning to learn'. Both declare the inevitable obsolescence of accumulated knowledge and prioritize the value of developing the skills and flexibility to acquire and put to use whatever is needed next.

The implications of this analysis for the issue of professional identity are interesting and far-reaching. Older forms of relations to knowledge enabled professional and academic identities to be centred in relatively stable identifications with (and loyalties to) clearly defined knowledge traditions which 'partook of the sacred' yet which were linked to practices in the world. However, as Bernstein observes, 'there appears to be an emptiness in the concept of trainability, an emptiness which makes the concept self-referential and therefore excluding' (in the sense of having no intrinsic content that allows self-definition or self recognition).[4] But if the concept is empty how does the actor recognize her/himself and others? Bernstein's answer is that this recognition is increasingly likely to be accomplished through 'the materialities of consumption'. In other words, relatively stable identities which previously were forged through subject loyalties are being progressively replaced by 'temporary stabilities (constructed) out of the products of the market' (ibid., p. 59).

Uncertain prospects for professional futures and identities

The conceptual tools developed by Bernstein that we have been using in this paper – notably the concepts of singulars, regions and generic modes – have a somewhat ambiguous status. From one point of view they seem to have been evolved by Bernstein himself from historically specific analysis of educational policy and change, mainly but not exclusively in Britain. But on the other hand, they have some of the properties of ideal types – formal analytical models, rarely encountered in their pure form, against which empirical developments can be examined and assessed. The following passage is indicative of this ambiguity:

> Finally, I have been considering these models and their modes as discrete, and as giving rise to distinct forms. It is crucial to understand that this may not always be the case. The models and modes may give rise to what could be called a pedagogic palette where mixes can take place.
>
> (Ibid., pp. 55–6)

Another possibility, however, would be to interpret the concepts as a framework for an ambitious theory of social and pedagogic change – a theory which implies a progressive de-specialization of institutions of formal education and a growing diffuseness and/or emptiness of academic and pedagogic identities. From this point of view, it could be seen as a pessimistic variant of 'the learning society' thesis.

A further important consideration for our purposes is that because Bernstein's analysis focuses primarily on pedagogic transmissions, it says relatively little about changes in occupations, and the complex and varying relations that may exist in different professions between their real world conditions of professional practice, the formal organization of the profession as a collegiate body, and university-based teaching and assessment of the professional disciplines. For example, the relationships between the occupations of engineering and accountancy and the respective university-based disciplines they relate to are not only very different from each other but also vary widely between different countries.

We are also conscious that in endorsing and extending Bernstein's analysis of these developments, we are liable to stand accused of self-interested apologetics on behalf of a conception of knowledge and expertise that, especially in an era of globalization, can be represented as indefensibly elitist, or as anachronistically self-absorbed, or both. Indeed, in suggesting that something of fundamental educational value may have been put at risk by the recent changes we have discussed, we lay ourselves open to criticism in equal measure from educational modernizers and postmodernists. The questioning by educational modernizers and marketizers of traditional assumptions about the knowledge-base of academic and professional work, has, after all, been given powerful (although not necessarily self-conscious) support by developments in social theory associated with postmodernism and social constructivism. Such perspectives reject the idea that professional or academic knowledge can make any kind of well-founded epistemological claim to objectivity or validity and see it as little more than an ideological device for protecting privileges and maintaining positions of domination. This kind of critique of professional and academic knowledge is not of course new. It has long been a familiar though not a central feature of Marxist thinking. What *is* new is that, unlike Marxism which has a strong, albeit highly contentious notion of knowledge and truth that is grounded in dialectical materialism, postmodernists reject the very idea that there could be a hierarchy of truth and knowledge on which professional relationships and certain kinds of professional authority might be based (Moore and Muller, 1999; Young 2000, Young, 2005).

These different sources of critique of academic and professional knowledge and autonomy pose a number of crucially important questions. Do they signify the end of a no longer defensible form of knowledge-based professionalism as we have come to know it? Do they point to the emergence of a new kind of professionalism with much weaker ties to the acquisition and production of knowledge in universities and much stronger links to practice in the real world? Even more radically, should the pretensions of professionals be exposed as little more than self-serving ideology – and their tasks deconstructed and reallocated on fundamentally different and, it may be claimed, more egalitarian principles? Or should both the universities and the professions simply be opened up to serious marketization and their state-protected 'labour-market shelters' and monopolies dismantled (Freedman, 1976, pp. 114–16; Freidson, 2001, p. 78)? The basic argument of this chapter is that although a whole range of changes, some of them global in scope, are undoubtedly challenging the once securely established legitimacy and autonomy of professional and academic work, the importance of the link between knowledge and professionalism and the key role of universities in this relationship remain both defensible and worth fighting for, albeit in terms that take account of the new circumstances.

A final general consideration is that as we have presented it so far, our (and Bernstein's) analysis of the prospects for professions continuing as occupations which retain some autonomy from both market forces and government regulation, which continue to enjoy a measure of autonomy to define their own knowledge-base, and which remain capable of forming a focus for identities centred in inner dedication, may appear unduly pessimistic. Such a view would, however, in our view be too one-dimensional. If things are in some ways bad, they are not uniformly so. Identifying a number of areas of both tension and challenge may help take forward one important part of the unfinished business we inherit from Basil Bernstein:

- Certainly there are professions – teaching in schools and colleges for example – where there have been strenuous efforts by government and its agencies to impose new modes of professional training in which genericism is dominant. In courses of initial teacher training, for instance, which are increasingly organized so that training institutions must comply with standards specifying tightly defined competencies, where there has been a marked shift of training sites from higher education to the workplace, where students have been successfully re-labelled as 'trainees', where intensive audit and inspection of 'providers' has become the norm, where training priorities change in response to a succession of government initiatives such as the National Literacy Strategy, it seems difficult to resist Bernstein's claim that the extension of generic modes 'institutionalises the concept of trainability *as the fundamental pedagogic objective*' (2000, p. 59, our italics). Moreover, the excision from such courses of all but the most instrumentally relevant forms of educational theory (especially the near elimination of philosophy, history and sociology of education) can be seen as illustrative of Bernstein's claim that generic modes involve a process of silencing – by denying trainees access to the forms of knowledge which permit alternative possibilities to be thought – thereby reproducing imaginary concepts of work and life which abstract real experiences from the power relations of their lived conditions and negate the possibilities of understanding and criticism (ibid., p. 53; Jones and Moore, 1993). Depressing though all this may be from a standpoint such as our own, it is important to recognize that teaching never succeeded, at least in England and Wales, in achieving full professional autonomy and may not be a paradigm for the restructuring of other professions – despite the enthusiasm of New Labour education ministers to depict it as a model for further reform within the public sector (see DfEE, 2001).[5] Moreover, efforts to stifle critical voices have been, to date, only partially successful, not least because attempts to assert greater controls over research and publication within university departments of education, such as the recently constituted National Forum for Educational Research, cannot be based on the same highly prescriptive model used by the Teacher Training Authority to control training.

- This brings us to a second consideration whose implications are harder to assess – that of the emergence of internal differences within professions. It seems probable that those who have felt most traumatized and hostile to marketization and the extension of external regulation are mainly professionals who enjoyed high levels of autonomy at earlier stages of their careers. But two other categories of professional employee have responded very differently, at least in some cases. First and most obviously, a proportion of professionals have enthusiastically embraced the new managerial opportunities that have been opened up and have indeed, pushed through the very restructuring that others so bitterly resent. It is important here that in many professional and academic spheres, the new managers have for the most part been recruited from within the ranks of the profession itself rather than imported from outside. As Newman and Clarke pointed out ten years ago, 'there has been a widespread transformation of bureau-professionals themselves into managers in the context of devolved or decentralised management systems' (1994, p. 24) – and this has continued. Furthermore, there is clear evidence that many in senior positions who are far less enthusiastic about the 'new directions' have felt in some measure 'co-opted' by audit cultures. The distinguished British social anthropologist Marilyn Strathern expressed the dilemma eloquently:

> It is ... no surprise that 'auditors' can be shown to be 'us' (cf. Brenneis, 1994). In the ways that academics are drawn into auditing practices, this is true at many levels. Peer reviews co-opt colleagues, willingly or otherwise. Those who devise and administer monitoring schemes are likely to come from the same of kind of professional background as those whose performance they scrutinize.
>
> (Strathern, 2000, p. 290)

A second important category is those who have recently begun their professional careers. Not only may their training have shaped their ambitions and expectations in new ways, their ideas of what may be strategic for career success may be based on more instrumental assumptions. Little is yet known about such intra-professional divisions and tensions, especially across a range of different occupations. Some recent studies of changing identities among primary school teachers have shown that many teachers in mid-career have found recent demands for 'performativity' traumatic (Ball, 1998; Broadfoot, 1998), though they have adjusted in complex ways rather than simply accommodated passively to the new regimes. Woods and Jeffrey conclude their recent study of one such group of teachers as follows: 'Will teachers simply grow more into their newly assigned social identity? Some will, no doubt, especially younger teachers who are fashioning personal identities in teaching for the first time. For our mid-career teachers, it is more a matter of gaining control ...' But, significantly, they conclude, in a way the echoes Bernstein's earlier observation: 'The new identities are much more volatile than the old.' (Woods and Jeffrey, 2002, p. 105)

- Thirdly, there are likely to be significant differences between those professionals who work, respectively, in the public or the private sector. This division, of course, cross cuts and even blurs many professional occupations, as private sector professionals such as accountants become increasingly involved in public sector contracts. The private/public division, however, still does represent another potential line of internal differences of experience and possible divisions of interest. Neither sector, however, has remained untouched by recent changes – and especially where a high proportion of a profession's members work for large organizations (whether public or private), similar pressures, especially heightened managerialism, accountancy-led forms of audit, etc. are likely to have been encountered.

- It is important to briefly mention the issue of expertise. Although it may be true that in some respects it is modern global markets that are undermining the conditions for professionalism, it is equally true that in many areas those same markets require an ever widening and deepening range of professional expertise if new products and services are to be developed. The possession of forms of expertise that are in demand does not of course guarantee that its possessors will choose, or will be able, to offer their services in the guise of professionalism. But other things being equal, it increases their leverage should they seek to do so. In this respect, Bernstein's epistemological agnosticism is not helpful in seeking to identify the areas of knowledge which may be the most robust in these respects. It was only in his last work, on 'vertical' and 'horizontal' knowledge structures, that he did begin to address these issues (see 2000, Ch. 9).

- Finally, from an ethical standpoint, highly publicized scandals such as the collapse of Enron have vividly illustrated the dangers of situations in which independent professional judgement becomes co-opted, intimidated or silenced by aggressive and triumphalist shareholder capitalism and unscrupulous senior management. If such developments convince a growing number of people that market forces and headlong privatization are not a panacea, the questions about the ethical and epistemological basis of different fields of professionalism in these new circumstances, with which this chapter began, may prove to be of far more than academic interest.

Chapter 6

'DIRECTED TIME': IDENTITY AND TIME IN NEW RIGHT AND NEW LABOUR POLICY DISCOURSE

Introduction – 'directing' time

'Directed time', at least in England and Wales, is a term which has become familiar to teachers since the imposition in 1987 of a requirement for teachers to work a stipulated number of hours per year performing contractually specified duties (Tomlinson, 1993, p. 58).[1] As Leaton Gray (2004) has suggested, the notion of directed time has metaphorical resonance far wider than teachers' contracts. First, this regulation of teachers' time-management was a symbolic marker of the new regimes of performativity and audit that began to be imposed in the 1980s. Secondly, directed time points to the fact that educational time itself can be variously punctuated and periodized, oriented to past or future, accelerated or slowed, according to the requirements of different policy discourses and agendas. This chapter offers a tentative exploration of contrasting orientations to time associated respectively with the political and educational priorities of New Right Conservatism and New Labour in Britain. It will seek to relate these orientations to official attempts to shape new educational and citizen identities.

Basil Bernstein suggested that a key part of the state's reassertion of control over education in England and Wales in the last three decades of the twentieth century involved efforts to project new 'official' educational identities – pupil and (future) citizen identities, and teacher identities. Briefly, he argued that a 're-centred state' was attempting to manage educational change in a context of new economic, cultural and moral challenges, by reasserting centralized control, with the explicit aim of reshaping the pedagogic identities of pupils and teachers in determinate ways (2000, pp. 66–8). Bernstein identified two contrasting types of such 'centred' identities, 'retrospective' and 'prospective', and it is the latter that will mainly concern us here. Prospective identities are future oriented – incorporating a specification of the person as a particular kind of economic producer, consumer and citizen. But with characteristic perceptiveness, Bernstein stresses that these identities are not purely future-orientated. Rather, they are formed by 'recontextualising selected features of the *past* to stabilise the future through engaging with contemporary change' (ibid. p. 68, original italics deleted, my italics inserted). Consequently, the shaping of such identities involves both reconfiguring the past (as well as the past's relation to the present) and also projecting a version of the future that is consistent with this imaginary past. Although Bernstein offered brief sketches of the prospective identities projected respectively by Thatcherism and by 'Blair's New Labour' (ibid. pp. 67–8), he did not elaborate them. In what follows, I shall attempt to fill in these outlines and explore some of the ways in which such identities incorporate particular orientations to time, within and beyond education.

'Thatcherism' And New Right Prospective Identities

Several commentators have argued that Thatcherism should be seen 'as an alliance of disparate forces around a self-contradictory programme' rather than as an ideologically unified and coherent political phenomenon (Jessop et al., 1984, p. 38). Similarly, the New Right educational agenda in the period between 1979 and 1997 has also been viewed as an attempt to unite two contradictory projects – those of neoconservative 'cultural restoration' (Ball, 1990; Wexler and Grabiner, 1986) and the marketizing, privatizing concerns of neoliberalism. Although certain of these apparent contradictions may not really have been as fundamental as they at first seemed (see Whitty, 1990), it is nevertheless hard to disagree with David Marquand's observation that

> The global market place which the new-style Tories celebrate is cold and hard; in a profound sense, it is also subversive. It uproots communities, disrupts families, mocks faiths and erodes the ties of place and history. It has created a demotic global culture contemptuous of tradition, hostile to established hierarchies and relativist in morality.
>
> (Marquand, 1995)

leveling does the same!

These considerations, however, suggest something problematic when we turn to consider the forms of identity which, if Bernstein is right, successive New Right administrations sought to project. How could a coherent identity grow from such forked roots? Admittedly, post-structuralists remind us that subjectivities are normally fragmented. Nevertheless, attempts to project official identities presuppose an endeavour to shape something possessing some degree of coherence. How might this have been accomplished? Interestingly, several writers use the term 'fusion' to explain this. For example:

- Ken Jones, began his book *Right Turn* as follows: 'Conservative education policy, Janus-headed, *fuses* the archaic and modern, mixes nostalgia with technology … ' (1989, p. 1, my italics).
- Bernstein himself, in his brief sketch of the prospective pedagogic identity projected under Thatcherism, suggests that 'a new collective social base was formed by *fusing* nation, family, individual responsibility and individual enterprise' (2000, p. 68, my italics).

This language of fusion does intuitively grasp something central to the Thatcherite project of identity formation but it is more than a little inexplicit. It could, variously interpreted, imply aggregation, coalescence, or reduction to an underlying essence.

A fruitful approach to unravelling these issues can be found in social anthropologist Marilyn Strathern's *After Nature* (1992). Strathern's overall concern in this text is to analyse the conditions that made possible the changing ways in which the English middle classes, across more than two hundred years, imagined themselves and their relationships – to one another, to convention, to family, and to society. One section of the book deals directly with Thatcherism and here Strathern's point of departure is Thatcher's assertion that: 'There is no such thing as society. There are individual men and women and there are families ...' (ibid., p. 158).

Against those who homed in on the supposed absence of morality and the 'sheer selfishness' implied in this claim, Strathern's interest is in how something that was a morality – a morality apparently independent of society – came to be constructed as a possible discursive object. She poses the question 'So where, then, does the morality now come from, how can it be seen?' (ibid. p. 159). She suggests that a key strategy involved was one of dislocating the individual from society by depicting collectivism, especially state-sponsored collectivism, as something artificial and alien to British instincts. This was counterpointed within Thatcherite discourse, by a 'naturalism' in which morality is installed as an inherent property of responsible individuals who simply know how to conduct themselves. Strathern speculates that:

> Perhaps that possibility draws on the ease with which the English have in the past personified convention: the 'forces' or 'principles' for morality, good conduct and the rest can be apostrophised as existing of themselves, so that people can respond to those forces without the intervention of (contrived, collectivist) human institutions. Morality is set free from such institutions ... People, we are told by the Government, do not need government to tell them what to do. Since ideas and values are seen to exert an influence by themselves, they do not have to be mediated by others, but can be taken for granted in the minds of right thinking individuals. All that individuals have to do is manage their lives properly ... What displaces the plurality of other persons who might be held to 'make society' is the single individual with means. 'Society' thereby becomes unimaginable.
>
> (Ibid., pp. 160–1)

Two crucial consequences of this are, first that 'it becomes impossible to invoke selfishness with the same axiomatic condemnation; attention to ones own interests is now a virtue' and second, 'since morality is within, then it must necessarily take the form that in turn typifies the individual: the capacity to exercise *choice*' (ibid., p. 161, my italics).

In all this, something rather strange and paradoxical happens to time. The naturalizing move seems to cancel temporal referents by eternalising certain dispositions as natural properties of individuals per se. Yet, this turns out to be not just any individual but rather one who is somehow innately British. John Quicke, for example, has drawn attention to the significance in New Right discourse, of recourse to certain givens supposedly 'lodged in the British Personality' (1988, p. 18). Strathern makes a similar connection: 'that people know what is right is taken for granted, rather like the stereotyped English gentleman who knows his duty even if he cannot say what it is until the moment is upon him' (op. cit., p. 159). Strathern is referring here to a lecture series delivered in 1929 by a certain Professor Dixon, concerning the 'English Genius'. Dixon suggested not only that the Englishman is typically an individualist but also that the Englishman's sense of duty is at once unreflective but instinctively sure – issuing in appropriate action: 'What is English here is the sense of conduct as the test of a man. Not what he thinks or feels ... Let others judge by the state of their emotions or of their minds ... Brushing all these aside as irrelevant, the Englishman judges simply by the act ...' (Dixon, 1938, pp. 78–80).

Or as Strathern satirically glosses this, 'the Englishman does his duty without quite knowing what it is', adding: 'this 1930s evocation of individual motivation anticipates a most interesting feature of the (neo-conservative) active citizen: that he or she is their own source of right acting' (op. cit., p. 153).

This analysis suggests that the construction of time in these discourses involves an amalgam of contradictory but efficacious fictions. On the one hand, time is cancelled by the appeal to naturalism. But it is enabled to reappear by associating this natural individualism with a conception of national character – one which in one sense is also 'eternalised' as the unchanging instincts of the Englishman, but that in another sense is necessarily historical, incorporating a vision of the national past. Here, perhaps, is a key element of the fusion of conflicting elements that has been seen as a hallmark of Thatcherism. The values which motivate this individual are at once purely individual and also timeless because natural, but at the same time they are historical because inseparable from a rugged but rooted Englishness. The consequences are significant. On the one hand, the resonance of this individualism with so-called Victorian values comes to appear self-evident as an expression of authentic English character in the past and thus also of tradition. But at the same time, what is licensed and legitimized is the innately morally responsible individual whose primary moral responsibility is to seek the good of themselves and their family through the exercise of marketized choices and enterprising behaviour.

The extent to which and the ways in which education (and more specifically pedagogic transmissions) may have contributed to a similar shaping of such 'dis-sociated' individualism is not easy to assess. Bernstein argued explicitly that the prospective pedagogic identity projected under Thatcherism was designed to shape 'what were considered to be appropriate attitudes, dispositions and performances relevant to a market culture and reduced state welfare' and (as we have seen) he suggests that this involved an attempt to create a 'new collective social base ... formed by fusing nation, family, individual responsibility and individual enterprise' (ibid., p. 68). The resonances with Strathern's analysis are clear. However, curricular constructions of the nation's past, even when surrounded by restorationist rhetoric, cannot be easily shaped to simply reinforce the sort of potent but unreflective commonsense Strathern describes, especially where the curriculum takes the form of a 'collection code' (Bernstein, 2000, pp. 10–11) which supports academic virtues such as respect for evidence and the importance of weighing competing interpretations of issues and events. Recognizing this tension, a number of other commentators have highlighted the significance of the role of the hidden curriculum as possibly a stronger influence on identity formation than either the content or pedagogy of the overt curriculum. For example, Whitty and Power have commented: 'while the content of lessons emphasises heritage and tradition, the form of their transmission is becoming increasingly commodified within the new education marketplace' (Whitty, 2002, p. 103). And Bernstein himself similarly suggested that context was likely to outweigh content in this contradictory pedagogic transmission:

> The culture of the pedagogic discourse of schools is retrospective, based on a past narrative of the dominance and significance of disciplines, whereas the management structure is *prospective*, pointing to the new entrepreneurialism and its instrumentalities. The state has therefore embedded a retrospective pedagogic culture into a prospective management culture. However, the emphasis on the performance of students and the steps taken to increase and maintain performance, for the survival of the institution, is likely to facilitate a state-promoted instrumentality. The intrinsic value of knowledge may well be eroded even though the collection code of the curriculum appears to support such a value.
>
> (op. cit., p. 61)

If this analysis is persuasive, Thatcherite conservatism sought to both project and ratify a new–old British identity centred in ostensibly self-made and self-supporting individuals and their families who had an intuitive sense of their links to a heritage of robust national and individual independence. This identity was thus able to combine a strong sense of continuity with a shared (if highly fictitious) national past which was also the foundation of a realistic orientation to a future in which markets and individual effort would rightly allocate resources and opportunities in an increasingly competitive world. The individual's sense of moral obligation towards the welfare of others would be expressed in voluntary effort rather than mediated by enterprise-sapping statist provision.

New Labour's Modernizing Agenda And New Prospective Identities

Before embarking on a discussion of identity formation under New Labour, it is worth recalling that Bernstein's analysis of identity was grounded in a broadly Durkheimian view that individual identity must be rooted in a 'collective social base'. It follows that any endeavour to construct identities therefore requires the parallel or prior construction of such a social base. In the case of New Labour's attempts to project centred prospective identities, what was explicitly foregrounded in contrast to Thatcherism, was social belonging – linked, however, to strong notions of individual enterprise and responsibility. The social base of these centred identities was thus 'An amalgam of notions of community (really communities) and local responsibilities to motivate and restore belonging in the cultural sphere, and a new participatory responsibility in the economic sphere.' (op. cit., p. 68)

In his broader discussion of pedagogic identities, however, Bernstein emphasized that at any historical moment, no one identity-project was likely to be hegemonic. And in his analyses of social and educational change in late twentieth century Britain, he saw the co-existence of contra-dictory forms of identity as characteristic of the period, in particular, the tension between centred identities projected by government and 'de-centred market' identities arising from the effects of market forces. For our purposes, it is significant that Bernstein did not examine in any detail the temporal aspects of the various forces that were reshaping identity as the twentieth century moved towards its close. In this section, therefore, I shall tentatively explore some of the ways in which New Labour has sought to construct a new version of the past's relation to the present, as a basis for an agenda of urgent modernization.[2]

In repositioning itself in the political landscape, it is significant that New Labour chose to re-brand itself by employing two key descriptors – New and modernize. Such terms are examples of what Bill Readings (1996) calls 'dereferentialization', i.e. words which are relatively content-less, but which, for that very reason can be mobilised to support whatever more specific goals an organization's current agendas may require. Readings cites the example of excellence, as used in mission statements and the like (but see also DfEE, 1997a, 1997b, 1999 and DfES, 2003). New and modernize are not, of course, wholly content-less. Both have a clear temporal reference: together they signify a future that will be radically different from the past though still linked to it: what was good will be conserved and the bad abandoned. In some respects, of course, the party leadership was content with nothing short of rupture – most clearly in expunging the old Clause 4 from the party's constitution. But for the most part, the modernizing initiatives have involved retaining both termi-nology and organizational forms from the past, whilst radically changing and sometimes inverting their meaning.

It will clearly not be possible to examine here the whole of New Labour's political or even educational discourse. Rather, I shall focus on just two areas of educational policy: first the 'modernisation of the teaching profession', and second, the intensification of the standards agenda. In each case, the discussion will draw mainly on education policy documents from a variety of sources. I shall also refer to a number of secondary commentaries.[3]

The modernization of the teaching profession

The 2001 Green Paper *Schools: Building on Success* felt able to celebrate the progress already achieved in modernizing the teaching profession:

> The changing economy is increasingly placing new demands on professionals in every field. In the 20th century, the professional could often expect to be treated as an authority, whose judgment was rarely questioned and who was therefore rarely held to account. Despite this ... particularly in the public sector, services were arranged to suit the producer rather than the user.
> Teaching, by contrast is already in many ways a 21st century profession. More perhaps than any other, the teaching profession accepts accountability, is open to the contributions that others can make and is keen to seek out best practice ... Growing acceptance of accountability means that the relationship between teachers and Government can build more than ever before on trust ... In this climate, in partnership with teachers, we will take forward the agenda of reform ... and complete the modernisation of the teaching profession.
>   (DfEE, 2001, paras 5.4, 5.5. and 5.6)

It is instructive to set this alongside a recent speech by Michael Barber, formerly the director of the DfES Standards and Effectiveness Unit and subsequently head of the prime minster's Delivery Unit:

> Until the mid-1980s what happened in schools and classrooms was left almost entirely to teachers to decide ... Almost all teachers had goodwill and many sought to develop themselves professionally, but, through no fault of their own, the profession itself was uninformed ... Under Thatcher, the system moved from *uninformed professional judgement to uninformed prescription.*
>   (Barber, 2001, cited in Alexander, 2004, pp. 15–16, italics in the
>   original)

Such statements are examples of a discursive strategy that seeks to construct an imaginary version of the past in an effort to shape conditions for a new consensus between teachers and government, and also to shape the identities of modern professionals. This strategy employs a dichotomous periodizing of educational time in order to create a pathological past set against an enlightened present. A pervasive feature of the discourse is its tendency to present highly contestable claims as if they were unquestionable truths.

Older forms of professional organization in which professions enjoyed greater autonomy are pathologized not merely as self-serving and unaccountable but also as professionally 'uninformed'. As Alexander has trenchantly remarked: 'Note how heavily professional ignorance features in this professional pathology, and how it is presented as an inevitable concomitant of professional autonomy. To be free to decide how to teach is to be uninformed.' He adds: 'it sets things up nicely, of course, for the transformation achieved by New Labour and the Utopia which is now in sight' (ibid., p. 16).

A related characteristic of the discourse is that it presents a range of crucially significant concepts as if they had only one legitimate interpretation. Thus we are told, baldly, that the modernized teaching profession accepts accountability – as if there was only one concept of accountability possible. It is ironic that those who accuse others of being uninformed can so conveniently overlook the debates of the 1980s on competing conceptions of accountability – for example, Bailey's discussion of the professional responsibilities of liberal educators (1984, pp. 236–40), or the work of the Cambridge Accountability Project (Elliott et al., 1981). By being positioned on the wrong side of the historical divide between pathology and enlightenment, such work is consigned to oblivion by the new modernizers, whose instrumental training-schedules allow no time for teachers to think in an informed manner about such issues. In these ways, the scope of professional debate is drastically narrowed and the professional conversations of the past are written out of history.

Pathologizing the past is, however, only half the story. Its counterpart is the deployment of a would-be inclusive language that seeks to co-opt teachers (and other professionals) as modern professionals. Here, modernization reveals its versatility. It can signal not only the new but suggest continuities with the past. The message is that teachers have always been in certain respects professional and now they are being 'helped' to become more so. Here, a further periodization becomes significant: between a Thatcherism that castigated teachers for their alleged inadequacies, replaced by a stance that recognizes teachers' longstanding professional commitment and seeks partnership with them. The new language, of 'shared vision', 'trust', 'goodwill', 'partnership', 'dialogue', is increasingly prominent in recent documents. Even where teachers are judged inadequate, e.g. by virtue of being uninformed, they are reassured that this was *through no fault of their own* (Barber op. cit., in Alexander, 2004 p. 16, my italics). This ostensibly post-Fordist turn in official discourse has helped New Labour to present its overall project as one of re-professionalization, not de-professionalization.

This invitation to partnership has been linked to a further claim: that New Labour's reforms have raised the status of the profession. The 2002 DfES document *Time for Standards*, under a subheading 'Teaching – A High Status Profession', claimed

In talking about what our best teachers are doing, we are describing a profession that is on the move ... We hope that teaching will emerge as the most admired profession of the 21st century, and the one young people are keenest to join ... Together, we can create a new and thoroughly deserved image for ... teachers as mind-shapers and not child-minders.

(DfES, 2002b, pp. 17–18)

Such rhetoric risks imploding into its own vacuity. Nevertheless, it signals a significant discursive shift from a culture of blame, to a culture of partnership and 'earned autonomy'. This presages a whole new era:

The 1997–2001 Blair Government inherited a system of *uninformed prescription* and replaced it with one of *informed prescription* ... The White Paper signals the next shift: from *informed prescription to informed professional judgement* ... The era of informed professional judgement could be the most successful so far in our educational history ...

(Barber, op. cit., quoted in Alexander, op. cit., 2004, p. 16, italics in the original)

At the heart of informed professional judgement is the idea of 'evidence-based teaching and learning'. Thus a 2002 DfES paper confidently declares:

Our best teachers are already using informed professional judgement. They are creating an evidence-based body of knowledge about teaching and learning. Establishing such a body of knowledge has always been a crucial step in marking out the top professions in our society. It will provide working models that other teachers will adopt and ensure that teaching is acknowledged for what it is: an innovative and expert profession.

(DfES, 2002b, p. 12)

Once again, the language of the discourse is as revealing as the content. It is 'our best' teachers who have created this body of knowledge – though, of course, crucially enabled by government. And, in an appeal to those older models of professionalism that the government is in other respects so keen to discredit, we are told that teaching may advance to the rank of a top profession by virtue of being based on such expert knowledge. What is more, teaching will win further recognition of its status through disseminating such 'proven best practice'. So far, so simplistic. It is ironic that what is being celebrated is professional judgement, when what is occurring is the narrowing of the scope of autonomous judgement about education and pedagogy in favour of a state-imposed technicism.

The creation (significantly by government itself) of the General Teaching Council for England in September 2000, was intended to be a key symbol of the claimed re-professionalization of teaching. The GTC is, in the words of its first chief executive, a body which has been given 'responsibility for advising the government and other bodies on education policy' and which has taken on certain functions of traditional professional associations including 'developing a code of professional practice with the full involvement of the profession' and also the regulation of professional misconduct (Adams, 2000). On closer analysis however, this professional re-empowerment turns out to be remarkably circumscribed. The GTC may advise on educational policy but it is government and its agencies that continue to operate the levers of power. Symptomatically, government spokesmen, when addressing the public at large, remain unabashed in declaring that it is they who are in charge and are 'driving through necessary change'. Thus Andrew Adonis could write in 2001: 'We have *imposed* a new national curriculum for initial teacher training, setting out the standards and content of training courses, which all providers *must* follow' (Adonis, 2001, quoted in Alexander, op. cit., p. 17, my italics), while Education Secretary David Blunkett declared 'I make no apologies for the *prescription* in the literacy and numeracy strategies; we had to deal with the failure of teacher training over decades' (2001a, p. 7, my italics). The italicized imperatives here provide a discordant counterpoint to the themes of trust and partnership so prominent elsewhere. As Alexander succinctly summarizes the situation, '… it is clear that in the post-2001 era of "informed professional judgement", to be "informed" is to know and acquiesce in what is provided, expected and/or required by government and its agencies – no less and, especially, no more' (op. cit., p. 17).

Making up for lost time: accelerating the 'standards agenda'

Although New Labour may allow itself some celebration of progress, there is no room (or time) for complacency. The latest imperative is to accelerate the pace of change. Michael Barber again:

> Our vision is of a world-class education service: one that matches the best anywhere … We want to see it achieved … as soon as possible within the decade that has just begun. Our sense of urgency comes … from the belief that time is running out for public education to prove its worth. (Barber, 2003)

Again, the discourse presents a set of speculative and contentious claims as unarguable imperatives. Thus, in a passage that directly follows that quoted above:

> The danger is that … more and more people will see private education for their children as a rational lifestyle option. If this were to occur, they would become less and less willing to fund public education, which would become … a poor service for poor people … Only if public education delivers, and is seen to deliver real quality, can this unwelcome prospect be avoided … successful reform is possible … and … need not take forever.

And a little later: 'In the modern world ... electorates are fickle and impatient ... They ... will not wait patiently for five or ten years to see if it delivers. They want immediate evidence that is on the way.' The clincher follows: 'Hence the central paradox facing education reformers in a democracy – a long-term strategy will only succeed if it delivers short-term results' (ibid).

As well as anxious parents and impatient electorates, contemporary education is also depicted as beset by inexorable globalization seen as shaping an economic environment in which educational institutions and national economies alike face a stark choice: adapt or perish. As David Blunkett (2000) put it: 'Universities need to adapt rapidly to the top-down influences of globalisation and the new technologies', adding menacingly that 'the "do-nothing" universities will not survive – and it will not be the job of government to bail them out'. Barber extends this diagnosis, employing further specious periodization, to announce the inevitability of educational globalization:

> Just as financial services globalised in the 1980s and media and communications in the 1990s, so in this decade we will see education reform globalising ... We, in England, will want to be sure that our 14 year olds are as well educated as students in the USA, Germany or Singapore, not least because they will ultimately be competing in a global job market. (op. cit.)

What is perhaps most striking about such claims (and they are legion – reiterated in almost every major government education policy document) is that 'no alternative is conceived, except that we, as a nation, might fail to keep up' and that 'few ends are considered for the nation and its education system, other than meeting the challenge and adapting' (Ahier, Beck and Moore, 2003, p. 82). In reality, however, globalization is not an unquestionable fact: rather, it is a contested concept whose definition and effects are vigorously disputed (see, for example, Beck 2000; Callinicos, 2001; Gray, 1999; Held and McGrew, 2002; and Hirst and Thompson, 1996).

New Labour's enthusiasts for change, however, are in no mood to allow mere academic arguments to impede the essential task of further and faster modernization. We must, we are urged, be decisive, innovative and pragmatic in dealing with these pressing challenges. Moreover, we must not cling to outdated delivery mechanisms:

> We must ask ourselves from where the energy, knowledge, imagination, skill and investment will come to meet the immense challenge of education reform over the next decade.
> For most of the 20th century, the drive for educational progress came from the public sector ... Towards the end of the 20th century, as frustration with existing systems grew, this legacy was challenged by a growing vibrant private sector ... The challenge for the 21st century is

surely to *seek out what works*. The issue is not whether the public, private or voluntary sector alone will shape the future but what partnerships and combinations of the three will make the most difference to student performance.

(Barber, 2003, my italics)

Yet again we encounter a pathologized past (of public provision) counterposed to a glowing future (of 'vibrant' private sector leadership and 'partnership'). And once more, complex issues of political philosophy and value are overridden by the supposed pragmatic imperatives of adopting whatever 'delivery systems' work best and quickest. Even issues as complex and controversial as expanding the provision of faith schools can, in this hurrying discourse, be treated almost entirely instrumentally – as little more than pragmatic mechanisms to help deliver the really important goal: driving up standards:

> We are intentionally breaking the mould in our relationships with the voluntary and religious sectors, by, for example, providing for the first time, state funding for Muslim, Sikh, and Seventh Day Adventist schools ...
> The central challenge is to build social coalitions in the drive for higher standards and radical reform. It is clear in Hong Kong and elsewhere that the business and religious sectors are strong allies. This is true in the USA too where ... the churches provide real energy and drive for educational progress ... Each a different combination, each fit for purpose ... (Ibid.)

Let us now consider the implications for identity of this headlong instrumentalism and pragmatism. They seem to point towards what Bernstein saw as a new sort of identity – whose most striking characteristic was that it was socially empty. Marketization and managerialization of education, he suggested, were likely to promote, at least in certain parts of the education system, generic pedagogic modes

> based on a new concept of 'work' and 'life' which might be called '*short-termism*'. This is where a skill, task, area of work, undergoes continuous development, disappearance or replacement; where life experience cannot be based on stable expectations of the future and one's location in it.

(Bernstein, op. cit., p. 59, my italics)

In such circumstances, Bernstein argues, a new kind of ability comes to be seen as particularly desirable – trainability – the capacity to accept and (ideally) embrace 'continuous pedagogic re-formations' requiring 'an ability to respond effectively to concurrent, subsequent, intermittent pedagogics'. Unlike more stable bases of identity formation, however, the identity produced by this combination of short-termism and trainability is intrinsically 'socially empty': 'there seems to be an emptiness in the concept of train-ability, an emptiness which makes the concept self-referential' (ibid. p. 59). It denotes, precisely, a vacant space waiting to be filled with whatever temporary contents market, or institutional, or governmental imperatives may dictate.[4]

A similar substantive emptiness seems to lie at the heart of New Labour's agenda of accelerating modernization. What is most striking about the modernizers' machismo – that there is no alternative but to respond to 'the challenge ahead through "step change", "tough", "new", "tough new", "world class", "best practice", "delivery", and so on' (DfEE, 2001, cited in Alexander, op. cit., p. 14) – is precisely that it too is so empty of principled or grounded educational content – largely as a result of being pragmatically orientated to short-term instrumental goals and adaptive responses. It is no less noteworthy that this change agenda is permeated with attempts (both discursive and practical) to reconfigure relationships between past, present and future, and that it seeks to do this in ways that would, if successful, render much of the past inaccessible and therefore unavailable as a basis for identity formation. In New Labour's rhetoric of adaptation and modern-ization, it is increasingly the case that those parts of the past that do not fit are either repudiated or repressed:

- repudiated as irrelevant because they offer no guide to challenges which are, by definition, unprecedented as well as pressing;
- repudiated as in various ways pathological and dysfunctional – a place of self-indulgence, or at best of well intentioned but inade-quately informed practice;
- repudiated as the site of discredited and inefficient forms of 'statist' provision;
- repressed by attempts to silence discourses critical of current policy and dismantle or restructure the organizational forms that carried them. Recent reforms of initial teacher training in England display both these tendencies.[5]

Conclusion

This orientation to the past by the party of government may be both an effect and a cause of what some have seen as a more general phenomenon of our times. As Eric Hobsbawm expressed it:

The destruction of the past, or rather of the social mechanisms that link one's contemporary experience to that of earlier generations, is one of the most characteristic and eerie phenomena of the late twentieth century. Most young men and women at the century's end grow up in a sort of permanent present lacking any organic relation to the public past of the times they live in. (1994, p. 3)

Such reflections return us to the theme of emptiness. As Bernstein saw it, something would be necessary to fill the empty identity-space produced by short-termism and trainability: 'If the identity produced by "trainability" is socially "empty", how does the actor recognise him/herself and others?' His answer was: 'by the materialities of consumption … the products of the market relay the signifiers whereby temporary stabilities, orientations, relations and evaluations are constructed' (op. cit. p. 59). If this analysis is persuasive, it may not be entirely far-fetched to suggest that New Labour's modernizers are tapping into but also shaping something that may indeed be an emergent sociocultural reality: an historically dissociated 'middle England' in which identity is increasingly centred in consumerist signifiers of value and personal worth. The tragedy (but paradoxically also the success) of New Labour may be that it so assiduously promotes this emergent sensibility rather than doing anything to question or challenge it.

Speaking out in this way against current shibboleths carries a certain risk. As Frank Kermode put it in relation to his own critical comments on 1960s literary modernism: 'To speak clearly on these issues is to attract the charge that one is simply no longer young enough or bright enough to grasp the exciting things that are going on.' (Kermode, 1966, p. 123) However, academics of a certain age may take some comfort from Kermode's affirmation: 'The critics should know their duty' (ibid., p. 124).

Chapter 7

THE SCHOOL CURRICULUM AND THE NATIONAL CURRICULUM: CONSERVATIVE AND NEW LABOUR REFORMS

What is meant by 'Curriculum'?

In thinking in general terms about the school curriculum, it may be useful initially to consider three basic issues that apply to any curriculum – those of scope, content and structure.

a) **The scope of 'curriculum'**
Several writers on the curriculum have distinguished between the overt and the hidden curriculum. The latter term has been used to refer to various aspects of how schools transmit the knowledge which is part of the formal curriculum: for example, how pupils are grouped for learning (setting, mixed-ability, etc.), how different forms of achievement are recognized (or not), the character of the school's pastoral system – all conveying messages about what the school really values and does not value (see, for example, Hargreaves, 1982, for a discussion of 'the hidden curriculum of the formal curriculum'). Various structural features of schooling can also convey unintended messages – for example, the existence of business sponsorship in some types of school, the effects of a faith ethos, etc. In what follows, the emphasis will mainly be on the overt curriculum but it is always important to be aware of the complex inter-relationships between the formal and hidden curriculum – for example: do similar principles underlie both or are there discrepancies or even contradictions?

b) **The content of the curriculum**
In terms of its contents, any curriculum is a selection from all the worthwhile knowledge that schooling could potentially transmit. This implies that questions about priorities are inseparable from curriculum design. An important issue, therefore, is to identify the principles that have been salient in shaping any particular curriculum. Five such historically significant principles are:

- children's and students' own interests and choices
- economic relevance
- vocational relevance

- shaping national identity and allegiance
- a humanistic conception of liberal education, emphasizing the value of knowledge and understanding for its own sake and in the development of self understanding and moral agency.

Linked to these underlying principles is the question of whether the curriculum should be similar for all pupils or whether it should differ for different types of pupil and if so, on what basis and from what age.

c) The structure of the curriculum

Curriculum structure has to do, at a fairly abstract level, with the nature of the elements that comprise it and their relationship to one another. Within the English national curriculum, for example, the fundamental elements are a set of discrete subjects, each normally separately timetabled and often, at least in secondary schools, taught by specialist teachers. However, in the 1960s and '70s, many innovative comprehensive schools organized their curricula within broad faculty structures such as integrated humanities, planning content around interdisciplinary topics like war, the developing world, the family, etc. More recently, the Qualifications and Curriculum Authority in its 2007 Secondary Review has urged schools to introduce a stronger emphasis on teaching across subject boundaries (QCA, 2007a). Progressive or child-centred education (or in modern parlance, personalized learning), typically involves structures that are even more flexible – for example, where individual pupil choice strongly influences what shall be learned, how much time shall be devoted to it, etc. Here, the elements of the curriculum could, for example, be pupil-chosen projects of various kinds, with teachers in the role of guides and enablers.

A key variable, therefore, is the definition and strength of the boundaries between the different elements. According to sociologist Basil Bernstein, strong boundaries indicate strong authority relationships – both in the structuring and transmission of knowledge and often in pedagogic relations too. Where boundaries are weak, authority relationships may be less secure and more open to change, and there is likely to be scope for learners to exercise greater control over what is learned, how, and at what pace – though even here there may be tacit or 'invisible' forms of control (see Bernstein, 2000, Introduction and Chapter 1). But the bottom line is that all forms of curriculum structure contain some set of principles that shape the selection and sequencing of knowledge and the pacing of learning. And for this reason, it is not sensible to draw too sharp a distinction between curriculum structure and curriculum content. Often, common principles shape both together – and also shape pedagogy in the sense of the character of the teaching–learning relationship.

Another important aspect of curriculum structure concerns the relationship between curriculum as specified nationally – e.g. in English National Curriculum Programmes of Study – and curriculum as interpreted in individual schools and classrooms. This is sometimes referred to as the delivery of the curriculum – but it is worth noticing that the very use of a term like delivery, itself contains significant messages, not least about control, over the structuring of knowledge and of teaching/learning, and about where such control is located.

The control of the curriculum

Because what children learn in school shapes the attitudes and beliefs of future generations, the content of the curriculum is often contested, especially in contemporary democratic societies which are both politically and culturally pluralistic. A range of key players compete (or cooperate) to influence what gets selected for transmission as educational knowledge. Among the most important of these are: politicians, state bureaucrats, think tanks, employers' organizations, trade unions, religious groups, the media, parents, academics and, of course, teachers themselves. All these groups (and subgroups within them) tend to have particular (some would say vested) interests – but each may easily assume that there is a natural correspondence between its own aims and the national interest or society's needs. This being so, there is often good reason to be sceptical about those who engage in needs talk – those who confidently assert that society, or our children, clearly need this or that or the other. Educational needs, we should remember, do not simply exist in the same sense as basic biological needs. Almost invariably, needs talk conceals hidden value judgements. Even if we accept this, however, all of the groups mentioned can all reasonably claim to have some degree of legitimate interest in the curriculum. But the extent to which the views of any one category, parents for example, should outweigh the views of others, opens up questions of considerable complexity. And given the value-laden nature of most decisions about schooling and the curriculum, such questions cannot be neatly settled by any simple appeal to reason or to evidence: equally reasonable and equally intelligent people using the same evidence, may reach very different conclusions. This is another way of saying that judge-ments about the curriculum are always value laden.

Since the introduction of a national curriculum in England in 1988, it is, of course, central government that has determined the basic structure and content of the curriculum in state schools – and countries like France have had a national curriculum for far longer. However, it is far from universally agreed that such state control is desirable. First, it is factually the case that affluent parents in England and Wales can bypass the national curriculum by sending their children to a range of independent schools which are not required to teach it (even though many do broadly follow its outlines). More fundamentally, various commentators, especially but not only on the political right, see significant dangers in government control over educational knowledge. Some of these critics argue that parents' and students' interests would be better served by creating an educational marketplace, in which parents as consumers could choose the kind of education they wanted for their children without interference by the state (see, for example, Tooley, 2000).

The introduction of a National Curriculum in England and Wales: differing rationales

For many decades, from the mid-1920s until 1988, there was very limited direct state prescription of curriculum structure or content in England and Wales. Support for the idea of a common core curriculum began to be politically canvassed from the mid-1970s when a Labour government Green Paper tentatively asked whether there should be a core or protected part of the curriculum common to all schools, perhaps comprising English, maths, science and maybe a foreign language (DES, 1977). From this hesitant beginning, there is a huge leap to the extensive and highly prescriptive national curriculum of core, foundation and basic subjects introduced by Kenneth Baker in 1988 when he was secretary of state for education. Moreover, even at the time, some within the government and many more outside it did not support so centralized, extensive and prescriptive an approach. Margaret Thatcher herself later had considerable reservations:

> ... the national curriculum ... the most important centralizing measure - soon ran into difficulties. I never envisaged that we would end up with the bureaucracy and the thicket of prescriptive measure that eventually emerged. I wanted the DES to concentrate on establishing a basic syllabus for English, mathematics and science with simple tests to show what pupils knew.
>
> (Thatcher, 1993, p. 593)

In the light of this, it is worth emphasizing that the simple fact of there now being a statutory national curriculum in England and Wales, does not in itself constitute a justification. Justification, after all, has to do with the quality of the arguments and relevant evidence that can be advanced – both for but also against an idea. We turn now, therefore, to examine some of the justifications that have been offered for a compulsory, common curriculum for all the nation's children (or, more often in fact, for all those in state schools).

a) Curriculum entitlement

One important justification was advanced by some of those who successfully advocated the introduction of comprehensive schooling. The establishment of a national system of non-selective comprehensive secondary schools in the 1960s and '70s, they argued, itself implied that such schools should provide broadly similar curricular experiences for all their pupils. One key argument here related to equality of educational opportunity. All pupils in such schools, it was contended, should have a common curriculum entitlement:

> Pupils should be entitled to the same opportunities wherever they go to school ... A national curriculum will help to raise standards of

attainment by ... ensuring that all pupils, regardless of sex, ethnic origin and geographical location, have access to broadly the same good and relevant curriculum ...

(DES, 1987, pp. 3–4)

Part of the justification here is to rule out arbitrary sources of unequal opportunity – and that clearly is important. Two qualifications, however, immediately come to mind. First, it is not self-evident that the principle of equality of opportunity always implies sameness for all. This is very clear if we consider children with special educational needs, who often require significantly unequal provision (e.g. individually focused learning support) if anything like equal opportunities are to be provided for them. Secondly, even if one broadly accepts the common entitlement argument, it is, at best, incomplete. There are certain fundamental questions which the notion of entitlement does not itself address. Most importantly, it provides no answers to the question 'entitlement to what?' – what, for example, might most appropriately constitute the same good and relevant curriculum referred to above?

b) 'Standards', continuity and progression

Among the arguments that were probably most powerful in winning support for a national curriculum in England and Wales were those relating to continuity and progression in learning. A prime concern here was to eliminate what Sir Keith Joseph, secretary of state for education in the mid-1980s, memorably called 'curriculum clutter' – the tendency endemic in a decentralized system for children to repeat similar content in different years and with different teachers (the 'not dinosaurs again, miss!' syndrome). More seriously, there is obviously a legitimate concern that children's learning is clearly sequenced and logically ordered, that it builds on prior achievements and that it avoids unnecessary repetition. A properly planned and quite highly prescriptive national curriculum is one effective way, at least at the macro level, of achieving these aims. It is, however, not the only way. Much less prescriptive and centralized approaches *can* achieve continuity and progression for individual students, as long as children's work and development is carefully monitored and guided. It is somewhat ironic that this has begun to be recognized as an implication of New Labour's recent conversion to personalized learning – which began to have a wider impact from around 2005 (see below).

What is sometimes called the standards agenda was probably of even greater significance in gaining support for the national curriculum than were concerns about continuity and progression. A main reason is that standards' were and are closely linked to a core preoccupation of recent governments – the perceived need to demonstrate that attainment in subjects seen as relevant to economic performance is high and is rising. In a world which, it is claimed, is increasingly globalized, the need to be able to score highly in international league tables of educational performance is seen as key, inter alia, to attracting and retaining inward investment, especially by multinational companies. Furthermore, the rise of the knowledge economy is taken to powerfully reinforce such arguments. Both these developments are, indeed, increasingly presented as unarguable imperatives. For example, a New Labour publication of 1998 asserted: 'we are in a new age – the age of information and global competition … We have no choice but to prepare for this new age', adding later, 'young people need to have high level skills for this complex new world of global markets and competition' (DfEE, 1998, p. 9 and p. 20). A highly prescriptive national curriculum linked to a strong and centralized system for assessing and reporting achievement is, of course, key to demonstrating in clear and accountable (if in some respects rather simplified) ways, what is happening to standards. It is no surprise therefore that New Labour has not fundamentally changed either the basic structure of the national curriculum nor the national system of assessment that is, from this point of view, its essential counterpart. When, in June 2007, the GTC (General Teaching Council) recommended that the 'burden' of national testing, especially on younger pupils should be reduced, ministers were quick to make it clear that such testing was here to stay. Tony Blair's mantra 'education, education, and education' at the time of the 1997 general election, is symbolic of the extent to which both main political parties in the UK have bought in to such highly instrumental views of education.

There are two essential points to note here. The first is simply to notice just how strongly instrumental this approach to education is. The term instrumental here simply means that education is seen less as an end in itself, something worthwhile pursued for its own sake; instead, educational is viewed mainly as a means to extrinsic ends – in this case the imperative of sustaining a competitive economy in a new globalized world. Although such instrumental views are strongly supported by politicians, by many in the media and by many parents anxious about their children's economic futures, it does not follow that there is an unassailable case for so strongly instrumental a view of education as that which is now being promoted. (The arguments discussed in the next two sections of this chapter will suggest significantly different priorities.) The second key point is that despite the force and influence of the rhetoric about unstoppable globalization, again, there are respected theorists who are sceptical about and critical of these tendencies:

> Many commentators have … pointed to the way globalization is used to promote only one future, and how globalization and its assumed impact on education is 'ideologically packaged' (Carnoy, 2000). Such rhetoric is used to justify only a particular set of policies, the apparently practical common-sense politics of fitting the nation to global reality, and modernizing the economy to fit the new situation. There is, in such visions, no place for citizens to stand back and protect themselves collectively from the demands of global change …
>
> (Ahier, Beck and Moore, 2003, p. 90)

Many environmentalists, of course, have similarly highlighted the (ironically) global risks to the environment that headlong pursuit of economic globalization seems likely to entail.

c) **Liberal education for all: promoting rational autonomy**
A quite different approach to justifying a broad, common curriculum is that offered by certain liberal philosophers of education, many of whom were associated with the University of London Institute of Education in the 1960s and 70s (see, for example, Hirst and Peters, 1970; Bailey, 1984). These writers argued that pupils of all abilities – and not just an academic minority – should be offered a broad liberal education. A key aim of this particular kind of liberal education is the development of rational autonomy. All young people should receive an education designed to help them to become more capable of making their own reasoned decisions about what might, for them, constitute 'the good life'. Liberal education would do this by developing in children and young people both a respect for reasoning and evidence, and a capacity to employ rational thought and argument to understand and interrogate the world around them. The disposition to ask: 'what's the evidence for that?', to seek reasoned justifications, and to reach justifiable conclusions based on relevant evidence, is therefore central to this particular conception of liberal education.

Such reasoning, however, cannot take place in a vacuum. To think seriously about such matters requires that young people acquire the kinds of knowledge and understanding relevant for these purposes. Exactly what forms of knowledge and understanding should have highest priority within this kind of liberal education has been (and continues to be) the subject of debate. But there is broad agreement that it is desirable that young people should understand the physical, non-human world (through mathematics and the natural sciences) and also the human world of society and culture – including their own place within it. Moral reasoning and understanding are also seen as central – not least because thinking seriously about what one ought and ought not to do, and why, is an essential element of individual moral agency and autonomy.

According to these philosophers of education therefore, children and young people should be offered a curriculum which is broad and balanced in the sense that it includes, in addition to mathematics, science and technology – humanistic, aesthetic, social, political and moral education as vitally important elements (not tokenistic add-ons). And crucially, in the light of the discussion in section (b) above, the primary purpose of being initiated into all these different forms of knowledge and understanding is not that they will help to pay the rent or create a prosperous economy – though they may in fact help to do so. It is that such an education is worthwhile for its own sake and that it is indispensable if young people are to have the chance of growing up to be thoughtful and relatively autonomous individuals, capable of exercising their own judgement and able to play an active role as citizens in a democracy. What was most genuinely radical about this approach to liberal education was the contention that it should be offered to all the nation's children. Previously, it was widely accepted that only an academic minority (such as those who went to grammar schools and the more academic independent schools) could cope with a curriculum of this kind – and that it was better to provide less able pupils with something less intellectually demanding and/or more vocationally relevant.

The 'right kind' of national curriculum, therefore, is something that at least some of the philosophers in this group might broadly be expected to have supported. The 1988 national curriculum arguably met their specification in some ways and to some extent, though far from perfectly. However, having the right kind of curriculum content is only part of the story. What is truly essential is that teachers understand and share the underlying aims and objectives of liberal education – and that they do so *autonomously*. This, of course, is a tall order – and it carries major implications for the education of teachers themselves and for teacher accountability. As Charles Bailey so clearly pointed out, liberal educators 'cannot be held accountable for not satisfying aims, or not achieving objectives which are themselves inimical to the purposes of liberal education' (op. cit., p. 236).

d) Neoconservative interpretations of liberal education
During the educational debates which surrounded the introduction of the national curriculum in England in the 1980s, however, other voices argued strongly for a somewhat different kind of liberal education. They too wanted to provide all children with a broad curriculum whose purposes were not merely economic or vocational. But their basic agenda was one of cultural restoration, with a strong emphasis on a particular conception of nationhood, the nation's cultural heritage, orthodox Christian doctrine and morality, and family values. As they saw it, Britain in the 1960s, '70s and '80s had experienced a dangerous decline in both educational and moral standards, and British culture was being undermined by 'an increasing politicization of the curriculum' resulting in indoctrination into 'anti-racism, anti-sexism, peace education ... and even heterosexism' (Hillgate Group, 1986, p. 6). Writers of this neoconservative persuasion included many of the contributors to a series of polemical 'Black Papers on Education' published between 1969 and 1977 (see Cox and Dyson; 1969; Cox and Boyson, 1977) and also the members of the Hillgate Group in the 1980s (see, for example, Scruton, 1987). The sometimes baleful tone of these polemics is caught in the following quotation from the Rev. Dr Edward Norman, then Dean of Peterhouse College, Cambridge: 'the values of this country are under threat; society discloses advanced symptoms of moral collapse ... a great moral chaos will accumulate within a few decades if the whole absurdity is allowed to go on that long' (Norman, 1977, p. 103).

There was similarly intense contestation within many subject areas of the curriculum. In history, for example, there was heated debate between supporters of the so-called 'new history' with its emphasis on world history, historical enquiry, empathy, etc. and traditionalists like Deuchar who contended that 'school history had tried "deliberately to deny British children the legitimate pride in themselves and their cultural heritage which is their birthright" and that "our civilization is threatened not only by cultures with different attitudes and values, but by destructive tendencies within ourselves"' (Deuchar, 1989, pp. 13–14, quoted in Phillips, 1998, p. 36).

Such neoconservative writers, then, generally supported the introduction of a national curriculum based on 'a settled range of proven subjects', with an emphasis on the cultural heritage of the British people and on traditional values. Some of them, however, had reservations about such a curriculum being state controlled:

> ... the best way to guarantee the continuance of a sound curriculum is not – or at least not initially – through state control ... Until a stable consensus emerges, the attempt to impose a national curriculum by law will be construed as yet another exercise in arbitrary state control ... While a legal guarantee of the curriculum (on the West German model) may be eventually desirable, it can be provided only against the background of a new consensus.
>
> (Hillgate Group, 1986, p. 7)

Others of a broadly neoconservative persuasion, including the then Secretary of State for Education Kenneth Baker, were happier to use state imposition as part of the project of cultural restoration. They were not unsuccessful. The inclusion of religious education as a 'basic subject' with at least 50 per cent of the available curriculum time devoted to teaching about Christianity, a stronger emphasis on British art and literature, more space given to British history and geography, were among their achievements when the national curriculum was introduced in 1988. In all these respects, therefore, neoconservatives were influential in establishing a version of a national curriculum that was, at least to begin with, academic rather than vocational, quite broad in its subject range, and which to some degree emphasized a traditionalist conception of national belonging and identity.

However, it is important to highlight an important difference between the underlying educational aims of neoconservatives, on the one hand, and those of liberal philosophers like Peters or Bailey, on the other. Whilst the latter are committed to intellectual openness – to widening pupils' intellectual horizons so that they may become more autonomous, the former are concerned, at least in some respects, to promote a kind of closure – to socialize children into the acceptance of a set of more specific and pre-selected beliefs and values – constructed around a highly selective, conservative, and idealized version of the nation's past (see Beck, 1998, Chapter 1 for a fuller discussion). The verdict of one distinguished left-wing commentator was: '... at the very moment when the so-called material basis of the old English identity is disappearing over the horizon ... Thatcherism brings Englishness into ... a narrower but firmer definition than it ever had before (Hall, 1991, p. 25).

Commonality, choice and market forces: some tensions affecting the national curriculum and secondary education since 1988

During the years of the Thatcher and Major governments (1979–97) discussions about the national curriculum were caught up in the wider tensions that existed between two significantly different strands of New Right ideology – those of neoconservatism and neoliberalism. As we have seen, neoconservatives were preoccupied with reinstating a particular version of British culture in the face of what they saw as subversive, immoral and alien tendencies that were allegedly undermining traditional beliefs and values. We have also seen that at least some neoconservatives were not averse to using strengthened state control to achieve their goals. The neoliberal project, on the other hand, was concerned with 'rolling back the state', in the sense of dismantling state provision of education, health, housing, etc. and replacing it with privatized or at least partially marketized provision. According to neoliberals, the only effective way to make services like education or health care really responsive to clients' concerns is to replace monopolistic state provision with free market competition. A much canvassed idea in education, for example, was that of educational vouchers, which parents could use to purchase the sort of education which they, and not self-styled educational experts, wanted for their children. Empowering the consumer, partly at least as a way of disempowering producers (i.e. the educational bureaucrats and professionals within the public sector) was therefore central to the neoliberal project.

But as many commentators have pointed out, these two tendencies within the New Right in many ways pulled in opposite directions. We have seen already that members of the Hillgate Group expressed significant reservations about a state-imposed curriculum. And for radical neoliberals, state control was complete anathema. According to Sheila Lawlor (1994), for example, 'the National Curriculum has become the organ for enforcing an educational consensus on all and crushing dissent by the weight of the law'. Even more fundamentally, as writers like David Marquand have pointed out, it is precisely market forces – especially when their reach is globally extended, which are most destructive of the things neoconservatives cherish:

> The global market place ... is cold and hard; in a profound sense it is also subversive. It uproots communities, disrupts families, mocks faiths and erodes the ties of place and history. It has created a demotic global culture, contemptuous of tradition, hostile to established hierarchies and relativist in morality.
>
> (Marquand, 1995)

A key part of the political achievement of Thatcherism was that successive Tory governments managed to combine these antithetical agendas in a way that was both popular and politically potent even though it was ideologically impure. Within education (and across the public sector), a

strengthened role for the central state was combined not with pure marketization but with the creation of quasi-markets, i.e., arrangements which set
organizations which were still publicly owned into competition with one
another.

- In terms of increased centralization, all schools were required to
  deliver the national curriculum and to administer centrally set
  national tests. All schools were also subjected to recurrent Ofsted
  inspections and teachers were regularly appraised. Teacher training
  was controlled through the imposition of national standards for ITT,
  combined with inspection.
- But at the same time, government created a kind of educational
  marketplace in which publicly funded schools competed with one
  another for customers and in which each school's income depended
  to a significant extent on recruitment. 'Performance indicators' such
  as league tables of results, enabled parents to become more informed
  choosers. Conservative governments also widened choice (for some)
  by creating new types of schools – grant maintained schools and city
  technology colleges for example – and also by establishing the
  Assisted Places Scheme which provided funding for less affluent
  pupils to take up places in the independent sector.

These measures, therefore, combined commonality of provision in some
respects with an emphasis on widening choice and promoting diversity in
others.

New Labour's reforms of schooling and the curriculum – some aspects

The coming to power of New Labour in 1997 did relatively little to
change the fundamentals of this potent if partially contradictory policy mix.
Geoff Whitty, surveying the Labour government's first term, argued that

> … many of New Labour's changes to the Conservative agenda were
> largely cosmetic. In some of its manifestations, New Labour's so-
> called Third Way looked remarkably similar to quasi-markets. The
> central thrust of the policies was probably closer to that of the
> Conservative agenda than to Labour's traditional approach … The
> main elements of the reforms of the 1980s and 1990s remained in place
> … (2002, p. 127)

More specifically, under New Labour, three interlinked policy orientations
have operated to reshape schooling and the curriculum – especially but not
only in secondary schools and colleges. These are: first, intensified instrumentalism; second, increased differentiation between different types of
schools; and third, a very significantly enhanced role for business in
education and the promotion of an enterprise culture. All three of these

developments have, inter alia, significantly eroded the commonality, breadth and balance of the common curriculum introduced by the 1988 Education Reform Act.

a) Increased instrumentalism: curricular prescription and curriculum stratification

Intensified instrumentalism has increasingly subordinated educational aims to perceived economic imperatives, in order, as Secretary of State for Education David Blunkett put it in 1998, 'to support and work with (industry) for skilling and re-skilling for what Tony Blair has described as the best economic policy we have – education' (quoted in Ball, 1999, p. 201). The most conspicuous examples of such directly instrumental interventions have probably been the National Literacy Strategy introduced from 1998 and the National Numeracy Strategy which was 'rolled out' a year later. A key (and to considerable degree successful) aim of both was to raise Britain's position in international numeracy and literacy league tables. Both initiatives, though technically non-statutory, represented a degree of government intervention into the curriculum that was unprecedented in recent times, in that the two strategies closely prescribed not only day-to-day curriculum content but also the required pedagogic means of delivery. Symptomatically, government and its agencies have repeatedly claimed that these interventions are research-based and 'disseminate proven best practice' (e.g. Barber and Sebba, 1999, p. 186). Critics, however, have taken leave to doubt whether, in so complex an enterprise as developing children's abilities in literacy or numeracy, it is really possible to uncontroversially identify best practice, let alone 'proven' best practice. But overconfidence is often the handmaiden of governmental instrumentalism, and undeterred by critical voices, the government went on in 2006 to prescribe even more rigidly the approach to be taken to the teaching of early reading – categorically endorsing the controversial and inadequately researched method of 'synthetic phonics' (Rose, 2006; and for a critical commentary see Wyse and Styles, 2007). The strengthened focus on 'the basics' that these two major strategies ushered in was facilitated by so-called 'new arrangements for curriculum flexibility' introduced in 1998. These allowed primary schools to partially disregard the Statutory Orders for the six foundation subjects (which meant devoting less time to them), thus significantly changing the balance of the curriculum and reinforcing the message about the kinds of knowledge that 'really matter'. The specification of demanding literacy and numeracy targets for individual schools further intensified the pressure to focus on the basics, and Colin Richards was only one of many critics who warned of the dangers of a return to a 'neo-elementary curriculum' (Richards, 1999). Subsequently, the government's Key Stage 3 Strategy, implemented between 2003 and 2006, in some ways extended this preoccupation with literacy and numeracy to the 11–13 age range. As far as ministers were concerned, however, the voices of the critics could be safely disregarded: the value of the initiatives was proven by the results:

... let us celebrate success. English 10 year olds are now ranked third in the world for literacy. 84,000 more pupils leaving primary school this year can read and write properly than in 1997 and 96,000 more children can do basic mathematics. 2006 saw the best ever primary school results.

(Blair, 2006a)

Increasing instrumentalism reinforced by a resurgence of vocationalism has also driven major changes to the curriculum at key stage 4. Few would question that the 1988 national curriculum suffered from content overload. This was probably mainly the result of allowing too much influence to subject specialists in the original National Curriculum Council subject working parties. Nevertheless, the aim of preserving substantial curriculum breadth was a cardinal (if always contested) feature of the original KS4 national curriculum. A succession of initiatives has, however, now radically eroded this common element, making it much easier for comprehensive schools to internally differentiate (and in many cases stratify) the curriculum for different types of pupils. One main consequence of the 1993 Dearing Report, with its proposals for academic, prevocational and vocational 'pathways' and its shrinking of the requirements for common provision (Dearing, 1993), was, according to former Chief HMI Eric Bolton (1994), to 'deconstruct the National Curriculum'. New Labour's vision for the 14–19 age range was set out in the Green Paper *14–19: Extending Opportunities, Raising Standards* (DfES, 2002a). Employing the usual rhetoric of life-long learning, flexibility and world class technical and vocational education, it proposed a radical restructuring of 14–19 education with the key cut-off point in terms of a broad common curriculum occurring at age 14 (or even 13). Post-14, it opened up possibilities of students following increasingly diversified routes, some mainly vocational, some combining academic and vocational subjects, some purely academic, and it also sought to raise the status of vocational subjects, for example by proposing the introduction of A2 level assessment in a range of these new vocational courses. From Year 10, all students would follow a much reduced core curriculum of English, mathematics, ICT and citizenship; some would take GCSEs at age 15 and others might skip GCSEs and move directly on to AS and A2 level courses.

For less academically successful students, these proposals were reiterated and further developed in the 2005 White Paper *14–19 Education and Skills* (DfES, 2005a) which, ironically in the context of the present discussion, stressed the government's intention of building its approach for these 'non-academic' students on what it termed 'a strong core' – which turned out to be centred principally on 'achieving (the) functional skills in English and maths ... essential for employment', with measures to 'ensure that no-one can get a C or better in English and maths without mastering the functional elements'. The key point here was to prevent schools 'going soft' on achievement in these basic subjects, for example by subsuming literacy and numeracy within less demanding 'vocational modules' and the like. To this end, the government announced its intention to 'toughen the GCSE Achievement and Attainment Tables' (i.e., the league tables comparing different schools' attainment levels) in order to clearly show 'what percentage of young people have achieved ... 5 A*–C grade GCSEs *including English and Maths*' (ibid. para. 8). The details of these various proposals are perhaps less important than the broad thrust (especially as there may be unforeseen further changes – such as the introduction of a British baccalaureate in some schools and colleges). But the overall principles guiding the direction of change for this age group are now quite clear: relevance, utility, employability, and separate tracking for different 'types' of student.

b) **Abandoning the comprehensive principle: institutional diversification**
Although, on coming into office in 1997, New Labour immediately abolished the Assisted Places Scheme which offered free or subsidized places at fee-paying schools to successful applicants from less well-off families, in other ways the incoming government very significantly extended the Conservatives' enthusiasm for specialist schools. On top of the tripartite division into community, foundation and faith schools introduced by the 1998 Schools Standards and Framework Act, the government strongly encouraged the creation of more and more specialist schools – i.e., comprehensive schools with a distinctive curricular specialism. In the Major years, the Conservatives had already developed a Specialist Schools Programme which included technology colleges and language colleges, further extended to include sports and arts colleges by 1996. New Labour's 1997 White Paper *Excellence in Schools* (DfES, 1997a) proposed further expansion as well as diversification of the types of permissible specialization, leading to proposals in 2002 to increase the number of specialist schools from the 181 which existed in May 1997 to at least 1,500 by 2005 and to 2,000 by 2006. Other initiatives have allowed existing specialist schools to bid for funding to create additional 'areas of excellence', some institutions now having as many as three designated specialisms. Although specialist schools were, until 2006, permitted to select up to 10 per cent of their intakes on the basis of aptitude in their designated specialism(s), relatively few actually did so. It would seem that for most of these schools, the main attraction was the additional resources that government made available as well as the institutional distinctiveness the specialist status conferred, rather than a desire to introduce formal selection by measured ability or aptitude. Inevitably, however, as a result of this accelerating growth, 'the "exclusive" legacy of the scheme, with some types of schools under- and others over-represented, was declining' (Fitz, Davies and Evans, 2006, p. 118; Gorard and Taylor, 2001).

The developing diversification agenda has also seen the creation, from 2002, of city academies (later re-christened simply 'academies') – schools mainly located (at least to begin with) in inner city areas, and in many cases replacing existing schools designated by Ofsted or local authorities as 'failing' or 'under-performing'. Like specialist schools, all academies are required to have a curriculum specialism (or more often, multiple specialisms – most have two or three). Unlike specialist schools, however, academies are also required to have substantial financial sponsorship (normally of the order of £2 million). To date, most of the sponsors have been individual entrepreneurs, companies or local consortia of business interests, and (less commonly) various religious foundations. The quid pro quo for the financial sponsorship is that government contributes the remainder of the capital costs of these new schools (typically of the order of a further £20 million), while the sponsors get to own the land and buildings, and gain control of the school's governing body with the power to appoint staff including the head teacher, as well as enjoying considerable freedom to impose more exacting contracts of employment and conditions of service than apply in mainstream state schools. The governing bodies in conjunction with the head-teacher also enjoy very considerable power to determine the character of the curriculum and pedagogy, provided they respect the minimum requirements of the national curriculum. According to the DfES Standards Site, in March 2007 a total of 46 academies had opened, and a further 86 were either in the 'implementation phase (having obtained funding agreement)' or in the 'feasibility stage (having submitted a formal expression of interest and undergoing investigation and consultation)'. Also in March 2007, Tony Blair and Gordon Brown jointly supported an aspirational (non-binding) eventual target of 400 academies, while Conservative leader David Cameron also expressed considerable enthusiasm for the academies programme.

Excellence in Schools (DfEE, 1997a) symptomatically portrayed New Labour's radical reforms of secondary schooling as '*modernising the comprehensive principle*'. We need here, of course, to remind ourselves that terms like modernizing are instances of dereferentialization – i.e., terms having virtually no intrinsic meaning but which sound good and can be mobilized to promote and legitimize initiatives favoured by politicians or corporate managers (Readings, 1996; see also Beck, 1999a, reprinted in this volume). However, by the time of his keynote speech to the annual Labour Party Conference in 2002, Tony Blair was ready to be a good deal more explicit about what such modernizing of comprehensive schooling actually involved, declaring: 'In education we need to move to the *post-comprehensive era* where schools keep the comprehensive principle of equality of opportunity but where we open the system to new and different forms of education built round the needs of the individual child ...' (Blair, 2002b, my italics).

The term post-comprehensive era had, inevitably, been spun for some time in the run-up to the conference speech – alongside slogans like 'we need an end to the "one size fits all" mass production public service'. The prime minster's speech highlighted the associated need to widen consumer choice: 'why shouldn't there be a range of schools for parents to choose from ... [all] offering excellent routes into university and skilled employment?' (Ibid.) Critics of these radical new directions, of course, argued that such policies might well prove to be internally contradictory – carrying grave risks of undermining equality of opportunity as between different types of nominally comprehensive schools – as well as severely eroding common curriculum entitlement for pupils. Such critics pointed out that different schools' specialisms might well result in increased differentiation in terms of both overt and hidden curriculum effects. Certain specialisms such as modern languages might well be perceived by parents as indicating a strongly academic ethos while others, like sport or performing arts or an absence of specialist designation, might be taken to indicate the opposite. Secondly, critics noted, specialist schools and academies tend to have superior (sometimes very superior) access to resources – including new buildings, state of the art information technology, science laboratories, etc. For example, Roy Hattersley, a former deputy leader of the Labour Party and a consistent critic of these school differentiation policies, warned in 2002: 'specialist schools and city academies, with massive extra resources, will be rated more highly in the public mind than ordinary comprehensives'.

The 2006 Education Act took school differentiation policies a stage further by introducing yet another new form of school organization – 'trust schools'. At the time of writing, it is too early to assess the impact of this further reform, not least because the first phase of implementation involved the establishment of 'pathfinder projects' designed to try out a diversity of ways of developing the potentialities of the trust idea. The core of it, however, involves associating individual schools, or more often groups of schools (perhaps locally based or in other cases spread across the country), in partnerships with a charitable foundation or trust. Trust schools will be funded in the same way as local authority schools, but are in other ways closer to foundation schools in that they will be able to employ their own staff, manage their own land and assets, and set their own admission arrangements; (these must, however, accord with the new Schools Admissions Code which was also introduced by the 2006 Act). Potential Trust partners include universities and further education colleges, educational charities, business foundations, local authorities, and community groups, and each trust can determine how many governors it wishes to appoint. Unlike academies, however, there is no requirement for the trust to provide significant funding. New state schools are empowered to include trust arrangements as part of their proposals for setting up – and the government is giving strong encouragement for them to do so. To facilitate the growth of both trust schools and academies, the government in 2007 appointed a new Schools Commissioner charged with this task and that of promoting wider local choice for parents. As Richard Hatcher has argued in a highly insightful analysis,

> Trusts represent an extension of the Academies policy ... the motivation for Trusts is identical to that of Academies ... In the words of the White Paper (*Higher standards, better schools for all*) 'Trusts will harness the external support and a success culture, bringing innovation and strong leadership to the school, improving standards and extending choice' (DfES, 2005b) para. 2.5).
>
> (Hatcher, 2006, p. 618)

This issue of the motives of both government and sponsors in promoting and supporting this array of school diversification reforms leads on to the last aspect of New Labour policy to be addressed in this chapter – the enhanced role for business people, business organizations, and business interests in the overall project of modernizing state education.

c) The growth of business influence over schooling and the curriculum: promoting 'enterprise culture'
i) control over schools
Where better to start in this regard than with Tony Blair's own summary of New Labour's aims in pursuing school diversification:

> Sometimes … we have failed to explain the end purpose of reform …
> The purpose is simple: fairness and opportunity for all. Public services exist so that those that cannot afford to buy good healthcare or schooling are not at a disadvantage … for the better off, the British education system is full of options. But for the middle and lower income family, whose local school is the option and which is underperforming, there is nothing they can do except take what they are given … over the past few years there has been much improvement … but it has relied, to a great extent, on central and local government direction. And it has tended to shy away from following through the logic of the reforms so far. The logic of changing to the specialist schools, of starting City Academies, of giving greater freedom to schools in who they hire, what they pay, how they run their school, is very clear. It is to escape the straightjacket of the traditional comprehensive school and embrace the idea of genuinely independent non fee-paying state schools. It is to break down the barriers to new providers, to schools associating with outside sponsors, to the ability to start and expand schools; and to give parental choice its proper place.
>
> (Blair, 2005)

Blair was honest enough to acknowledge in this speech that 'This will never mean that every parent has the place they want for their child (ibid.). But although it is parental choice and opportunity that are foregrounded in these comments, it is arguable that the dominant agenda is something else – to further reshape the control of schools and the workforce in schools, particularly by weakening the remaining power and voice of local authorities and the teacher unions. In these respects, it arguably amounts to a sustained effort to complete the work begun by the 1988 Education Reform Act (see Simon, 1988).

The key control mechanism, across the whole period from 1988 but considerably intensified under New Labour, has been what Ken Jones and Richard Hatcher have called '*re-agenting*' – the creation and empowering of new agents to control education and to deliver it at local levels. As Jones has noted: 'Around its project of transformation, New Labour seeks to create new kinds of educational alliance … There is no place in this new system for the forces associated with the earlier periods of reform.'(2003, p. 160)

The new agents are, of course, on the one hand the not so new but all too 'fit for purpose' quangos – such as Ofsted, the QCA, and TDA – and on the other hand, the new agencies and groups that are driving forward the more recent developments, notably the Specialist Schools and Academies Trust (SSAT), and the clusters of business and religious interests who are only too eager to embrace the opportunities government is offering. The involvement of a diversity of sponsoring organizations is, of course, crucial to the government's strategy. To be credible, the 'new educational alliance' Jones speaks of must include, and be seen to include, interests significantly wider than just those of business. The alliance embraces both individual and collective active citizens including: individual philanthropists, entrepreneurs and sports stars; universities and colleges; independent schools; and an array of religious bodies, business corporations and corporate foundations. Indeed, it is significant that the single organization that, in 2007, was sponsoring the largest number of academies was a religious not a business foundation – the blandly named 'United Learning Trust' which, according to its own website

> ... has been created to manage a number of Academies spread across the country. ULT is a subsidiary charity of the not-for-profit charity, United Church Schools Trusts (UCST) and shares with it the objective of managing schools which offer students a good education based on Christian principles ...
>
> (UCST, 2007)

It is also worth noting that a key aspect of the trust schools initiative is to further widen the range of groups involved in controlling school provision, most significantly by creating new forms of participation that do not require substantial financial sponsorship.

Despite this diversity of providers, there are, nevertheless, clear signs that among the various constituencies supporting these new initiatives, especially academies, it is business interests that predominate. For example, of the 46 academies that had been opened by September 2006, no fewer than 25 had either business or enterprise as one of their designated specialisms. (The next largest category of specialisms [14] was sport, while there were 10 cases of a specialism in technology or ICT.) Similarly, among the sponsors, a clear majority of the 46 institutions were sponsored by individual entrepreneurs, or companies, or what Hatcher has termed 'collective business organizations ... bodies such as the Corporation of the City of London and Manchester Science Park' (op. cit., p. 610). In a number of cases, there is co-sponsorship by business in conjunction with religious or education foundations of various kinds.

In the light of such evidence, it is, however, important to avoid the trap of seeing these developments as signs of an imminent wholesale takeover of education by commercial organizations seeking to run more and more schools on a for-profit basis. There is, for one thing, some evidence that sections of 'edu-business' are resentful of the protections and privileges that New Labour has given to its favoured quango in this area – the Specialist Schools and Academies Trust. As a recent article in the UK's leading neoliberal economic journal, *The Economist*, put it:

> The SSAT is growing fast ... (and) is winning increasing sums for 'additional programmes' ... Rival education businesses accuse SSAT of 'mission-creep' (and are concerned that) ... the SSAT is being given wodges of cash that could have been put out to tender ... (and) ... that the SSAT may have an unfair edge when contracts are put out to tender (because) ... from its core grant funded work, it holds precious data about schools that its rivals cannot buy and is thus at an advantage in bidding (and is getting work directly from schools). Its overheads, too, are lower because it is a charity.
>
> (*The Economist*, 2006, p. 32)

More generally, as Hatcher argues, whilst a 'possible future scenario of the business takeover of schools for profit is real and a legitimate concern ... it should not be the principal lens through which we analyse the actual developments taking place today, which concern the role of business and other interests as key agents in the transformation of the school system to conform to the *government's* agenda ...' (op. cit., pp. 614–15, my italics). In Hatcher's view, the current situation is more complex: the role of business (and some allied interests) is two-fold: 'the colonization of government education policy implementation and delivery of national and local educational services by private companies for profit' but also 'the reshaping of schools through non-profit sponsorship, which in the case of Academies amounts to *a non-profit form of privatization*' (Ibid., my italics).

ii) The curriculum and the promotion of 'enterprise'
For New Labour, it is clearly not sufficient for business interests to be given a very considerably enhanced role in the control of schooling. Business values and especially the promotion of enterprise are also seen as increasingly important. One aspect of this is the ambition to re-shape the ethos of schools in appropriate ways:

> What really makes Academies different is their ethos, their sense of purpose, the strength of their leaders ... And much of that comes from the can-do attitude of their principals and staff, and the drive that their business and educational sponsors bring to their development – backed by their willingness to innovate. In practice, that combination means that things can be done differently if that's what's going to get results.
>
> (Blair, op. cit., 2005)

But, for New Labour, an appropriate ethos needs to be complemented by seeking to re-shape educational knowledge in relevant ways. In part, as we have seen, this is to be accomplished in certain schools by centring their mission on curriculum specialisms like business and enterprise. But to have general impact, more extensive curricular remodelling is clearly desirable. There is not space here to discuss recent developments in this area at length. But it is appropriate to conclude this chapter with a brief analysis of some of the changes initiated by the Qualifications and Curriculum Authority for a significant restructuring of the national curriculum in secondary education, centred on comprehensively revised statutory programmes of study. These were communicated to schools in autumn 2007 ready for implementation from autumn 2008.

Taken as a whole, these reforms were in part framed within the government's heightened focus on personalization and personalized learning (aspects of which are discussed briefly in Chapters 2 and 3 of this volume). This has led to the 'statements of attainment' in various specialist subject areas becoming somewhat less detailed and prescriptive. In addition, in developing their curricula for the 2008 implementation date, schools have been exhorted to be more flexible, especially in linking subjects across the curriculum as well as in personalizing learning:

> Flexibility and opportunity are at the heart of the QCA's secondary curriculum review … A modern curriculum needs to focus on what young people learn and how they learn and experience their subjects. It needs to show how subjects link together and to a clear set of aims for the curriculum…
> Schools can already tailor the curriculum to meet the needs of their young people. Some are doing this, others have asked for further advice on personalising the curriculum and approaches to assessment.
> (QCA, 2007a)

In planning how they will do this, schools have been advised to view their curricula through three separate 'curriculum *lenses*': 'curriculum aims', 'personal development' and 'skills'. Also, schools were further required to take account of four new 'curriculum *dimensions*' – 'the global dimension', 'creativity', 'cultural understanding and diversity', and finally, 'enterprise'.

It is worth at this stage making two important general points before focusing more closely on the new QCA guidance on 'economic well-being' and its links to 'enterprise'. The first point is that the declared reorientation towards greater flexibility, reduced prescription, and on personalizing the curriculum, learning and assessment, reflects the influence of a wide diversity of interests. The emphasis on personalization, for example, has clearly been shaped in part by New Labour's 'organic intellectuals' including Charles Leadbeater (see Chapter 2, note 4). But it is also the case that this emphasis on giving pupils a greater voice in their learning and greater freedom to develop their own learning styles and agenda, has been encouraged and welcomed by a very broad range of educationalists including many with impeccably progressive credentials. At an earlier stage in the development of the Secondary Review, for example, the QCA's Futures Unit sponsored a series of short films, one of which was about 'the need for greater personalisation and innovation'; and the associated website published a range of statements by leading UK educationalists emphasizing the value of reorienting the national curriculum in these directions. Professor Jean Rudduck, for example, commented

> We need to respond to the kinds of things young people say they want in school, which is more opportunities for decision-making, more choice, more responsibility ... Pupil voice is actually supporting in an indirect way the standards agenda by helping pupils to strengthen their motivation, by their feeling that they belong and that they matter.
>
> (QCA, 2005)

Neil McLean, executive director of Becta (the British Educational Communications and Technology Agency) commented in the same publication 'The first step towards a personalised curriculum is to engage the users of the curriculum, i.e. the learners, in the description of the curriculum. It isn't something you parcel up and package to them and then your approach isn't personalised.'(Ibid.)

It is important to note here, however, that not only did QCA issue an official disclaimer to the effect that 'This film is intended to stimulate debate; views expressed are not necessarily those of QCA', but also that its then head of research, Tim Oates, in the same publication, offered a much less student-centred interpretation of personalized learning:

> I think personalised learning is about thinking about a core curriculum of those things that are going to be valuable for all people to progress into society and then into work. And then use personalised learning to think about how you would deliver that in a way that is motivating for the individual so that they would engage with that content. It's not about an educational free-for-all ... It's about thinking about how we can make the curriculum motivate.
>
> (Ibid.)

The second general point that is worth emphasizing is that although, as will be demonstrated below, the QCA has written into its curriculum guidance a very considerably strengthened emphasis on education for enterprise and for economic well-being, it is important to bear in mind that the impact of these sorts of cross-curricular initiatives, even where they are made statutory as with citizenship, has always been blunted by two things: by sheer curriculum overload and by the marginal importance that many head teachers, school governors and parents think attaches to these peripheral and often non-assessed areas of the curriculum. HMI Adrian Lyons, one of Ofsted's leading proponents of enterprise education, candidly acknowledged this in a speech to the Association for European Economics Education in Ghent in 2005:

> Ofsted found that 'headteachers often cite initiative overload, a shortage of curriculum time and pressure to raise standards as reasons for not making enterprise education more of a priority in their schools' (Ofsted, 2005). In England tables are published showing the performance of schools based on GCSE scores. As enterprise does not directly contribute to GCSE scores some headteachers regard it as a distraction.
>
> (Lyons, 2005, p. 6)

For these and other reasons, it will clearly only be possible to examine – and that only briefly – certain QCA documents on enterprise and economic well-being as policy texts that, to an as yet unknowable degree, may shape thinking and practice in different schools in various ways – in some cases perhaps encountering considerable modification or resistance (see Ball, 1993). And even within this limitation, it will not be possible to subject the text of the selected documents to the kind of close-textured dissection characteristic of the work of sophisticated sociolinguists like Norman Fairclough (1992, 2000) or Ruqaiya Hasan (2006). Even within these limitations, however, there is a strong case for judging the QCA's proposals in this area to be insidiously indoctrinatory. What is perhaps most objectionable is what Charles Bailey, in a discussion of similar educational documents that were influential over twenty years ago, called their unwarrantable 'assumption of non-controversiality' (Bailey, 1984, p. 177).

The potentially indoctrinatory character of these curricular documents is, to a significant extent, a consequence of their discourse – most especially the language, the content and various symptomatic absences that are characteristic of these texts. The problem is epitomized by one of the key organizing concepts employed: the notion of economic well-being – which turns out to be a prime example of what Ruqaiya Hasan has called glibspeak. Hasan defines glibspeak (rather technically) as 'an attempt to separate a signifier from its legitimate signified – i.e. from that signified which is treated by the speech community in general as legitimate' (Hasan, 2006, p. 214). In this case, as we shall see, the ordinary language meaning of well-being is, in these texts, annexed to a highly particular pedagogic and ideological agenda that appears calculated to shape future worker-citizens of a quite particular kind.

In terms of the overall restructuring of the national curriculum, the new programmes of study that are the focus of concern here redefine and expand the existing non-statutory cross-curricular area known as PSHE (personal, social and health education). The restructuring splits the area into two equally weighted core elements: *personal* well-being and *economic* well-being. The former remains focused on traditional PSHE issues like sex and relationships education, drugs and alcohol education; while the latter expands existing areas like careers education, to include economic and business understanding, enterprise and financial capability. The area as a whole has been redesignated as 'PSHEE': i.e., personal, social, health and economic education. In what follows, the focus will be mainly on two specific documents: the new programmes of study proposed for key stages 3 and 4 on economic well-being (QCA, 2007b) and the parallel and closely linked proposals for the new curriculum dimension of enterprise (QCA, 2007c). At the time of writing, only the versions of these texts published as part of the 'consultation' exercise (January–April 2007) were available – but the final versions proved to be only marginally different. Occasional reference will also be made to other texts that are cross-referenced in these two main documents.

Here, then, is a sample from the first of these documents – its definition of 'The importance of economic well-being':

> Education for economic well-being is concerned with equipping pupils with the knowledge, skills and attributes to make the most of the rapidly changing opportunities in learning and work … It helps pupils to aim high. Pupils build a positive and realistic view of their needs and capabilities so that they can make effective learning plans, decisions and transitions … Pupils learn to be enterprising. They develop the ability to handle uncertainty and respond positively to change, to create and implement new ideas and ways of doing things. They learn how to make reasonable risk/reward assessments and act upon them, and develop a 'can-do' attitude and the drive to make ideas happen. They develop their ability to be informed and critical consumers of financial services and to manage their finances effectively.
>
> (QCA, 2007b)

The companion document on 'Enterprise' foregrounds what is termed '*enterprise capability*' which involves much the same cluster of desired attributes, including: 'innovation, creativity, risk-management, having a "can-do" approach and the drive to make things happen'; while 'enterprise understanding' includes 'innovation, risk, teamwork, managing change and personal effectiveness' (QCA, 2007c). In other sections of the economic well-being programme of study, students at key stage 4 are exhorted, inter alia, to 'demonstrate the main qualities and skills needed to enter and thrive in the working world'; to 'take action to improve their life chances'; to develop 'knowledge of opportunities in learning and work skills and qualities in relation to employers' needs', to learn about 'personal budgeting, money management and debt', and so on (op. cit.).

From one point of view, this agenda of 'desirable' qualities, capabilities and forms of understanding, could be seen as sound common sense – reflecting the contingencies many young people in Britain are increasingly likely to face in a globalizing world characterized by growing uncertainty – and as setting out the qualities needed to cope with these challenges. But that is precisely the effect such discourse is designed to produce – both in onlookers and in its recipients. Closer inspection of both the form and content of these texts reveals that they work more subtly and insidiously – by positioning their addressees in very particular ways. Most significantly, the addressee is the generic pupil – each a separate individual but at the same time undifferentiated by gender, ethnicity, social class or unequal opportunity. One of the most significant ways the discourse achieves this effect of abstracting its addressees from their real social locatedness is through the reiterated use of the generic (pseudo-inclusive) term pupils (used four times in the first extract cited above), and subsequently in the same passage, through the gender-undifferentiated pronoun they (used three times). It is worth noticing also how the discourse constructs the pedagogy as powerful: as enabling and as empowering these individuals in a variety of ways. Not only this, but the combination of present tense and active voice, employed throughout the first extract quoted above, is implicitly behaviourist. The pedagogic aims and their intended outcomes are conjoined as already achieved behaviours: 'pupils *build* a positive and realistic view ...'; 'pupils *learn* to be enterprising'; 'they *develop* the drive ...'; and so on. These features (present tense, active voice, active verbs) have in recent years become universal characteristics of the language of national curriculum programmes of study – but their effects seem particularly insidious and problematic here, where they display marked affinities with the discourses of competency training sponsored by leading industrial training lobbies in the 1980s and trenchantly critiqued by Jones and Moore (1993).

If we look more closely at the relationship between the form and the content of the discourse, it quickly becomes apparent that a key discursive effect is to position each individual learner as s/he who is personally responsible for their own success or failure – in education and training, and in life. Each student individually carries the responsibility to 'make the most' of what they are being offered in the brave new world of personalized and economically relevant learning opportunities. Of particular interest here is the linking of the themes of 'opportunity' and 'responsibility' with a wider discourse concerned with 'risk'. Thus, each student has the responsibility to develop the sort of enterprise capability that will equip them to 'assess, undertake and manage risk in a range of contexts' and 'take action to improve their life chances' (QCA, 2007b). They are also encouraged to develop the financial capability to become competent investors in themselves and their own futures – for example by understanding 'risk and reward, and how money can make money' and in appropriate cases, by developing their 'awareness of the issues and strategies involved for coping with a period of extended study' (ibid.).

In these sorts of ways, both the world of work, and the economy more generally, are portrayed as depoliticized spaces in which there is almost no scope for, say, collective action to improve life chances, or to question let alone challenge the increasing dominance of the marketized provision of goods and services, including financial services. The examination of risk in these documents has none of the complexity or awareness of political tensions that is to be found in, say, Ulrich Beck's analysis of *Risk Society* (1992). Instead, the discourse of risk in these texts is underpinned by an implicit mythology of meritocracy, where rewards commensurate with abilities flow to those 'deserving' individuals who develop the knowledge and capability to make prudent life plans and to take calculated risks. And correspondingly, this is a world where those who fail to make and keep themselves 'employable' have only themselves to blame. (For a critical commentary concerning discourses of employability see Hesketh, 2003). There is also no recognition anywhere in these texts of the ways in which a range of recent government policies such as increasing tuition fees in higher education actually at once diminish equality of educational opportunity and increase the differential levels of risk faced by unequally privileged individuals. Nor is there recognition that such policies may be the objects of legitimate criticism – not least by students themselves (see Ahier et al., 2003).

The proposals concerning economic understanding in these QCA documents are similarly deficient. There is, first, a tendency to couple economic understanding with business understanding, and treat both under the rubric of enterprise education:

> *Enterprise*
> Enterprise education consists of enterprise capability, supported by financial capability and business understanding ... Economic and business understanding is the ability to understand the business context and make informed choices between alternative uses of scarce resources.
>
> (2007b)

More specific aims relating to economic understanding include:

> *knowledge* of a range of economic concepts such as market, competition, price, efficiency, and economic growth ... understanding of *how the economy functions*, including the role of business and the financial services ... understanding of a range of financial concepts such as money, credit, wages and investment ... how businesses use finance and how to draw up a business plan ...
>
> (Ibid., my italics)

This is both an intellectually impoverished and disturbingly uncritical way in which to characterize objectives for enabling young people to develop an understanding of economic issues in a rapidly changing society and a globalizing world. It is true that a small number of somewhat more critical aims are suggested, for example consideration of rights as well as responsibilities at work, and 'social and moral dilemmas about the use of money' (ibid.). Even so, the proposals as a whole are manifestly inadequate and tend strongly towards the inculcation of attitudes uncritically favourable to the dominance of market forces and enterprise ideology. In these respects they contrast very unfavourably with the much more balanced and critical conception of 'political literacy' that, since the Crick Report of 1998, has been a key element in the QCA's progammes of study for citizenship (Advisory Group on Citizenship, 1998). And it is worth noting that this critical orientation is strongly preserved, indeed in some ways enhanced (see the final section of Chapter 8 of this book), in the most recent programmes of study for citizenship (QCA, 2007d). It is also symptomatic of the weaknesses of the proposals for economic well-being and enterprise that they contain virtually no cross-references to citizenship education – as if the spheres of business and the economy are somehow areas on which issues of citizenship have no bearing (see also the discussion of 'active citizenship' in Chapter 3 of this volume).

How might we explain these biases and lacunae? They result partly, I think, from the ways in which economic understanding has been framed as part of a non-statutory curriculum area that sees itself as focusing primarily on personal development. On the positive side, this has always been a strength of PSHE – trying to sustain, within a curriculum mainly devoted to the acquisition and competitive assessment of instrumental knowledge, a balancing dimension in which the development of 'the whole child' is central (Best, 1996, but see also McLaughlin, 1996). This partly perhaps explains why both main strands of the new PSHEE are structured around the organizing notion of 'well-being'. But particularly in the areas under discussion here, this focus on the developing individual can, if not carefully and critically handled, become educationally disabling. The economic well-being proposals do preserve an emphasis on what are undeniably important issues for young people: thinking about and preparing themselves for working life and future careers. But at the same time, as has been shown, the proposals graft on to these legitimate concerns a highly questionable way of defining individual economic well-being, essentially as the expression and outcome of enterprise and enterprise culture. This, as we have seen, inappropriately 'responsibilizes' individuals (Rose, 1999b), encouraging them to see their success or failure in life as almost entirely a result of either their own achievements or their individual inadequacies. It is because of the ease with which positively toned ordinary language terms such as well-being, can, as here, be misappropriated by sectional groups to promote specific interests, that Hasan critiques them as instances of glibspeak (see above).

As a form of mainly 'experiential' pedagogy, enterprise learning, as characterized in these texts, also cuts its recipients off from access to more critical and elaborated forms of knowledge – say a more politically informed study of economic issues – that would better equip them to understand the social-structural (and much more potent) forces that actually shape their economic destinies. In these respects, the enterprise and economic well-being proposals display marked similarities to the social and life skills courses developed for the young jobless in the 1980s by the Manpower Services Commission (for a thoughtful critique, see Moore, 1990).

The second main source of the educational deficiencies of the QCA's economy and enterprise proposals is that they appear to reflect the ways in which, and the extent to which, enterprise lobby groups now feel confident of their right to shape education in their own interests. New Labour, of course, has been the enthusiastic midwife in this process – in the various ways examined in different chapters of this book. It comes then as no surprise that the QCA's enterprise proposals unblushingly include a major subsection entitled 'Developing a curriculum that *supports* enterprise', and which cites Ofsted documents recommending schools to 'establish a clear definition of enterprise learning and ensure that it is *understood* by staff, learners and other stakeholders' (2007c, my italics). Symptomatically, on the very day I was writing these comments, there appeared in my post, an invitation to a major national conference – the '2nd Annual Conference: Embedding an Enterprise Culture in Education', sponsored by the National Education Business Partnership Network and a range of other bodies including Universities UK. The conference prospectus revealed that this was indeed a 'can-do' event – with keynote speakers advocating the 'embedding of enterprise culture at all levels of education', and a major panel debate on '*How* can we embed an enterprise culture in education?'.

The key educational objections to arrogance and hubris of this kind were eloquently expressed, more than twenty years ago, by Charles Bailey. It is appropriate to conclude this chapter with an extended quotation from Bailey's book:

> Running through the discussions ... is an unspoken consensus about society, values and education. The assumed consensus is that of continually accepted technological change and development ... all taking place in the context of a competitive free market economy, and in a wider context of international competitive trade. Also assumed is the undeniable value of wealth creation, ostensibly as a necessary condition of all else that might be valued, but in fact by its emphasis seen as a valued end in itself. Education, in this model, becomes a commodity both for the individual person and for society as a whole, to be assessed like any other commodity in terms of its profitability or usefulness. The education favoured for the individual is one leading to a well-paid job; for the employer it is one producing well-disposed and capable workers and potential managers; and for the state it is one making the country strong in economic competitive power ... That such a consensus exists as anything more concrete than an assumption or necessary presupposition is highly questionable. The value of continued technological growth, especially when dictated and operated by a profit mechanism, is challenged by many people ... Similarly the background context of the free competitive market as the determinant of resource allocation is anything but a consensus view of how society should most desirably operate.

With regard to education, Bailey insists that:

> For educators to influence the minds of pupils in the sole direction of the economic utility model of education ... would be highly indoctri-

natory and therefore inimical to the development of rational and moral autonomy which is the duty of the liberal educator ... Politicians and employers have every right, in a democracy, to argue their case; but it does not follow from this that any of them have the right, least of all in a democracy, to impose their particular view on the education system. Such a system, insofar as it tries to bring about political and economic understanding in the minds of the pupils entrusted to it, must treat controversial matters *as* controversial.

(Bailey, 1984, pp. 177–9)

Part III

CULTURAL, RELIGIOUS AND ETHNIC DIVERSITY: CHALLENGES AND POSSIBILITIES

Chapter 8

CULTURAL COEXISTENCE AND IDENTITY POLITICS IN AN AGE OF ANXIETY: DILEMMAS OF NATIONHOOD AND CITIZENSHIP

Introduction

To begin, an anecdote. In 2006, while Christmas shopping in Cambridge (England), I happened to go into the social science section of Borders bookstore where my attention was caught by a display of recently published work. It was hard to know whether to be more impressed by the galaxy of world renowned authors exhibited or by the chilling titles of the books they had written. These ranged from Bruce Ackerman's *Before the Next Attack* (2006), through Amartya Sen's *Identity and Violence* (2006), to Zygmut Bauman's *Liquid Fear* (2006). Other works included Michael Mann's *The Dark Side of Democracy* (2005), Noam Chomsky's *Hegemony or Survival* (2005), John Gray's *Al Qaeda and What it Means to be Modern* (2003), Malise Ruthven's *Fundamentalism* (2004), Benjamin Barber's *Jihad versus McWorld* (2003), Terry Eagleton's *Holy Terror* (2005) and Melanie Phillips' *Londonistan* (2006). All these books were published or republished between 2003 and 2006. All in their different ways, address the issue of resurgent religious fundamentalism, its relation to acts of terror, and the anxieties these developments have inspired across the world in the opening years of the twenty-first century.

The globally relayed spectacle of the destruction of the twin towers of the World Trade Center on 11 September 2001 was, of course, only the most dramatic of a succession of terrorist atrocities that have extended from Bali to Washington, from Mombasa to London, from Baghdad to Madrid. There is no need to detail the sad catalogue of these events; they are part of our vicarious shared history as global, media-consuming citizens. Such horrors and their media portrayal have, perhaps inevitably, played a key part in provoking governments across the world to reassess their approach to issues of immigration and asylum, cultural and ethnic diversity, and nationhood and citizenship – as well as heightening concerns about 'homeland security'. In the process, however, several of these governments have, to varying degrees, become snared in nets of contradictions partly of their own making. To recognize this is not, of course, to suggest that the problems involved are anything less than extraordinarily complex and intractable; some indeed may be insoluble. And educational solutions may be particularly hard to devise or, where attempted, be likely to prove relatively ineffectual.

New Labour's 'integration' agenda

In Britain, one dominant reaction to these events (and to other evidence of growing separatism and antagonism between different cultural groups) has been to argue that *'it's time to move on from multiculturalism'* (quoted in Toynbee, 2004, my italics). These are the words of Trevor Phillips, then the chairperson of Britain's Commission for Racial Eqality[1] in a high profile speech delivered in 2004. A year later, in the aftermath of the suicide bombings in London on three tube trains and a bus by four young British Muslim men (an event referred to in the UK as '7/7'), Trevor Phillips delivered another highly publicized speech entitled *Sleepwalking to Segregation*:

> ... the aftermath of 7/7 forces us to assess where we are. And here is where I think we are: we are sleepwalking our way to segregation. We are becoming strangers to each other, and we are leaving communities to be marooned outside the mainstream ... those marooned communities will steadily drift away from the rest of us, evolving their own lifestyles, playing by their own rules and increasingly regarding the codes of behaviour, loyalty and respect that the rest of us take for granted, as outdated behaviour that no longer applies to them. We know what follows: crime, no-go areas and chronic cultural conflict.
>
> (Phillips, 2005)

The alternative to multiculturalism, Phillips had argued in his earlier speech, should be integration, which he was at pains to distinguish from assimilation:

> My ambition is not for assimilation. My aim is to better manage the tensions that naturally flow from aspects of difference so we can all live more harmoniously. We need to achieve an integrated society based on 'shared values' and 'shared loyalties' which allows for 'diversity and difference'.
>
> (op. cit., 2004)

And, further clarifying his approach to multiculturalism:

> Multicultural Britain in already a fact of life. But it is not enough. The philosophy of multiculturalism begins by defining people as different and then treating them differently. This lazy ambition, where we have a rich diversity of peoples who make little or no effort to reach out to each other, is insufficient and will surely lead to an American-style future of segregation.
>
> (Ibid.)

Recognizing various 'barriers impeding successful integration', including in some quarters a 'genuine confusion and anger about the perceived collapse of British identity', and in others the fact that 'many immigrants do not feel accepted as British even when they want to be', Phillips nevertheless went on to suggest that *'people need to be encouraged to feel British and be properly welcomed as British'* (ibid., my italics).

Both of these speeches were thoughtful, if contentious, contributions to what Phillips himself recognized as a complex set of debates. Perhaps as a former journalist however, he should have been more aware that what would register most strongly, especially in the media, were the key sound-bites – the arguably overstated diagnosis of a whole nation sleepwalking to segregation and the programmatic response of shaping a common identity whose key principle of cohesion was acceptance of a qualified degree of cultural diversity accompanied by integration around a set of shared values characterized as British. A multitude of other voices, of course, have joined in the debate. Some, like prominent *Guardian* journalist Polly Toynbee, immediately applauded Phillips for his courage, as chair of the CRE, in daring to say the unsayable (Toynbee, op. cit.). Others, including London Mayor Ken Livingstone and his official adviser on equality and policing Lee Jasper (also general secretary of the National Assembly Against Racism), accused the CRE of 'fuelling general hostility to ethnic minorities by attacking the principle of multiculturalism' (see Hinsliff, 2006).[2] And despite Phillips' expressions of confidence that 'we can find a mature lexicon and a positive tone in which to seek out ways of dealing with difference' (op. cit., 2004), events to date have suggested that efforts to promote consensus around this particular vision of integration could prove more divisive than otherwise.

Late in 2006, Tony Blair himself entered the lists. In a high profile speech in his legacy-forming series of lectures entitled 'Our Nation's Future – lectures from the PM on vital issues', Blair pointedly located his analysis in the context of the aftermath of 7/7, despite stressing that various advisers had warned him not to do so.

> Others warned me against putting this issue in the context of 7/7, of terrorism, of our Muslim community. After all, extremism is not confined to Muslims ... But the reason we are having this debate is not generalised extremism. It is a new and virulent form of ideology associated with a minority of our Muslim community ... a minority ... particularly originating from certain countries.
>
> (Blair, 2006b)

The prime minister, however, also went out of his way to avoid outright repudiation of multiculturalism: 'it is not that we need to dispense with multicultural Britain; on the contrary we should continue celebrating it', adding in his conclusion 'we know migration has been good for Britain'. This endorsement, though, was immediately qualified by a very much stronger emphasis on integration – rooted in what he repeatedly characterized as shared values.

Here, it is worth highlighting a significant ambivalence within the discourse of the speech. At one point the prime minister made a highly pertinent distinction between on the one hand, culture as the basis of identity and on the other, the duties of common citizenship in a democratic polity: 'Integration in this context, is not about culture or lifestyle. It is about values ... It isn't about what defines us as people, but as citizens, the rights and duties that go with being a member of our society.' (Ibid.)

But in most of what followed, these civic values were, with increasing emphasis, repeatedly characterized as British:

> The right to be in a multicultural society was always implicitly balanced by a duty to integrate, to be part of Britain, to be British and Asian, British and black, British and white ... When it comes to our essential values – belief in democracy, the rule of law, tolerance, equal treatment for all, respect for this country and its shared heritage – then that is where we come together ... it is what gives us the right to call ourselves British ...

And in a ringing peroration:

> Our tolerance is is part of what makes Britain, Britain. So conform to it; or don't come here ... If you come here lawfully, we welcome you. If you are permitted to stay here permanently, you become an equal member of our community and become one of us. Then you, and all of us, who want to, can worship God in our own way, take pride in our different cultures after our own fashion ... but do so in a shared space of shared values in which we take no less pride and show no less respect. The right to be different. The duty to integrate. That is what being British means. And neither racists nor extremists should be allowed to destroy it. (Ibid.)

Despite or perhaps because of its rhetorical potency, language of this sort threatens to blur precisely the key demarcation that, in my view, is most essential to maintain in these debates – that between on the one hand assimilation into an imagined national culture and on the other hand, certain demands that may legitimately be made upon all reasonable citizens in a liberal, democratic polity. The appeal to nation, heritage and 'shared British values' almost inevitably conjures up, even when this is not intended, an historically false and self-serving image of British culture as the unquestionable repository of freedom, civility, tolerance and fair-mindedness – imagery resonating with those Burkean fantasies of 'our' national past celebrated with such enthusiasm by, among others, David Blunkett and Gordon Brown (see Chapter 3 of this book).

The risk of such rhetoric encouraging a blurring of crucially important distinctions – between integration and assimilation, between civic duties and subscribing to an historically rooted national culture – was manifested in the glee with which the Conservative media seized on Blair's speech, portraying it as evidence that both he and New Labour had finally seen the light and were at long last supporting neoconservative assimilationism. A leading article in the *Daily Telegraph*, for example, welcomed the speech in the following terms:

> ... we are delighted that Mr. Blair has come round to the view that this newspaper has always held and that our countrymen have clung to through the decades of official bullying and hectoring.
> What, though, are the 'British values' that Mr. Blair wants everyone to accept? It will not do to cant about freedom, fairness and tolerance ... British values, surely, are bound up with our institutions: common law, a sovereign parliament, *habeas corpus*, counties, army regiments: the very institutions that have often been traduced by this ministry.
>
> (*Daily Telegraph*, 2006b)

In the same edition, Philip Johnston, the paper's home affairs editor, offered the following gloss on the prime minister's speech:

> ... Mr Blair said that what was meant by multiculturalism was not what it became. It was really intended to be a classic British fudge, a toleration of other people's ways, religions, cuisines, languages and dress, yes. But it was supposed to be a two-way street: *immigrants were expected to subscribe to the value system of the host nation*. That bit got lost somewhere along the way ...
>
> (Johnston, 2006, my italics)

He added, with heavy irony, that in the light of developments since 2001 and especially 7/7, 'Labour ministers ... now ... queue up to espouse respect for the monarchy, demand that immigrants learn English, praise British history and insist on the primacy of the law' (ibid).

Despite the political point-scoring inseparable from such comments, they do highlight the core problem with the ambiguous term 'integration': the fact that it can so easily become, or be perceived to be, a cover for crypto-assimilationism. However, we would all do well to recognize that none of the most widely used terms and concepts in this area is uncontroversial – and all are likely to remain contested. Some may even be 'essentially contested'.[3]

Multiculturalism, identity and the politics of recognition

The concepts of both multiculturalism and multicultural education are good examples of this tendency for key terms to be repeatedly contested and in the process, redefined. For example, much of what passed for multicultural education in British schools in the 1970s was quite rapidly, and with considerable justification, attacked by antiracist writers. It was held to be tokenistic – at worst the so-called 'three S's' of saris, samosas and steel bands. It was also widely seen as patronizing and exoticizing. And it was said to be increasingly time-warped in the sense of taking little account of the contemporary realities of the lives of different ethnic communities within the UK – rapidly changing communities experiencing racism of various kinds but also exhibiting increasing internal diversity and sometimes internal conflict. There is no space here to recapitulate these debates. Suffice it to say that partly in response to various forms of antiracist critique, some writers moved on to develop the concept of '*critical* multiculturalism' – characterized by Stephen May as 'a theory of multicultural/antiracist education which incorporates both a *critical* and *non-essentialist* approach to cultural difference' (1999a, p. 13). Of course, this stance too is both contestable and contested.[4]

The analysis I shall offer here, itself inevitably controversial, follows at least in some respects, the approach taken by radical antiracist theorists such as Kenan Malik and A. Sivanandan. These writers argue that the endorsement of a certain type of multiculturalism (and sometimes 'antiracism') by both central and local government in Britain, especially since the 1980s, has had a key role in amplifying and legitimizing divisive forms of cultural and ethnic identity politics. Sivanandan argues that this resulted from a protracted set of developments which diverted what had, until the early 1980s, been a common fight against racism and discrimination, into 'a struggle *for* culture' (Sivanandan, 2006, my italics). In similar vein, Kenan Malik, discussing Afro-American identity politics in the USA from the 1960s onwards, says that black self-organization against racism 'soon gave way to the idea of black *identity*; black people had to organize separately not as a strategy but as a *cultural* necessity' (Malik, 2005, p. 55, my italics). It was not long before

> ... not just black people but everyone had an identity that was uniquely theirs and that separated them not just from the white man, but from every other kind of man and from men in general. 'The demand is not for inclusion within the fold of universal human kind on the basis of shared human attributes; nor is it for respect in spite of one's differences', wrote feminist sociologist Sonia Kruks. 'Rather, what is demanded is respect for oneself as different'.
>
> (Ibid., p. 55)

Malik goes on to illustrate this major reorientation in the politics of race and culture, by focusing on the specific example of the adoption of a new multicultural and antiracist strategy by the local council in the northern English city of Bradford during the early 1980s.

> Bradford's race relations plan declared that every section of the 'multiracial, multicultural city' had 'an equal right to maintain its own identity, culture, language, religion and customs'. At the heart of this multicultural strategy was a redefinition of racism built on the insights of identity politics. Racism now meant not simply the denial of equal rights but the denial of the right to be different ... By the late-1980s the

focus of antiracist protest in Bradford had shifted from political issues such as policing and immigration, to religious and cultural issues: a demand for Muslim schools and separate education for girls, a campaign for halal meat in school, and the confrontation over *The Satanic Verses*. As different groups began asserting their identities ever more fiercely, so the shift from the political to the cultural arena helped to create a more tribal city. Secular Muslims were regarded as having betrayed their culture.

(Ibid. p. 56)

Sivanandan offers a very similar, though more general, analysis:

As the antiracist component of the struggle ebbed, multiculturalism as policy began to degenerate into what I would term *cultural ethnicism*, it became part and parcel of a competitive fight for central and local government favours, and moved the struggle from the streets to the town halls ... When antiracism was taken out of the equation ... all that was left was culturalism and ethnicism. The result was cultural and ethnic enclaves with their own cultural and ethnic politics.

(op. cit., my italics)

Sivanandan's concept of 'cultural ethnicism' is, in some ways at least, quite close to what Amartya Sen calls 'plural monoculturism' (2006, especially Chapter 8). I will return in due course to a fuller discussion of these ideas in relation to some aspects of New Labour's policy proposals.

For the moment, however, let us pick up on Malik's point (quoted above) about 'different groups asserting their identities ever more fiercely ...' In a justly celebrated discussion of identity politics and its links to the 'politics of recognition', Canadian philosopher Charles Taylor offered a careful and detailed explanation of how, across a period of more than 200 years, it became increasingly important to people of all cultures and social classes at least in westernized nations, to feel that others in their society had a duty to accord them not only dignity as fellow human beings but also recognition of the value of the cultures that shaped and informed their different identities (Taylor, 1992). Drawing on the insights of the American founder of symbolic interactionism George Herbert Mead, Taylor highlighted the point that people's sense of identity is not monodic but dialogical – in the sense that it depends upon the images of ourselves that others, and especially 'significant others' reflect back to us. If the culture of certain groups in a society is strongly dominant and that of others arbitrarily and compreheneisvely disparaged or marginalized, then it can reasonably be held, Taylor argued, that culpable injury has been done to these subordinated groups. They have been denied legitimate recognition of things central to what makes them what they are.

It is crucial to appreciate, however, that in developing these and related arguments, Taylor went out of his way to emphasize that he was not thereby endorsing thoroughgoing cultural relativism. For one thing, he pointed out that even those forms of liberalism that are hospitable to recognizing cultural differences are nevertheless *not culturally neutral.* Rather, they are grounded in certain substantive liberal values and for that reason cannot be completely impartial as between all cultures and subcultures, or between all diverse theories of the good life. Discussing these issues in the context of certain reactions to the publication of Salman Rushdie's highly controversial novel *The Satanic Verses* in 1988,[5] Taylor commented:

> All this is to say that liberalism can't and shouldn't claim complete cultural neutrality. Liberalism is also a fighting creed. The hospitable variant I espouse, as well as the most rigid forms, has to draw the line. There will be variations when it comes to applying a schedule of rights, but not where assassination is concerned. But this should not be seen as a contradiction. Substantive distinctions of this kind are inescapable in politics, and at least the nonprocedural liberalism I was describing is fully ready to accept this.
>
> (op. cit., pp. 62–3)

Taylor went on to point out that many contemporary societies are becoming both more culturally diverse and also more 'porous', in the sense of 'more open to multi-national migration' both inward and outward (ibid., p. 63), and he went on to argue:

> In these circumstances, there is something awkward about replying simply, 'This is how we do things here'. This reply must be made in cases like the Rushdie controversy, where 'how we do things' covers issues such as the right to life and to freedom of speech. The awkwardness arises from the fact that there are substantial numbers of people who are citizens and also belong to the culture that calls into question our philosophical boundaries. The challenge is to deal with their sense of marginalization without compromising our basic political principles.
>
> (Ibid., p. 63)

Having made this point, Taylor concluded his article by confronting head on the isssue of demands for recognition of the equal worth of different cultures. 'The further demand we are looking at here is that we all *recognize* the equal value of different cultures; that we not only let them survive, but acknowledge their *worth*' (ibid., p. 64). His response was characteristically nuanced and thoughtful but, once again, it did not even come close to unconditionally supporting the view that 'we owe equal respect to *all* cultures' (ibid., p. 64) His suggestion was the significantly more limited one that people should approach cultures other than their own, or at least 'cultures that have animated whole societies over some considerable period of time', with an initial presumption that 'they have something important to say to all human beings' and that they may therefore prove, in these respects at least, worthy of recognition (ibid., p. 66). Taylor, as a philosopher strongly influenced by the hermeneutic tradition, was also more aware than many commentators on these issues, of the formidable problems relating not only to developing a sufficiently informed understanding of another culture, but also of then going on to forming judgements about the worth of various aspects of that culture. But he concluded his discussion unequivocally:

> It makes sense to demand as a matter of right that we approach the study of certain cultures with a presumption of their value, as described above. But it can't make sense to demand as a matter of right that we come up with a final concluding judgement that their value is as great, or equal to others. That is, if the judgement of value is to register something independent of our own wills and desires, it cannot be dictated by a principle of ethics.
>
> (Ibid., p. 69)

I have presented Taylor's arguments at some length because they seem to me in various ways exemplary: in their open-mindedness, in their demarcation of key boundaries and sticking points, and in taking as a fundamental point of reference not nations but polities and the 'basic political principles' of certain kinds of liberalism. Distressingly, however, the approach Taylor so thoughtfully advocated seems less and less in evidence in many aspects of contempoary debates, in Britain and elsewhere.

Identity politics in modern Britain: growing polarization

In this section, I will examine a number of developments which suggest that we are currently witnessing a significant growth in the tendency on the part of people with strong investments in identity politics, to fail to listen to one another, to misrepesent one another's arguments, and in some cases even to go out of their way to seek confrontation. Not infrequently, these contestations are couched in terms of a language of rights and involve accusations of 'hurt' to cherished beliefs, symbols, and identities.

Two terms that have assumed increasing prominence as part of the discourse of certain kinds of contemporary identity politics are *Islamophobia* and *homophobia*. In critically discussing these terms, it is essential to acknowledge at the outset that both can be legitimately used to designate a range of real, obnoxious and widespread social attitudes and behaviours, including:

- irrational hostility,
- prejudice,
- various forms of discrimination,
- abuse and violence,
- a failure to display the kinds of tolerance of legitimate difference that a democratic liberal polity justifiably requires of all its citizens within the public sphere.

The *Concise Oxford English Dictionary* defines phobia as 'an abnormal or morbid fear or aversion', and homophobia as 'hatred or fear of homosexuals'. To affix phobia to either Islam or homo is therefore, in terms of dictionary definition, justifiable – at least within certain limits. There are individuals and groups of people who irrationally fear or loathe homosexual impulses, within themselves or in others; and there is, in some quarters, unreasoning fear and hatred of Islam and of Muslims. However, a considerable danger associated with these terms, (or from another point of view their attractive versatility), is that they can easily suggest that each and every form of criticism of Islam or of homosexual practices can be no more than an expression of irrational prejudice or even a form of psychopathology. Employed in these ways, both terms can become part of discourses whose underlying aim is to censor or silence all criticism or expression of dissenting beliefs.

One area where attitudes of this kind have recently become increasingly polarized has to do with religion on campus, specifically the role and rights of Christian Union groups in certain British universities and colleges. I propose here to examine some aspects of the basic issues that are at stake in these disputes, rather than the details of any particular case. In the last few years, there have been several instances in UK universities in which branches of the student Christian Union (whose origins go back to 1923) have been subjected to of a range of sanctions – including disaffiliation, freezing of bank accounts, denial of use of campus facilities – that have been imposed by the overarching student union authorities or by the university administrators of their respective institutions. The types of issue involved were summarized in an article in *The Times* in November 2006:

> Tensions between Christian Unions and student authorities have been rising since January, when the CU at Birmingham University was suspended by the Guild of Students after it refused to allow its meetings to be led or addressed by anyone not prepared to sign up to its ten-point statement of beliefs. It also refused to alter its constitution to include references to people who were gay, lesbian, bi-sexual or 'transgender' ... In Edinburgh, (a) six-week course, entitled 'Pure', was forbidden by the university from being taught on campus after claims that it promoted the 'healing' of homosexuality ... The (Edinburgh) CU's vice-president said: 'we would deny absolutely that we are homophobic. The Pure course lists homosexuality in the same category as fornication and adultery, so it doesn't single it out and say it is worse than anything else. According to the Bible we have all sinned'.
> Much of the opposition to the Christian Union stems from its ten-point statement of beliefs or 'Doctrinal Basis', which states that 'the whole of humankind is sinful and guilty', and has to be affirmed by all committee members and speakers.
>
> (Lister, 2006)

Various forms of ongoing controversy and litigation continue to surround these disputes, and again, I shall not discuss specific cases. More to the point is to consider the issues and arguments involved. At the heart of these is the question of the legitimate limits to be placed on the right, in a liberal and pluralistic democracy, to cause offence to others. Incitement to racial hatred is, by general consent, behaviour meriting strong legal sanctions. But, as Rowan Williams, the current Archbishop of Canterbury has stated, beyond issues of this kind, 'we sometimes seem to be unclear':

> Quite often in discussion of Christian attitudes to homosexuality (and this is often the presenting issue where Christian Unions are concerned), it is taken for granted that any statement that a form of behaviour might be sinful is on a par with the expression of hate, so that it is impossible for a conservative Christian, Catholic or Protestant or, for that matter, an orthodox Muslim to state the traditional position of their faith without being accused of something akin to holocaust denial or racial bigotry ... Yet the truth surely is that while it is wholly indefensible to deny respect to a person as such, any person's choices are bound to be open to challenge. Any kind of behaviour or policy freely opted for by a responsible adult is likely to be challenged from somewhere; it isn't as though sexual activity were different from any other area of conscious choice. And to challenge behaviour may be deeply unwelcome and offensive in a personal sense, but it is not a matter for legislative action.
>
> (Williams, 2006)

Some opponents of this sort of argument, of course, hold that homophobic views are simply intolerable in modern society and that student authorities are fully justified in denying recognition and resources to homophobic student groups or organizations. But it is at points like this that certain of the dangers associated with terms like homophobic become evident. At least some religious conservatives hold a thoughtful, considered and sincere belief that homosexual acts are sinful. This belief is part of a self-consistent set of wider convictions to which they subscribe and which in some cases form the basis of how they live what are in many cases good lives, contributing in many ways to the wider public good. It seems to me perverse to think that people of this kind are on a par with those who have a visceral and irrational fear or loathing of homosexuality and homosexuals, or who would engage in behaviour either disadvantaging or directly injuring gay or lesbian or bisexual or transsexual people. Attempts to ban religious conservatives of this sort from expressing their whole set of beliefs, or to deny them rights of association under the umbrella of student unions, seem to me a highly undesirable form of censorship and a denial of legit-imate freedom of speech. As Rowan Williams put it: 'If disagreement is to be silenced because offence may be caused, that is not good for intellectual life; it personalises and "psychologises" all conflict of ideas and denies the possibility of appropriate detachment in debating issues' (ibid.). Such arguments, should apply with particular force in institutions of higher education.

Unfortunately, the kind of argument I have developed in the previous paragraph is not at all helped by evidence of a growing tendency among the more fundamentalist sections of several faith communities, to demonize and victimize homosexuals in ways that unarguably do merit the label homophobic. Malise Ruthven has vividly described such tendencies among certain fundamentalist Muslims and Islamic nations and states:

> ... in the world of Islam ... the traditional tolerance of homosexuality as being less threatening to 'family values' than heterosexual (especially female) infidelity is now being replaced by active homophobia, with homosexuality stereotyped (quite inaccurately) as an 'imported' Western vice ... The Taliban who ruled in Afghanistan executed homosexuals by lapidation, bulldozing walls to crush their bodies. In Iran, after the revolution, homosexuals were hanged; in Egypt, under fundamentalist pressure, discos frequented by gays have been closed down and participants arrested.
>
> (Ruthven, 2004, p. 121)

Efforts to promote dialogue and mutual tolerance are similarly undermined within the UK by the efforts of some religious activists to censor the expression of views which they regard as hurtful and insulting to their religious sensibilities. Recent and highly publicized examples have involved protests – sometimes involving violence or incitement to violence – on the part of Sikhs, evangelical Christians and Muslims. These instances included first the de facto banning in 2004 in Birmingham of the performance of a play that some members of the local Sikh community found offensive; secondly, threats in January 2005 by the lobby group Christian Voice to instigate a blasphemy action against the BBC (British Broadcasting Corporation) over the screening of *Jerry Springer: The Opera*; and thirdly, a demonstration in February 2006 outside the Danish embassy in London by a small but vociferous group of Muslims protesting about the publication in Denmark of a set of cartoons depicting the Prophet Mohammed; some of the protesters carried placards reading 'Behead those who insult Islam' and 'Whoever Insults the Prophet, kill him'. Before discussing the first of these cases in more detail, it is essential to emphasize that in each instance, many of the co-religionists of the protesters, both locally and nationally, strongly disapproved of the form these protests took. There was also significant internal disagreement within each of the relevant faith communities about the substantive issues involved.

In Britain's second city Birmingham in December 2004, the play *Behzti* (Dishonour) by Sikh writer Gurpreet Kaur Bhatti was cancelled by the management of Birmingham Repertory Theatre following protests by more than 400 mainly male Sikhs. The violent protests involved the throwing of missiles at the glass-fronted building, thereby endangering patrons and employees. The theatre's executive director, explaining why, with the greatest reluctance, all further scheduled performances of *Behzti* had been cancelled, pointed to the management's legal 'duty of care':

We are determined not to go down the road of censorship but when one stands in the foyer with 800 women and children and sees stones being thrown and police officers injured, then security and safety issues come to the fore. We are certainly not bowing to censorship, we have refused to change the play.

(quoted in Kirby, 2004, p. 4)

The play was set in a Sikh *gurdwara* (place of worship) and depicted scenes of sexual abuse, violence and murder involving members of a fictitious Sikh community. The objections to the play focused partly on the 'negative portayal' of members of the Sikh community but more particularly on the offence caused by the action being set mainly within a (fictional) *gurdwara*. Attempts had been made, during prior discussions with community representatives, to persuade the writer and theatre company to rewrite the play, setting the incidents in a non-sacred context – but this pressure was steadfastly resisted.

Comments from spokespersons on each side of the debate reveal the gulf that, in the aftermath of these events, still separated certain community leaders from those arguing for freedom of expression. One prominent Sikh member of Birmingham City Council responded to the cancelling of the performances by saying

'I welcome and respect this decision, which is a very honourable course for the theatre to take. It means that relations with the local community can be restored.' He warned that any attempt to stage the play anywhere in the world would be likely to result in similar protests.

(Ibid., p. 4)

Another Sikh from a south Birmingham *gurdwara* added: 'It's a sad fact but it is a very good thing that they have seen common sense; but it has taken things to become violent before it happened' (ibid., p. 4). On the other hand, the chair of the British Writers Guild commented:

If you can get a big enough crowd, then you can suppress something. That's a terrible principle. Over the next months and years, it makes it less likely that they're going to take the plunge with anything slightly challenging or controversial, about any subject at all where a mob might be whipped up'.

(Ibid., p. 5)

It would be superfluous to add to these examples. But the picture they reveal is not encouraging. Far from progressing towards greater tolerance and mutual understanding, the zealous prosecution of identity politics on the part of multiple special interest groups seems, at least in some contexts, to be adding significantly to a climate of mutual distrust and adversarialism. And it is not only the various opposing interest groups themselves who are contributing to this situation. In a recent article on the role of the media, the philosopher A. C. Grayling has highlighted what he sees as the increasing prevalence of '*contrarianism*', which he defines as 'disputation for the sake of disputation' (Grayling, 2007). One of the key points he makes is that the more sensationalist sectors of the media frequently manufacture (or at least amplify) tendencies to polarization in public debate – for example by deliberately searching out spokespersons who speak from polar-opposite stances, and by passing over potential contributors with more complex and nuanced views. More subtly, Grayling also points out that 'the admirable aim of organizations like the BBC to scrupulously achieve balance in discussions' can, not uncommonly, itself result in distortions 'because it gives the impression that the world divides 50:50 on every topic, whereas the proponents of opposing views (may) represent very different actual weightings of opinion' (ibid.).

What *kind* of multiculturalism?

Amartya Sen has recently argued that as far as modern Britain is concerned 'the real issue is not whether "multiculturalism has gone too far" ... but what particular form multiculturalism should take' (op. cit., p. 152). As has already been argued, in the UK since the 1980s, the dominant agendas of many multicultural and even of some antiracist activists have propelled us in the direction of the wrong kind of multiculturalism – a terrain of cultural essentialisms. mutually antagonistic 'master identities', and what Sen himself calls 'plural monoculture' (ibid.). Moreover, a range of government policies and funding strategies, wittingly or not, have played a significant part in encouraging these developments. Charles Taylor was of course right to have emphasized that identities that derive from collective affiliations can be foundational to our sense of who we are, and that they can be the source of some of our deepest commitments. This is one main reason why issues of respect and recognition need be taken very seriously. It is, however, also very important to remember that such identities are by no means always religious or ethnic, nor even some combination of the two. Political belonging and commitment, and various kinds of secular ethical beliefs can be just as foundational of strong and enduring identities and commitments – and have at least as respectable cultural pedigrees. Moreover, and especially in a pluralistic society, it is not legitimate to expect, let alone to require, that identities should remain fixed. Indeed, for theorists like the political philosopher John Rawls, it is precisely the capacity and the freedom to reconsider and revise our comprehensive theories of the good life that is fundamental to identity formation in modern liberal societies.[6] Moreover, it is this capacity for ongoing self-interrogation and revision of one's beliefs that is, arguably, now most in need of protection – particularly from those who are intent on foisting on others their stipulative versions of acceptable master identities.

Such advocacy of a more open and self-critical form of multiculturalism will, of course, discomfort some – including certain community leaders whose influence and authority has been entrenched by some of the multi-cultural/antiracist policy initiatives of recent decades. But we need to remember here that there are many *other* people within these same communities whose freedom to define *their* identities has been restricted due to increasing cultural authoritarianism. For example, as Priyamvada Gopal has recently argued, during the last two decades the shared identity 'British Asian' has dissolved into divisive identity politics – sometimes with disastrous consequences for freedom of expression.

> Too many of us have been busy unhooking ourselves from the collective term 'British Asians' and dividing ourselves into Hindus, Sikhs, Muslims, Indians, Pakistanis and Bangladeshis ... where were the angry voices ... when a Sikh playwright, Gurpreet Bhatti was bullied by loud voices within her own community and even subjected to death threats? ... Where were the custodians of Asian dignity when crews filming Monica Ali's eponymous novel were hounded out of Brick Lane? When artist M. F. Hussain's exhibition was shut down because of vandalism by goons apparently representing hurt Hindu sentiments?
>
> (Gopal, 2007)

Like Malik and Sivanandan (discussed above), Gopal attributes such developments in large measure to the growing influence of those kinds of multi-culturalism and antiracism that have, at least in certain places, helped entrench the power of unrepresentative traditionalists and even extremists:

> A large part of the problem is that apart from the sterling work done by a few dedicated individuals and organizations, antiracist politics has become a facile 'representation' game that involves appeasing the fragile sensitivities of the vocal few claiming to represent the whole community. It is about harassing artists and writers, demanding that they conform to 'right' ways of representing the community.
>
> (Ibid.)

At this point, it is worth introducing a further crucial issue into the discussion – that of the types and range of 'cultural differences' we should take into account in thinking about the future of our diversely multicultural society. Specifically, I suggest, we need to examine our attitudes to social class and to class-cultural differences at least as self-critically as our attitudes to ethnic and religious difference. An instructive case in point here is the furore that arose in Britain in January 2007 over certain incidents screened as part of the UK reality TV show *Celebrity Big Brother* (Channel 4 TV). In one of the episodes of this programme, the famous Indian Bollywood star Shilpa Shetty was subjected to bullying and racist taunts by three white British contestants, the most prominent being Ms Jade Goody. All three minor celebs involved in this bullying were white, nouveaux riches, working-class women. The programme provoked a wholly unprecedented number of complaints (more than 44,000) to the TV watchdog Ofcom, mainly but by no means only from viewers whose family origins were in the Indian subcontinent. It also led to heated public protests in India itself, which happened to take place during a tour of the country by the then UK prime-minister-in-waiting, Gordon Brown. Carphone Warehouse, the main commercial sponsor of *Big Brother*, withdrew its funding and the firm's chief executive commented 'We are totally against all forms of racism and bullying; as a result we feel that, as long as this continues, we are unable to associate our brand' (in Gibson, Wray and McVeigh, 2007). New and old Labour MPs and several ministers joined in the chorus of condemnation. Others, including Gordon Brown during his Indian tour, sought to cool the incident by representing Britain as a nation of tolerant and fair-minded people who all deeply regretted the actions of this 'unrepresentative' group of deplorably ignorant women. Media pundits aplenty added their voices.

Yet arguably, the programme, precisely because of its populist character, actually held up a mirror to the nation – and this was even more true of much of the media reaction. What went on inside the *Big Brother* house, for all the contrived sensationalism inseparable from this type of reality TV, seems to have actually involved a complex mix of personality clashes, cultural antagonism, class envy, career envy, as well as strong elements of racism.[7] No less revealing, though, was the classism that was so evident in the rush to condemn these 'ignorant working-class racist women' – especially by sections of the media and political elites. A single edition of one of Britain's most liberal newspapers, *The Guardian*, contained the following comments in three separate articles:

> The Big Brother house remains one of hate, divided between ugly, thick, white Britain and one imperturbably dignified Indian woman ... Jade Goody defended herself by saying ... 'its not in me to be racial about anybody' ... The word you want, Jade, is not racial, but racist: do spend some of that estimated £8 million you have earned on a remedial education rather than boob jobs and liposuction ...
>
> (Jeffries, 2007)

> Former Tory Minister Edwina Currie told BBC 1's 'Question Time' last night: 'They [Goody and Lloyd] are crude young women having a go at another young woman in the most horrendous fashion. She [Shetty] is a beautiful young lady and they are slags'.
>
> (McVeigh, Wray and Ramesh, 2007)

> While the comments were probably made more inflammatory by editing juxtapositions, the stupid hatred of these white women for a brown one was real enough.
>
> (Lawson, 2007)

Mark Lawson, however, proved to be one of very few commentators to also recognize that

... one worrying consequence is that those exposed as bigots may now themselves be exposed to another form of bigotry – the middle-class denigration of the working classes as 'white trash', the one remaining openly racist phrase in common usage. The libelling of a large part of the British population in some parts of the media is a strange way of preaching tolerance. (Ibid.)

A few days later, Johann Hari in the *Independent* newpaper, made a similar point about the vicious class stereotypes that had been widely employed to denigrate Jade Goody and 'people like her'. Hari's comments are particularly pertinent here because of the connection he makes between such outbursts of racist classism and the myth of Britain as a meritocracy.

We wanted a Jade. We wanted to be told the 'underclass' were uneducated imbeciles who think there is a foreign country called East Angular ... Ordinary people ... want to think their higher social status is earned. So they look to Jade, and reassure themselves that Britain is a meritocracy after all... Snobbery is a more toxic force in Britain today than racism ... It lets us convince ourselves the 'stupid', 'racist' working class are not like us.

(Hari, 2007)

Not only this, but some of the reactions, as illustrated graphically above, involved a deeply unappealing combination of classism and sexism. Having, like Hari, noted the disturbing way in which 'Jade and her "chav" milieu provide[d] grist for the mill of self-congratulatory political correctness among upper- and middle-class white Britons', Priyamvada Gopal also drew attention to the no less 'nauseating ... play-off between ugly white slags and beautiful Indian princesses' – the invoking, as she pointed out, of 'a familiar Orientalist male fantasy' (op. cit).

All this highlights an uncomfortable truth: that it is neither an exaggeration nor a misuse of language to regard at least certain sorts of classism as a species of racism. Both racism and classism, after all, frequently manifest themselves in various forms of social exclusion and even segregation – in housing, education, patterns of sociality, and endogamy. Both involve imputations of inferiority and otherness which, in the politically correct society Britain has increasingly become, are rarely expressed outside the closed milieux concerned. And both remain pervasive – not only in the UK but also across the Indian subcontinent. It may be, then, that there is a hidden double standard operating here and that the myth of meritocracy helps legitimize it – in India as much as in Britain. Gopal argues in this regard that modern Indian elites are 'increasingly obsessed with disseminating the myth of the nation as fundamentally middle-class, professional and successful' and adds that this task 'has partly fallen on the feminine shoulders of India's flourishing glamour industry' (ibid.).

Perhaps the most important lesson to be drawn from this unedifying but revealing episode is that people who wouldn't be seen dead in *Big Brother* houses should not throw stones. More seriously, cases of this sort highlight the importance of attending to the complex intersections between ethnicity, class and gender (see, for example, Bradley, 1996). Facing up to the divisions arising from these intersections of identities may, if nothing else, help us towards a clearer sense of the depth and scope of the problems we now face.

Integration around 'shared British values'?

a) The problem of 'Britishness'
We have seen already that New Labour's approach to these problems seems to be increasingly focused on attempts to promote integration through the fostering of shared British values. This strategy, at least couched in these terms, seems, unpromising. Its basic problem is that it remains stuck on the very terrain we need to vacate: the terrain of particularistic culturalism. What this version of integration does is to continue to insist on the centrality of Britishness as the prime focus of identity and allegiance, whilst at the same time seeking to redefine Britishness as inclusive – for example, as embracing a range of hybrid or hyphenated identities such as 'British and Asian, British and black, British and white' (Blair, 2006b, op. cit.). But as we have seen, these values are promoted not only as core political virtues that all British citizens should endorse but also as somehow having their origins and essence in British culture. In Gordon Brown's words, they are said to be 'the enduring ideas *that Britain gave the world* – a commitment to liberty ... a belief in fairness' (Brown, 2006, my italics). But an all too obvious drawback of such self-congratulatory rhetoric is that Britishness is also, and inextricably, associated with a colonial past that is indelibly marked by a conspicuous absence of liberty and fairness – most obviously in centuries of racial exploitation, to say nothing of contemporary manifestations of racism. What is more, many of the core symbols of Britishness are similarly impossible to separate from this legacy of oppression, discrimination and separatism. One result of this is that the same signifier can be at once a source of legitimate national pride and an evocation of associations many would wish to disown. Paul Gilroy's phrase 'there ain't no black in the Union Jack' (Gilroy, 1987) memorably encapsulates this problem.

The divisive potential of discussions centred on Britishness was further manifested in the reception given to the *Parekh Report* (2000). This report, which was entitled *The Future of Multi-Ethnic Britain* and which was sponsored by the Runnymede Trust,[8] held out a vision of the future of the UK as a strongly multicultural 'community of communities' and perhaps even as a country that was en route to becoming 'a multicultural post-nation'. In assessing various obstacles to further movement in such directions, the authors of the report argued that

... there is one major and so far insuperable barrier. Britishness, as much as Englishness, has systematic, largely unspoken, racial connotations. Whiteness nowhere features as an explicit condition of being British, but it is widely understood that Englishness, and therefore by extension Britishness, is racially coded ...

They then added: 'Unless these deep-rooted antagonisms to racial and cultural difference can be defeated in practice, as well as symbolically written out of the national story, the idea of a multicultural post-nation remains an empty promise' (Commission on the Future of Multi-Ethnic Britain, 2000, pp. 38–9).

These claims provoked the following intransigent riposte from *Daily Mail* columnist Paul Johnson:

The Runnymede Trust report, calling for a total rewrite of our history and the banning of such terms as 'English' and 'British' as racist, looks like the first move in a New Labour brain-washing exercise to destroy our sense of nationhood ... Britain was the first truly free country in world history and because our history has always been free, we can trust it. And what does it tell us? It tells us that the New Labour Runnymede Trust version is tendentious rubbish. It is simply not true that Britain is a racist country with an oppressive past ...

(Johnson, 2000)

Widespread reactions of this kind led New Labour ministers, including the then Home Secretary Jack Straw, to very rapidly distance themselves from both the vision and the recommendations of the *Parekh Report*. And now, after 9/11, 7/7 and the rest, prospects for restoring these more radical multicultural visions to the mainstream agenda seem blighted – whatever one may think of them in principle.

Nevertheless, the appeal of British values to many New Labour ministers seems undiminished. As recently as June 2007, then Immigration Minister Liam Byrne and Communities Secretary Ruth Kelly launched a jointly authored pamphlet in which they called for the introduction of a national Britain Day to promote a clearer sense of British identity, as well as proposing Australian-style 'earned citizenship' for new immigrants, involving a points system to reward 'deserving' applicants and penalise the 'underserving' (Kelly and Byrne, 2007). Interviewed by the BBC, Mr Byrne stated:

At a time when we face the threat of a new extremism ... it's important now for the law-abiding majority to stand up for the values we've got in common. One of the ways we can do that is just taking a bit of time out each year to actually celebrate what we're proudest of in this country.

(BBC News, 2007)

Shared British values are also central to the discourse of the pamphlet itself: 'our diversity has always been underwritten by a subscription to a common set of values including our traditions of fairness and open-mindedness ...' (cited in *Evening Standard*, 2007). Reactions to these proposals were, of course, diverse – but they included the following predictably vehement reaction from *Daily Mail* columnist Andrew Roberts: 'since New Labour has spent the past decade doing its best to undermine what is truly distinctive about being British, isn't this one of the most grotesque demonstrations of gesture politics this tarnished government has yet come up with?' (Roberts, 2007). Several liberal commentators, however, were scarcely less sceptical – even if their style was more nuanced and their arguments more considered. Jonathan Freedland writing in *The Guardian*, perceptively commented:

> What of the proposed British Day? No one's going to say no to a day off, but something about this idea still prompts an embarrassed cringe ... The Americans have July 4, the French Bastille Day, but those mark genuine moments in the national narrative. What date could we pluck out the calendar that would not feel contrived? ... This goes to the core of the problem. Kelly and Byrne – and Brown – see that societies like the US have a mechanism for integration: their founding myths allow for the kind of civic, rather than ethnic, nationalism that anyone can join. The government would like some of that inclusive magic over here. But it's not so easy. You can't just pick off the cherries you like, like a national day. You have to plant the whole tree.
>
> (Freedland, 2007)

Freedland went on to suggest that 'planting the whole tree' would, in the case of the UK, need to involve reforms as radical as the construction of a written constitution and perhaps even, Britain becoming a republic.

b) **The problem of 'shared values'**
The second main problem area in assessing New Labour's integration agenda is the issue of shared values. It is a common assumption of many in government (and of some of their neoconservative critics), that societies can only be stable and ordered if there is a widely shared underpinning value consensus. The corollary of such a view is that social cohesion will be seriously imperilled if this foundational value consensus is undermined. Those who have the temerity to question such assumptions are likely to be attacked and misrepresented by both sides. I was myself criticized for such heresy by that scourge of both multiculturalists and New Labour, the neoconservative polemicist Melanie Phillips. Referring to something I wrote more than ten years ago, Ms Phillips recently glossed my views in the following terms: 'An education lecturer approvingly quoted writers who questioned whether there could be any shared values at all' (Phillips, 2006, p. 114).

What I actually said was rather more complex and did not involve denying the *possibility* of there being any shared values. My point was, rather, that such orderliness and stability as exists in complex societies has multiple sources, and often results in part from various balances of power between social groups whose values, far from being consensual, may be mutually antagonistic. Here is a somewhat abbreviated version of what I wrote:

As John Thompson has pointed out, the view that shared values are a kind of necessary social cement ... is highly questionable:

> There is little evidence to suggest that certain values and beliefs are shared by all (or even most) members of modern industrial societies. Moreover, there is little reason to suppose that the stability of complex industrial societies requires or depends upon a consensus concerning particular values and norms. Insofar as societies are 'stable' social orders, this stability could just as easily be the outcome of a diversity of values and beliefs, a proliferation of divisions between individuals and groups, a lack of consensus at the very point where oppositional attitudes might be translated into political action.
> (Thompson, 1990, p. 8)

To briefly elaborate:

a) Social institutions have powerful *non-normative* means of securing their own reproduction: industrial and commercial organizations, for example, have definite legal and political as well as economic conditions of existence. Such institutions also wield impressive power which very effectively constrains the actions of individuals and groups – for example, employees limiting their trade union militancy for fear that new investment will be channelled elsewhere ...

b) The remarkable orderliness of ... everyday social interaction does not rest primarily on a sharing of *values*. As ethnomethodologists demonstrated ... such orderliness is (rather) ... dependent upon ... 'background expectancies'. Harold Garfinkel brought these hidden sources of stability and predictability to light – for example, by encouraging his students to engage in calculated acts of *disruption* of these expectancies – such as trying to haggle over the price of toothpaste at a super-market checkout (Garfinkel, 1967).

c) Social action and inter-action is ... shaped and even determined by a whole range of *discourses* ... (but) such discourses ... are not unified, nor are they ultimately traceable or reducible to some 'core' of fundamental common beliefs. Quite the contrary: they are multiple and in many ways contradictory. The writings of Michel Foucault have been of decisive importance in demonstrating the ever-widening significance of the discursive regulation of social action and individual identity in modern societies ... The work he has inspired is, however, in important respects different from theories which employ the concepts of normative order or … dominant ideology. In particular, although for Foucault, discourses create 'regimes of truth', and although they do not merely regulate but in important ways actually *constitute* social subjects, the power exercised through them has no unified location or basis. It is not the sole property of any social class (or of the State) nor are discourses a set of instruments which can be appropriated by … any one section of society … As a result, the 'subject positions' which this multiplicity of dispersed, de-centralised discourses creates are inevitably *contradictory* to some degree … Our actions are the products of processes much less unified and much more contradictory than any theory of internalization of a system of common values would suggest.

(Beck, 1996, reprinted in Beck, 1998 pp. 19–20)

The increasing influence of theories of late/second modernity and the growing individualization that goes with it (e.g. Giddens, 1991, Beck and Beck-Gernsheim, 2002), as well as the proliferation of postmodernist and post-structuralist writing on social and personal morality (e.g. Bauman, 1995, Weeks, 1995), present a further range of challenges to those who aspire to restore, or to construct anew, some unifying value consensus in modern societies. The Dutch sociologists Jansen, Chioncel and Dekkers have recently characterized these challenges in the following way:

The impact of globalization, individualization and diversification leads to the conclusion that late modernity 'eats away the very foundations on which value communities can feed and constantly renew themselves' (Beck and Beck-Gernsheim, 2002, p. 17). A morally inspired ordering of society is no longer conceivable as the outcome of consensual community values. Instead, the focus of social cohesion shifts from consensus to the art of *coping with diversity and dissensus*. This shift requires a social morality that changes its agenda from 'how to justify Us' to 'how to be with Others' (cf. Bauman, 1989).

(Jansen, Chioncel and Dekkers, 2006, pp. 190–1)

Prospects for progress towards greater mutual understanding

To acknowledge that social order in complex societies is not necessarily or even normally founded upon an extensive value consensus does not, however, imply that values are unimportant. Far from it. But the evidence reviewed so far does suggest that we need a lot more honesty and realism, and less rhetoric, if we are to make progress in thinking productively about such values issues. A key part of this realism involves more openly acknowledging the degree to which our society is internally divided – not only by attachments to competing beliefs and the identity politics associated with them, but also by growing economic and class inequality. In many areas, we face one another as 'men mistrustfully interlinked' (Roth, 1996, p. 374) rather than as willing participants in a Habermasian 'ideal speech situation' of open and undistorted communication (Habermas, 1991).[9] This suggests that developing 'the mature lexicon' and 'positive tone' Trevor Phillips recommended as the route to trying to resolve our cultural and social differences is likely to prove very arduous.

As far as a shared lexicon is concerned, we need to begin by saying that linguistic barriers themselves can be one major source of problems. Over twenty-five years ago, the American sociologists Brigitte and Peter Berger analysed the 'war over the family' in the USA in the 1960s and '70s, and examined various ways in which linguistic differences helped intensify the divisisions between, on the one side, supporters of traditional family structures, and on the other, various sorts of feminists intent on under-mining this 'bastion of patriarchy'. Berger and Berger termed these opposed ways of using language 'Goshtalk' and 'Femspeak'. Goshtalk was the euphemistic language of the moral majority and more widely of 'all these people who say "gosh" instead of God, "heck" instead of "hell" ... and who "step out for a moment" '(Berger and Berger, 1984, p. 54). Commenting on the ways in which Goshtalkers become increasingly 'enraged by the "militant obscenity" of the Free Speech Movement at Berkeley' in the late 1960s, Berger and Berger not only illuminate how intimately language informs identity but also why conflicts over language can become so intractable.

> Imagine them facing each other, two typical representatives of the critical and the neo-traditionalist camps: It is as difficult to imagine the latter stepping out to take a shit as to imagine the former asking coyly to go to the bathroom ... Neo-traditonalists ... correctly (albeit instinctively) understand that the language of their adversaries stands for much more than a rebellion against trivial conventions ... Goshtalk is the language of an embattled bourgoisie linked in conflict ... with the rising knowledge class and its drive for power. Ideas are weapons. So is language. Linguistic victories are translated into political victories, and vice versa ... And all participants in these events sense this even if they lack the social scientific concepts to describe their intuitions accurately.
>
> (Ibid. p. 56)

In other areas, linguistic differences may sometimes be even more unbridgeable – for example where particular terms in one language and type of discourse may have no counterpart in another. In such cases, differing definitions of the situation may be incommensurable. A case in point, that I myself debated with Mark Halstead and Katarzyna Lewicka some years ago (Beck, 1999b), concerns the category 'sexual orientation'. This is not the place to rehearse the whole of that debate, but Halstead and Lewicka's main contention remains thought-provoking. They argued that

> ... Muslims cannot enter into the debate about the causes of homosex-uality, because from an Islamic perspective there is no such thing as

a homosexual orientation, just homosexual acts. If pushed, they might claim that the western concept of homosexuality, which has, after all, only been in existence since the end of the nineteenth century, is an attempt at rationalising a pattern of behaviour which is in conflict with divine law.

(Halstead and Lewicka, 1998, p. 59)

The obstacles to a meeting of minds on this issue, as between many in the gay and lesbian community and many orthodox Muslims, are here seen as profound – for many reasons but partly because accordingly to this interpretation 'the notion of homosexuality as a lifestyle at all, let alone a natural and equally valid one, is … incoherent from a Muslim perspective' (ibid., p. 29). Yet if the views of such orthodox Muslims are simply written off by their adversaries as blatantly homophobic, and those who hold such views dismissed as people with whom communication is pointless, then the already fragile possibilities for dialogue are likely to be further diminished.

To move from issues of language to issues of substance, we need to be clearer than we often are, that in debates of the kind we have been discussing, neither side can realistically expect the other to accord respect to the substantive beliefs and values of their opponents. Probably the best we can hope to achieve is a teeth-gritting acceptance by both sides that they have a civic duty to respect the rights of the other, in a liberal society, to hold and to be free to express (within the law) values and beliefs that others find offensive – even deeply offensive. Each side, moreover, needs if possible to see that in such matters offence is likely to be reciprocal. And this reminds us that tolerance, properly understood, is a strenuous civic virtue. It is not at all the same thing as easy-going permissiveness or a casual laissez faire outlook. We are only really called upon to exercise tolerance in cases where we find certain practices or beliefs objectionable or worse.[10] Depressingly, as several of the examples of cultural and identity conflict discussed above suggest, we seem as a society to be becoming more intolerant of one another – as competing groups of very diverse kinds insist upon their rights not to be hurt by others, or seek to press their rights beyond the limits of what others see as reasonable.

And this is where values really do come in. Even, or perhaps especially where there is in fact an absence of shared values, society, in the form of the democratic state (and if necessary employing its monopoly of legitimate violence for purposes of guaranteeing certain legally enshrined rights and liberties), must as far as possible uphold the foundational values of a liberal democratic polity. The most important of these core values (which we need to keep remembering are not in practice endorsed by all citizens, 'communities', or organizations), are those that provide a range of vital protections for individuals as free and equal citizens of a liberal polity.[11] Such values, in a liberal and pluralistic society, rightly prioritize fundamental individual freedoms. As Amartya Sen has put it in relation to multiculturalism:

Unless it is defined very oddly, multiculturalism cannot override the right of a person to participate in civil society, or to take part in national politics, or to lead a socially non-conformist life. And ... it cannot lead automatically to giving priority to the dictates of traditional culture over all else ... Britain can hardly be seen as a collection of ethnic *communities*. However, the 'federational' view has gained much support in contemporary Britain. Indeed, despite the tyrannical implications of putting persons into rigid boxes of given 'communities', that view is frequently interpreted, rather bafflingly, as an ally of individual freedom ... But must a person's relation to Britain be *mediated through* the 'culture' of the family in which he or she has been born? A person may decide to seek closeness with more than one of these predefined cultures or, just as plausibly, with none. Also, a person may well decide that her ethnic or cultural identity is less important to her than, say, her political convictions, or her professional commitments, or her literary persuasions. It is a choice for her to make no matter what her place is in the strangely imagined 'federation of cultures'.

(op. cit., p. 158)

One of the further strengths of this argument is that it applies with equal force to the claims of those 'home grown' cultural restorationists who want to assimilate everybody to what they define (always highly selectively) as the culture and traditions of the host community.

The key democratic values in question here are 'public values'. But they are public in the sense that they are the principles properly foundational of the public sphere in a liberal democratic polity. These values include respect for persons, values protective of individual liberties (e.g. freedom of thought and belief), values protecting legitimate collective forms of association and expression (e.g. freedom of asociation, press and media freedom). It is of particular importance to emphasize that *these values are not, in any simple way, appropriately identified as national values*. This is partly because they function to some degree as ideals – even in those cases where they are enshrined in documents such as written constitutions. But also, and crucially, they are also not the property or unique legacy of any one nation or culture – because they have very diverse sources. Amartya Sen (ibid.), for example, discusses the values of religious and political tolerance, and shows how they are rooted in a remarkably wide range of diverse ethnic, national, faith and philosophical traditions that have developed over many centuries. Attempts to appropriate such values as the exclusive legacy of one particular national culture are, partly for this reason, both unconvincing and potentially divisive. The really difficult task is to persuade more people from across the whole spectrum of social classes and communities to actually respect these values more consistently in their daily lives – at least within the public sphere (though this may have signficant implications for individual liberties within the non-public sphere as well). Although they are not in reality by any means universally endorsed, these public values should, nevertheless, be treated as non-negotiable by liberal democracies and by those who hold public office within them (especially in politics and in the judiciary). From time to time, various retreats and evasions can be expected to occur – as in the case of the play *Behzti* discussed above. But people should, as far as possible, be educated to understand why such instances are retreats from the principles that a liberal democracy should apply in such cases.

How far and how effectively educational institutions can play this kind of role is, of course, debatable. This book has suggested many reasons for pessimism. Nevertheless, some recent contributions to debates about citizenship education and cultural diversity in England have displayed an impressive combination of thoughtfulness, realism and hopefulness. Of particular value here has been the 'Ajegbo Report' entitled *Curriculum Review: Diversity and Citizenship* (DfES, 2007), written by Sir Keith Ajegbo and Seema Sharmar (respectively former head teacher and exisiting assistant head teacher of Deptford Green School in south east London), and Dr Dina Kiwan, lecturer in citizenship education at Birkbeck College, London. The Review Group members took extensive soundings among a wide range of interested parties, and formulated their findings with impressive clarity, honesty and realism. Although unwavering in its view that citizenship education should promote strongly inclusive conceptions of UK citizenship, the report never underestimates the extent and complexity of the challenges involved. For example, discussing Britishness, the writers report that

> The term 'British' means different things to different people. In addition, identities are typically constructed as multiple and plural. Throughout our consultations, concerns were expressed … about defining 'Britishness', about the term's divisiveness and how it can be used to exclude others.
>
> (Ibid., p. 8)

Consistently with this, although the authors emphasize that their brief was to 'examine whether and how a new "fourth strand" (of citizenship education within the National Curriculum) could provide pupils with … learning opportunities around the … themes of diversity on the one hand, and unity or "shared values" on the other …' (ibid., p. 89), they felt compelled to suggest that the notion of shared British values might prove to be as much a hindrance as a help:

> … how do debates on 'Britishness' relate to 'values' and 'shared values'? There is considerable debate about what 'shared values' are, as well as whether they are indeed specific to the UK – and whether it matters if they are also shared by other nations. We must also be wary of using 'shared values' to somehow challenge or question the acceptability of the expression of diversity.
>
> (Ibid., p. 93)

The report goes on to quote Chris Waller, professional officer of the Association for Citizenship Teaching, who argues that citizenship education in these areas is only likely to be effective if it encourages genuinely open and critical debate, rather than being constrained by, for example, the agendas of various politicians:

'The character of Citizenship must retain its critical and practical focus. Citizenship is about grey areas. It's not about whether I'm right or wrong; it's about me trying to understand my own explanations and explain those to others' (Waller). The overarching aim is to develop 'active citizenship' that is informed by relevant evidence, drawing on contemporary history to examine issues of contemporary importance around themes of identity and diversity in a political context in the UK.
(Ibid., p. 95)

Also strongly endorsed in the report is John Annette's idea of 'the importance of developing *"civic listening"* in citizenship in order that we all learn to listen to and evaluate the views and arguments of others' (ibid., p. 96, my italics). It is very encouraging that most of the main recommendations of the Ajegbo Report, and especially its proposal for the addition of an explicit focus on 'identities and diversity' as a key element of national curriculum citizenship education, have been enthusiastically endorsed by the Qualifications and Curriculum Authority (QCA). The new Programmes of Study for citizenship will come into effect in September 2008 – and they highlight the importance of enhanced political literacy as central to young people developing a critically informed understanding of issues relating to diversity, as called for by the authors of the Ajegbo Report.

Despite such positive developments, however, optimism about the prospects for significant change, even within education let alone more widely, must remain qualified. In the first place, as Sir Keith Ajegbo's own Foreword to the report candidly acknowledges: 'As a headteacher ... I know the sinking feeling when another weighty report lands on the desk. My first thought was "when will I have time to read it, let alone act on it?"' (ibid., p. 4).

As the discussion in the final part of Chapter 7 of this book has already suggested, the combination of the relatively low status of curriculum areas like citizenship and PSHEE on the one hand, and the 'innovation overload' and 'performativity' demands placed on schools on the other, means that there are major obstacles to the take-up of even the most desirable innovations – especially in these peripheral areas of the curriculum. Furthermore, as was also noted in Chapter 7, the marked lack of 'joined up thinking' between different elements of the QCA's own programmes – such as the almost complete absence of citizenship in the POS's for 'Economic well-being' and 'Enterprise' – is a further serious problem. And this remains true notwithstanding the QCA's exhortations to schools to emphasize overall curriculum integration more strongly. Also, of course, there is also the predictably hostile and sensationalizing reaction that almost any progressive innovation in education evokes from certain sections of the British media – an antagonism that is likely to inhibit some schools from venturing into such controversial areas, while encouraging others to default on their responsibilities. It was symptomatic, in this regard, that the publication of the Ajegbo Report was greeted by a *Times* leader headlined 'School Britannia: The latest recommendations will not help to establish a national identity' (*The Times*, 2007), while a *Daily Mail* columnist fumed 'New curriculum will make every lesson politically correct' – adding, 'children will be taught race relations and multiculturalism with every subject they study ...' (Clarke, 2007).

However, attempts to strengthen these curriculum reforms by resorting to centralized prescription can also rebound on their sponsors. Once again, this is partly due to professional battle fatigue in the face of the never-ceasing cascade of government initiatives. In May 2007, New Labour Schools Minister, Jim Knight, addressing the Annual Conference of the NAHT (the primary school head teachers' association), revealed that with effect from September 2007, schools would have a new statutory duty to promote community cohesion – particularly between racial and religious groups. The new guidance also made it clear that schools' compliance with this new set of responsibilities would be subject to inspection by Ofsted. The reaction on behalf of hard-pressed heads was both understandable and all too predictable. NAHT general secretary, Mick Brookes, while accepting that 'schools at the heart of the community is a great idea', commented: 'I winced. My heart sank. It seems like another stick to beat schools with. They think of something and they make it law and then Ofsted kicks in and – if you don't do it – you lose your job' (quoted in Garner, 2007).

A similar reaction came from John Durnford, general secretary of the Association of School and College Leaders, which speaks for most secondary school heads: 'It is an unnecessary statutory responsibility for schools in an area where schools are already in the front line' (ibid.).

Conclusion

This chapter has offered a wide-ranging though far from exhaustive survey of some of the most pressing problems we face in this fraught area of inter-cultural and inter-ethnic relations in modern Britain. Trevor Huddleston's memorable phrase 'naught for your comfort'[12] comes irresistibly to mind, even if it suggests a degree of pessimism that the facts do not yet wholly justify. Nevertheless, it is increasingly difficult to see the glass as half full rather than as half empty.

Notes

Notes for Chapter 2

1   As will be seen later in this chapter, in some of his more recent work, Giddens has modified his position to some degree, becoming more critical of the limitations of New Labour's approaches to reducing inequality, both at the bottom but especially at the top of society.
2   Those interested in the presentational and discursive aspects of New Labour's policy discourse should consult the work of Fairclough (2000), Hasan (2006) and Levitas (1998).
3   The government White Paper *Excellence in Schools* expressed an uncompromising commitment to improving children's life-chances through school improvement, for example via a set of 'non-negotiable' demands on schools, teachers, and LEAs.

> Our aim is excellence for everyone ... Hence our commitment to zero tolerance of underperformance ... Schools that have been found to be failing will have to improve, make a fresh start, or close ... The principle of zero tolerance will also apply to local education authorities. Our policy will be driven by the recognition that children only get one chance. We intend to create an education service in which every school is either excellent, or improving or both.
>
> (DfEE, 1997; and in Chadwick and Heffernan, 2003, p. 147)

4   The concept of 'personalisation' was developed and elaborated by Charles Leadbeater, an influential New Labour policy adviser and writer for the think tank Demos, in *Personalisation through Participation* (Leadbeater, 2004). For Leadbeater, the central idea was 'putting users at the heart of public services, enabling them to become participants in the design and delivery' (ibid., p. 19).
5   Even so, New Labour has consistently exaggerated the degree to which its successive reforms have really improved overall school effectiveness. It is salutary to note in this regard, that only two months before Blair delivered this 'educational legacy' speech, the first Annual Report of the new Chief Inspector of Schools for England, Mrs

Christine Gilbert, indicated plenty of cause for continuing concern. The report revealed that in the year to September 2006, 13 per cent of secondary schools had been classed overall as 'inadequate' and a further 38 per cent as only 'satisfactory'. The report stated:

> I would share the view of predecessors that 'satisfactory' is not good enough. Better education and care make a difference to the life chances of young people. It is a cliché to say that children have only one chance at school, but the cliché is right ... More needs to be done and swiftly to reduce the number found to be inadequate.
>
> *(Daily Telegraph,* 2006)

(There is an unintentional and ironic symmetry here between Mrs Gilbert's use of the 'only one chance' mantra and its appearance in both *Excellence in Schools* and Blair's education legacy speech.)

6   The promotion of this model of leadership, in education as in many other spheres, has been reinforced by turning the most 'outstanding' school leaders into a species of celebrity – for example by conferring knighthoods upon them. Thus Blair, in the education legacy speech cited above, highlighted the achievements of two schools that had been 'turned round' under New Labour:

> Ten years ago, Shireland was rated merely 'satisfactory' by Ofsted. A few weeks ago under Sir Mark Grundy's leadership the inspectors called it 'outstanding'.
> Or take Mossbourne Academy in Hackney. In 1995, Hackney Downs School was so bad that the last government sent in a hit squad to close it down. Today in award-winning new buildings, under what Ofsted calls the 'visionary and astute leadership of Sir Michael Wilshaw', Mossbourne Academy is a school transformed.
>
> (Blair, 2006a)

Whilst not wishing to decry the real achievements of some outstanding individuals, it is nevertheless salutary to remember, as John Fitz, Brian Davies and John Evans have recently pointed out, that if we wish realistically to judge the effects of policy innovation on the structure of opportunity, it is essential both to strive for objectivity and to take the long view:

> For anyone in need of measured accounts of the impact of major educational policy changes on the structure of opportunity or changes in life chances or employment prospects of children from different classes, a dip into social mobility studies is a much needed antidote to the claims of government optimists and their boosters, school management gurus, school effectiveness transformers and sundry educational entrepreneurs. When it comes to the big stuff,

like closing attainment gaps ... or opening up employment opportunity for students in Ebbw Vale or Sunderland, having read and
marked the social mobility literature, in the spirit of Monty Python,
we should ask 'What did the National College of School
Leadership and its mojo ever do for you?'.

(Fitz, Davies and Evans, 2006, pp. 134–5)

7   Such belief in the pre-eminent importance of 'leadership quality' seems
     to be sacrosanct even in areas where there is a looming crisis of finding
     enough leaders with the requisite qualities. This seems increasingly
     likely to be the case, for instance, in primary education in England and
     Wales during the next decade, as demographic factors severely shrink
     the pool of experienced leadership candidates willing to take on the
     every-increasing burdens.

8   The ambivalences in which leaders of the most prestigious universities
     are caught here are illustrated by the following comments made by
     Professor Richard in an interview in *Cam* – Cambridge University's
     alumni magazine:

We need to invest to stay at the top of our game. Cambridge
appears at or near the top of all the international league tables and
is determined to say there ... I do take league tables with several
pinches of salt: they relate to past performance ... and they
measure only what is easily measurable. You can't measure ideas,
which are the most interesting and vital part of any great university.
But, that said, I don't think it's by accident that we coming out in
the top handful of universities and I want to be sure we stay
there.

(Richard, 2006b, p. 9)

9   At the end of October 2006, a report by Bahram Bekhradnia and Tom
     Sastry, published by the Higher Education Policy Institute, highlighted
     the greater reliance of old universities on teaching undertaken by
     graduate students. Interviewed by Donald MacLeod for the *Education
     Guardian*, Bekhradnia commented:

One of the most interesting things to emerge is how the new
universities outperform the old universities in many respects. They
offer more teaching and they have less teaching in large groups.
On top of that, the teaching is by proper academic staff. You
would expect the old universities to have more graduate students
teaching because they have more of them and it is part of their
training to be an academic, but you don't want it as a substitute.

(MacLeod, 2006)

10   The incorrigibility of many senior civil servants' assumptions on these
     matters has been recently highlighted by Ivor Goodson in a discussion

of the privatization of the railway network in the UK in the 1980s and what he sees as the erosion of employee loyalty and dedication that went with it. Goodson describes a series of safety failures, dramatized by a succession of major accidents during the 1990s, which arguably resulted from the demise of 'the Sergeant Major of the track ... the dedicated railwayman who used to inspect a ten-mile length of track and knew what was wrong' (Green, 2001, p. 28 in Goodson, 2007). Goodson goes on to highlight the way many influential government advisers have none the less persisted in claiming that there is only one possible remedy: better and more effectively incentivized senior management. He cites the following remarks by Sir Steve Robson, a former second permanent secretary in the UK Treasury, who was heavily involved in rail privatization: 'What about Railtrack? Where should we go now? The basic issue is the same – management and management incentives. Rail infrastructure needs to be run by top quality managers who are incentivized, and empowered to do a good job' (Robson, 2001, p. 28).
Goodson's comment is caustic.

> The myopic absurdity of this diagnosis is breathtaking in the light of what has happened to the railways. It is as if the workforce and its inherited and ongoing expertise are of no importance in the delivery of the railway services. Again, they return to the problem of how to incentivize the elite. This elite has been superannuated and incentivized to an absurd level, and the result has been a catastrophic failure of delivery. One wonders what kinds of experiences will be required for the learning curve of certain sectors of Government to move upwards.
>
> (Goodson, 2007, p. 140)

11   Data from Incomes Data Services for the twelve months to July 2006 revealed dramatically rising differentials between the rewards of the chief executives of leading companies in the UK and those of their employees.

> The pay gap between FTSE 100 chief executives and their average full-time members of staff has widened this decade to a point where the heads of Britain's biggest companies now earn 98 times as much on average as their employees ... FTSE 100 chiefs saw their total earnings jump by an average of more that 40 per cent to £2.89 million in the 12 month period.
>
> Richard Lambert, the CBI Director-General said: 'Senior executive pay has increased in line with international benchmarks while lower-skilled employees have found themselves competing with low-cost workers overseas'.
>
> The gap between the chief executive and the rank and file has more than doubled so far this decade. The average FTSE 100 chief

executive earned 39 times the amount of their average employee in 2000. The IDS (Incomes Data Services) report says that most of the gap is a result of the dramatic rise in bonuses, as companies seek to give incentives to top managers.

(Bawden and Duncan, 2006)

Other sources providing an abundance of recent evidence about the widening gap in income, wealth and influence in Britain include Lansley (2006) and Williams (2006).

12   The research on which this quotation is based employed John Goldthorpe's three-fold classification of 'service', intermediate and working classes. The still relatively unfamiliar term 'service class' (sometimes referred to as 'the salariat') is defined as including higher-grade and lower-grade professionals, administrators and managers, proprietors, supervisors, and higher-grade technicians. (See Halsey et al., 1980, pp. 16–19 for a fuller exposition.)

Notes for Chapter 3

1   Despite its prestigious academic pedigree (for example, in Giddens, 1998), the phrase never really caught on – perhaps not least because, as Andrew Marr suggested at the time, it involved 'a negative definition of politics – the Third Way can be described ... only by what it is not' (Marr, 1998).

2   Consider, for example, the contradictions inherent in simultaneous exhortations to support multiculturalism but to be unabashed in celebrating a supposedly historically rooted 'modern patriotism': '... identity and belonging need to be linked to our commitment to nationhood and a modern form of patriotism ... That is why ... Gordon Brown has put forward a clear view of British values, stemming from both our history and our beliefs as a people' (Blunkett, 2005).
    The conditional character, and clear sense of 'othering', in Blunkett's ostensibly inclusive modern patriotism, are caught in the following:

> ... debating our identity and sense of belonging is not to be nostalgic, but to address the world of the 21st century ... A debate, therefore ... about how we develop a common home that is welcoming to others is vital for our well-being and for developing, through patriotism, our embrace of those whose culture, colour, religion and lifestyle are different. First-generation immigrants can be proud to be Pakistani and British or African and British, and those rooted here proud to be English and British ... (Ibid.)

3   'De-centred' identities are the counterpart of those that are 'centred' – most significantly for analyses of modern Britain, what Bernstein

terms 'de-centred *market* identities', though the typology also includes de-centred 'therapeutic' identities. It is important to appreciate that Bernstein treated these categories as akin to 'ideal types', arguing that they were rarely encountered in their pure form and in particular, that schools in Tony Blair's Britain, would tend to promote various mixes of these identity types.

4   For a detailed account of the career of the term 'hard-working families', see Oscar Reyes, 2004.

5   The Power Commission, an independent enquiry supported by the Joseph Rowntree Foundation, was set up in 2004. The ten-member panel chaired by Dame Helena Kennedy QC, published its report *Power to the People* (also known as the Power Report) on 17 February 2006. The report documented the marked decline in recent years in the UK, in participation in mainstream politics, including voting and party membership. It went on to summarize evidence of widespread disenchantment with the political system among Britain's citizens – notwithstanding evidence of strong involvement in single-issue causes. It linked this disengagement and alienation to 'the weakening mandate of legitimacy for elected governments ... the weakening of political equality ... and the rise of undemocratic political forces' (The Power Commission, p. 15). Dame Helena Kennedy, interviewed by The *Guardian* newspaper on the day the report was published, commented:

> Politics and government are increasingly in the hands of privileged elites, as if democracy has run out of steam ... Too often, citizens are being evicted from decision-making – rarely asked to get involved and rarely listened to. As a result, they see no point in voting, joining a party or engaging with formal politics ... Parliament has had many of its teeth removed and government is conducted from Downing Street.
>
> (quoted in Branigan, 2006, p. 4)

6   The reference here is, of course, to T. H. Marshall's classic text *Citizenship and Social Class* (1950). (For more extended discussions of tensions between 'Marshallian' and neoliberal citizenship see, inter alia: Ahier, Beck and Moore, 2003; Faulks, 1998; and Gamble and Wright, 2004.)

7   Such moralism is highly selective, for example, in condemning those said to be 'de-moralised' by 'dependency culture' whilst remaining insouciant about the widening divisions of wealth and income in the UK and the increasing self-aggrandisement of various elite groups (see Lansley, 2006; Williams, 2006; also Chapter 2 of this volume).

8   The phrase is, of course, an adaptation of the term 'really useful knowledge', employed by Richard Johnson, following the usage of various English nineteenth century radicals. 'Chartists and Owenites in particular espoused education – *really* useful knowledge – in much the way in which Gramsci espoused it as a latter-day "Jacobin" and

educator for Italian communism. It was tied into political strategies and infused with power and meaning.' (Johnson, 1976, p. 50)

9   As we have seen, Blair's preoccupation with respect goes back at least to his 'My vision for Britain' speech of 2002, and it is not entirely clear how or when it began to be elaborated into a coherent policy agenda. There is little doubt, however, that it was quite soon recognized as such. For example, *Observer* columnist Jay Rayner sees Christian socialist Labour MP Frank Field as one key source, arguing that Field's book *'Neighbours from Hell*, published in 2003, is now seen ... as a direct influence on Tony Blair's much trumpeted respect agenda' (Rayner, 2006).

10   The term '*social* entrepreneur' was promoted by the think tank Demos and popularized in the run-up to the 1997 general election by, among others, the Rev. Peter Thomson – said to be one of Tony Blair's spiritual gurus, who characterized it in the following terms: 'what social entrepreneurship is about is empowering people at the bottom to feel they can make a difference' (Rowe, 1997).

11   The concepts of pseudo-mutuality and double-bind were developed by radical anthropologist Gregory Bateson and radical psychiatrist R. D. Laing in the late 1950s, as key concepts in their attempts to develop an alternative theory of the genesis of schizophrenia and related conditions (see Bateson, et al., 1956; Laing, 1959). As far as I am aware, it is not a concept used by Sennett himself but it seems highly apposite.

12   This decisive departure from the tentativeness about citizenship education displayed by all previous UK governments occurred after David Blunkett became secretary of state for education in Tony Blair's first administration in 1997. One of Blunkett's first acts as minister was to set up an Advisory Group on Citizenship, chaired by his former politics tutor at Sheffield University, Bernard Crick, a long-time advocate of political education in schools (see Crick and Porter, 1978). The Advisory Group's remit was to provide 'advice on effective education for citizenship in schools, to include the nature and practices of participation in democracy; the duties, responsibilities and rights of individuals as citizens; and the value to individuals and society of community activity' (Advisory Group on Citizenship, 1998, p. 4). Accepting this guidance, the group's Final Report highlighted three key elements of citizenship education: social and moral responsibility; community involvement; and political literacy. The report was favourably received by ministers and the upshot was that, with effect from September 2002, citizenship became a statutory foundation subject of the national curriculum in all state secondary schools and part of the non-statutory 'framework for PSHE' (personal, social and health education) in primary schools. Since then, schools have received an abundance of further official guidance and exemplars of good practice, to help them in the task of developing the new subject effectively (e.g. QCA, 2000; QCA, 2001). Schools were, by design, allowed considerable autonomy in deciding such matters as how they would

deliver citizenship, whether the new subject would be formally assessed for any or all of their pupils, and so on.

13 An emphasis on promoting 'education with character' as part of 'helping young people to develop into active citizens' was one element in what was a very heterogeneous government White Paper *Schools: achieving success* (DfES, 2001, pp. 27–9). James Arthur has pointed out, however, that in Britain in marked contrast to the USA, character education has never taken root and that this White Paper appears to contain 'the first reference to character education in government documents for nearly 50 years' (2005, p. 245).

14 Each core and foundation subject in the national curriculum for England has its prescribed content specified in a Programme of Study (POS). In the case of citizenship, however, the content and pedagogic approaches specified are deliberately 'indicative' or 'light touch' rather than mandatory since the aim is to allow individual schools and colleges to design an approach that, while respecting the POS's, also meets their own distinctive needs and priorities as they define them.

15 Robin Alexander highlights both the absurdity but also the potency of the discourse of the strategy's key policy document:

> First there's the soft sell of that title: *Excellence and enjoyment.* The default vocabulary for education policy since 1997 highlights 'standards', 'driving up standards', 'underperforming' ... 'hard-hitting', 'the challenge ahead', 'step change', 'tough', 'new', 'tough new', 'world class', 'best practice', 'delivery', and so on (DfEE, 2001).
>
> (Alexander, 2004, p. 14)

Notes for Chapter 4

1 This £10 million recruitment campaign was launched by the TTA in October 1997. The 'No-one forgets a good teacher' poster campaign was backed up by cinema advertisements in which a series of celebrities named their favourite teacher. Ironically enough, in a parallel move, Tony Blair found it necessary to appoint Alec Reed, chairman of the UK's largest private employment agency Reed Executive, to spear-head the effort to solve the growing crisis in teacher recruitment which was threatening to undermine the government's much publicized efforts to boost national standards in numeracy and literacy by the year 2000 (see Rafferty and Dean, 1997).

2 In introducing these aspects of Bernstein's work, it is important to point out that in his more recent writings, the category pedagogy has become an overarching concept – subsuming not only:

(a) his own earlier analytical framework which treated 'curriculum, pedagogy and evaluation' as three separate (though interrelated) elements (Bernstein, 1971), but also
(b) a complex apparatus of intellectual fields – notably:
i) the field of the creation of academic and other discourses (mainly the province of universities in modern societies), and
ii) two recontextualizing fields which between them structure the transmission of reconstructed versions of these higher discourses. These two recontextualizing fields Bernstein labels respectively the ORF and the PRF. The ORF (Official Recontexualizing Field) in modern societies is normally dominated by the educational and training agencies of the state, while the PRF (Professional Recontextualizing Field) consists of 'pedagogues in schools and colleges and departments of education, specialized journals, private research foundations', etc. (Bernstein, 1996, p. 48).

It is the internal structuring of these fields as well as the changing relationships between them that is a central focus of Bernstein's analysis – but this is also analysed with reference to the way change internal to these pedagogic fields is shaped by wider economic, political and cultural influences.

3   The manner in which Bernstein derives inspiration from major social theorists of the past is an intriguing issue in itself. For example, many of his core preoccupations are strongly Durkheimian – yet, as his treatment of the category of the sacred illustrates, he is far from systematic in the ways he derives this concept from Durkheim and his use of it goes beyond what any strict mode of theoretical derivation would endorse. This is similarly true of his indebtedness to Marx and Weber – and also more recent theorists like Foucault or Bourdieu. However, in reading Bernstein, it seems to me profitable not to carp about theoretical rectitude – but rather to value the insights and the fecundity of the ideas.

4   The fact that actual practitioners and professional bodies have not uncommonly fallen short of this conception of a profession as a calling – in Max Weber's sense of that term (Weber, 1948) – does not significantly damage the point being made here. It is not necessary to conjure up a non-existent golden age of purely altruistic professions wholly dedicated both to the pursuit of knowledge and the interests of their clients, to nevertheless maintain that the guardianship of traditions of scholarship and ethical autonomous practice by professional communities is very much more than a self-serving myth. Furthermore, the relative autonomy of these professions and their organic links with relatively autonomous communities of scholarship within universities were an essential structural condition of the formation of subjective identities which were centred to a very important extent in the valuing of learning for its own sake and the exercise of independent judgement in the service of the best interests of clients.

5   As far as schools and the training of teachers are concerned, these processes have, in Bernstein's own language, inexorably eroded the autonomy of the PRF and subordinated it to the prescriptions, audits and inspections emanating from the ORF (see Bernstein, 1996, pp. 70–5).

6   A source of potential misunderstanding of this aspect of Bernstein's work is his idiosyncratic definition of the term 'competence' when discussing teacher-training reforms. The mainstream use of the term is as I have employed it, i.e. competency-based training, is training structured in accordance with batteries of closely specified behavioural outcomes – the most recent example in the UK being the 'Standards for the Award of Qualified Teacher Status' (DfEE, 1997). Bernstein, however, employs the term competence in precisely the opposite sense. He derives this usage from the well-known distinction in linguistics between linguistic competence (referring to a generalized and creative capacity) and linguistic performance (specific and context-bound utterances). There is no ambiguity in his discussion so long as this is appreciated.

7   The Teacher Training Agency's developing framework of National Professional Qualifications (NPQs) exemplifies these developments very clearly. It extends from initial teacher training, via the training of Advanced Skills Teachers, Subject Leaders, and Special Educational Needs Coordinators – to training for headship. At each stage, the training programmes' objectives are specified as sets of nationally applicable competencies (National Standards) – which all providers must closely follow.

8   It is important to recognize, although there is no space to discuss it here, that Bernstein also examines a range of alternative (and in some cases competing) identities – which different groups of teachers and lecturers, differently located in various ways, might embrace. He groups these into three broad categories: de-centred, retrospective and prospective identities (see Bernstein, 1996, pp. 75–81).

9   Interestingly, Newman and Clarke, in their perceptive analysis of managerialization across public sector institutions in the UK, also draw attention to the fact that 'much of the resistance to the process of managerialization' has 'focused on the emptiness or hollowness of its language' (Newman and Clarke, 1994, p. 28). Insightfully, they suggest that this emptiness is more than a matter of the rhetorical hollowness of the mystificatory language of mission, empowerment, ownership and the like, and that:

> The basis of this emptiness of managerialism as a discourse is to be found in management's social location. It is derived from management's position as a recipient of devolved social and economic power – historically rooted in the separation of ownership and control in private enterprise. In that sense, management possesses no super-ordinate goals or values of its

own. The pursuit of efficiency may be the mission statement of management – but this is efficiency in the achievement of objectives which others define ...

(Ibid., p. 29)

10   Clarke, Cochrane and McLaughlin, in their recent authoritative survey of the impact of managerialization across the whole field of social policy in the UK, contend that the objective of controlling and reducing public expenditure has consistently been accorded the highest priority in the managerialist reforms of recent years – to the extent that the goals of efficiency and effectiveness, which form the key legitimations of managerialization, have often been seriously compromised. They further comment:

these overarching political objectives have also pushed other concerns – questions of equity or social justice, for example – off the social policy agenda. Despite some of the grander claims, therefore, fiscal considerations have placed budgetary control at the core of managerial discipline ...
(Clarke, Cochrane and McLaughlin, 1994, pp. 226–7)

11   Under New Labour, devolution of real powers to new national bodies in Scotland and Wales (and to a lesser extent to regional bodies) qualifies this – but not fundamentally.

12   Such attempts are, however, by no means always successful. As Clarke, Cochrane and McLaughlin have pointed out, 'attempts to de-politicize social policy by stressing the apparently super-ordinate, and neutral criteria of "economy, efficiency and effectiveness" that are to be achieved by the new management, have only been partially successful' (op. cit., p. 231). Such problems of legitimation arise in part precisely because of the necessarily semi-devolved nature of these state regimes:

Attempts to maintain 'arm's length' or 'hands off' governance of agencies have been undermined by the constant temptation and, in certain instances, political necessity to intervene in order to reaffirm policy directions, reconsider the direction of reform or to deal with emergent problems of process and practice.
(Ibid., p. 231)

13   Moore and Muller have described this phenomenon as follows:

Today, the most common form of this approach is that which, drawing upon postmodernist and poststructuralist perspectives, adopts a discursive concern with the explication of 'voice'. Its major distinction is that between the dominant voice and those ('Others') silenced or marginalized by hegemony ... The main move is to attach knowledge to categories of knowers and to their experience and subjectivities. This privileges and specializes the subject in terms of its membership category as a subordinated voice.

(Moore and Muller, 1999, p. 190)

Notes for Chapter 5

1   For most of his career, Bernstein adopted an 'agnostic' stance on these epistemological issues – a stance which he only partially abandoned in his late (and in this respect still somewhat ambiguous) paper on 'vertical and horizontal discourse' (2000, Ch. 9).

2   As the philosopher of education Charles Bailey once pointed out, 'what an autonomous teacher' (and we would include here certain other kinds of professional) 'could not do, and retain autonomy, would be to consider (their) role simply as that of agent for someone else's decision-making, especially where such another was not a professional ... ' (Bailey, 1984, p. 237).

3   Since the establishment of the Learning and Skills Council to manage all post-16 pre-university education in England, the term 'further education' referring to provision in the colleges has been replaced by the Learning and Skills Sector which, significantly, includes work based learning and provision by private training providers.

4   Bill Readings highlighted an analogous emptiness in the proliferation in American universities of what he called 'de-referentialized discourse', i.e. terms like 'excellence, empty of intrinsic meaning but which are (ironically) mobilized for 'image-building' purposes. (Readings 1996). Beck has observed that something similar applies to the use by New Labour of terms like modernize (1999, 2002, 2005).

5   See, for example, the Green Paper *Schools: Building on Success* (2001) which sets out a vision of teaching as a modernized profession and claims that it provides a model for others within the public sector:

> The changing economy is increasingly placing new demands on professionals in every field. In the 20th century, the professional could often expect to be treated as an authority, whose judgment was rarely questioned and who was therefore rarely held to account. Despite this ... particularly in the public sector, services were arranged to suit the producer rather than the user ... Teaching, by contrast is already in many ways a 21st century profession. More perhaps than any other, the teaching profession accepts accountability ... and growing acceptance of accountability means that the relationship between teachers and Government can build more than ever before on trust ... In this climate, in partnership with teachers, we will take forward the agenda of reform ... and complete the modernization of the teaching profession.
>
> (DfEE, 2001, paras 5.4, 5.5. and 5.6)

For a more developed discussion of efforts to restructure the teaching profession in England and Wales, especially under New Labour, see Beck, 2006 (reprinted as Chapter 6 in this volume).

Notes for Chapter 6

1   The imposition of new statutory pay and conditions of service requirements under the Teachers' Pay and Conditions Act of 1987 followed 'a prolonged and bitter dispute between the DES, teachers unions and LEAs' between 1984 and 1987 (Tomlinson, 1993, p. 49). The School Teachers' Pay and Conditions Act 1991 modified the statutory framework in various ways. In addition to 'directed time', teachers' contracts also contained provision for 'additional contractual obligation time' and a much smaller element of 'self-directed time' (Tomlinson, 1993, p. 58).

2   This chapter will not attempt to assess the extent to which this was accomplished. The discussion is mainly concerned with analysing educational and other discourses rather than estimating their efficacy.

3   I have, in particular, made extensive reference to Robin Alexander's paper 'Still No Pedagogy?' (2004), in which he developed a trenchant critique of the government's 2003 Primary Strategy, via a detailed analysis of the DfES document *Excellence and Enjoyment: a strategy for primary schools* (DfES, 2003).

4   Although generic modes are treated by Bernstein as linked to 'de-centred market' identities (Bernstein, 2000, Chapter 3), we need to remind ourselves that he recognized that in reality, more hybrid forms are encountered. It certainly seems plausible that under New Labour, hybrid identities of this kind are being shaped and that they are the product not only of direct market imperatives but also of centred (i.e. governmental) initiatives intended to 'functionalise' the education system to more effectively meet perceived market demands. Centrally imposed reforms of teacher training under both Conservative and Labour governments since the 1980s have arguably resulted in a significantly stronger emphasis on trainability (see Beck, 2002; and Beck and Young, 2005 – reprinted as Chapter 5 in this volume).

5   It was Moore and Jones who first drew attention to the ways in which the introduction of competency-based paradigms into teacher training in England in the 1990s threatened to deny 'trainees' access to more critical kinds of academic discourse, notably, insights developed within the philosophy and sociology of education. As these writers also pointed out, competency-based training tended to conceal its own grounding in theoretical knowledge (mainly in behaviourist psychology), and it did this by representing itself as simply common sense and thus as an alternative to what the secretary of state for education at the time, Kenneth Clarke, memorably called 'barmy theory' (Jones and Moore 1995).

Notes for Chapter 8

1   Early in 2007, Trevor Phillips became the chair of the newly created Commission for Equality and Human Rights, which incorporated a range of previously separate equality agencies into a single organization. The creation of this new body was itself highly contentious, some seeing it, for example, as evidence of the government 'going soft' on effective promotion of anti-racist policies and initiatives.

2   The public stances adopted by Phillips and Livingstone during these years became increasingly polarized. Private exchanges between the the two camps were said to be even more acrimonious: 'In a private letter to Phillips seen by *The Observer*, Livingstone ... concluded: "your activity already means your credibility is at an all-time low among those who are victims of racism, and is falling further with each statement you make"' (quoted in Hinsliff, 2006).

3   The idea of essentially contested concepts was first introduced by the philosopher W. B. Gallie who defined the term as follows: essentially contested concepts are ideas 'which inevitably involve endless disputes about their proper use on the part of users' (1955, p. 169).

4   To follow the twists and turns of these complex debates would involve too great a digression from the main line of argument. It would also entail grappling with the abstruse discourse of postmodernist and post-colonial theory as well as the many varieties of antiracism. These debates are, of course, of very considerable relevance to the issues under discussion here but they are so complex and contested as to prohibit brief exegesis in a book of this kind. The interested reader is referred to the excellent collections edited by May (1999b) and Ladson-Billings and Gillborn (2004).

5   Salman Rushdie's controversial novel was published by Penguin late in 1988. The book was burnt in public in Bradford in January 1989. A *fatwah* on Rushdie was imposed in Iran by Ayatollah Khomeni on 14 February. Sayed Abdul Quddus, the then secretary of the Bradford Council of Mosques, is reported as having said 'Muslims here would kill him and I would willingly sacrifice my own life and that of my children to carry out the Ayatollah's wishes should the opportunity arise' (Tendler, McEwan and Beeston, 1989, cited in Phillips, 2006, p. 46).

6   The second of Rawls' two 'moral powers' of citizens pursuing justice as fairness, and engaging in social cooperation in agreeing the principles underpinning the basic structure of a just, liberal and democratic society, is:

> ... a capacity for a conception of the good: it is the capacity to have, to revise, and rationally pursue a conception of the good. Such a conception is an ordered family of final ends and aims which specifies a person's conception of what is of value in human life or, alternatively, of what is regarded as a fully worthwhile life.
> (Rawls, 2001, p. 19)

Rawls adds in relation to the freedoms of citizens in such a society, that

> ... as citizens, they are seen as capable of revising and changing (their conception) of the good on reasonable and rational grounds, and they may do this if they so desire. As free persons, citizens claim the right to view their persons as independent from and not identified with any particular conception of the good or final ends.
>
> (Ibid., p. 21)

7   In fact, Channel 4 executives persisted for some time in denying that there had been a racist component in the behaviour of the white 'residents' of the *Big Brother* house. However, as Priyamvada Gopal devastingly observed, contestant Jade Goody's reference to Shilpa Shetty as Shilpa "Fuckawallah" was 'not the innocent concoction of someone straining to recall a surname', as was later claimed by the programme makers (Gopal, 2007). In May 2007, the media watchdog Ofcom published a censorious report on the incidents and required Channel 4 to issue a series of formal apologies.

8   The Parekh Report, *The Future of Multi-Ethnic Britain*, was produced by The Commission on the Future of Multi-Ethnic Britain, a group of 'the great and the good' involved in multicultural issues which was chaired by Professor Bhiku Parekh. The Commission was established by the Runnymede Trust, a charitable organization with a track record of supporting progressive developments in the fields of multiculturalism and antiracism.

9   As the Cambridge sociologist Patrick Baert explains, the German critical theorist Jurgen Habermas

> ... talked about 'undistorted communication' whenever people can openly criticize and defend each other with regard to validity claims. It occurs when there are hardly any barriers to open debate. Habermas coined 'ideal speech situation' (*ideale Sprechsituation*) to refer to the ideal-typical situation in which there are no such barriers at all. Everybody is entitled to argue their case, to question what others have said, and to raise new topics. The ideal speech situation is entirely dominated by the principle of the 'force of the better argument'.
>
> (Baert, 2005, p. 122)

10 Even in John Rawls' account of reasonable citizens engaged together in the use of public reason to determine fundamental constitutional principles of a liberal and pluralistic polity, there is recognition that those holding differing comprehensive theories of the good life will recurrently have to take upon themselves what he calls 'the burdens of judgement' – for example in deciding hard cases, in accommodating their diverse value stances on issues of significant complexity, and the like (see, for example, Rawls, 2001, pp. 35–6).

11   For an illuminating discussion of protection in relation to issues of liberal democratic citizenship, see David Hogan (1997).
12   'Naught for your Comfort' is the title of a famous account by Trevor Huddleston of racial injustice in Johannesburg and the township of Sophiatown under the South African apartheid regime in the early 1950s. Huddleston, a tireless campaigner against apartheid, was a member of the Community of the Resurrection; he later became Archbishop of the Anglican Province of the Indian Ocean. He died on 20 April, 1998.

Bibliography

Ackerman, B. (2006), *Before the Next Attack: Preserving Civil Liberties in an Age of Terrorism*. Newhaven, CT: Yale University Press.

Adams, C. (2000), 'Statement by Carol Adams, Chief Executive of the General Teachers' Council for England', in *The GTC: Listening to Teachers*. London: General Teaching Council for England.

Adonis, A. (2001), *High Challenge, High Support*. London: Policy Network.

Advisory Group on Citizenship (1998), *Education for citizenship and the teaching of democracy in schools* (The Crick Report). London: Qualifications and Curriculum Authority.

Ahier, J., Beck J. and Moore, R. (2003), *Graduate Citizens? Issues of citizenship and higher education*. London: RoutledgeFalmer.

Alexander, R. (2004), 'Still No Pedagogy? Principle, pragmatism and compliance in primary education', *Cambridge Journal of Education*, 34 (1), 7–33.

Althusser, L. (1971), 'Ideology and the Ideological State Apparatuses', in *Lenin and Philosophy and Other Essays*. London: New Left Books, pp. 123–73.

Anderson, P. (1990), 'A culture in contra-flow – I', *New Left Review*, 180, 41–78.

Arthur, J. (2005), 'The re-emergence of character education in British education policy', *British Journal of Educational Studies*, 53 (3), 239–54.

Atkinson, P. (1997), 'Review Symposium – Basil Bernstein: Pedagogy, Symbolic Control and Identity: theory, research, critique', *British Journal of Sociology of Education*, 18 (1), 115–19.

Avis J. (1996a), 'The Myth of the Post-Fordist Society', in J. Avis, M. Bloomer, G. Esland, D. Gleeson and P. Hodkinson, *Knowledge and Nationhood: Education, Politics and Work*. London: Cassell, pp. 71–82.

Avis, J. (1996b), 'The Enemy Within: Quality and Managerialism in Education', in J. Avis, M. Bloomer, G. Esland, D. Gleeson and P. Hodkinson, *Knowledge and Nationhood: Education, Politics and Work*. London: Cassell, pp. 105–20.

Baert, P. (2005), *Philosophy of the Social Sciences: Towards Pragmatism*. Cambridge: Polity.

Bailey, C. H. (1984), *Beyond the Present and the Particular: A Theory of Liberal Education*. London: Routledge and Kegan Paul.

Ball, S. J. (1990), *Politics and Policy Making in Education: Explorations in Policy Sociology*. London: Routledge.

Ball, S. J. (1993), 'What is policy? Texts, trajectories and toolboxes', *Discourse*, 13 (2), 10–17, and in S. J. Ball (2006) *Education, Policy and Social Class: The selected works of Stephen J. Ball*. London: Routledge, pp. 43–53.

Ball, S. J. (1998), 'Performativity and fragmentation in "Postmodern" schooling', in J. Carter (ed.) *Postmodernity and the Fragmentation of Welfare*. London: Routledge, pp. 118–27.

Ball, S. J. (1999), 'Labour, learning and the economy: a "policy sociology" perspective', *Cambridge Journal of Education*, 29 (2), 195–206.

Ball, S. J. (2001), 'Performativities and Fabrications in the Education Economy: Towards a performative society', in D. Gleeson and C. Husbands (eds) *The Performing School: Managing, Teaching and Learning in a Performance Culture*. London: RoutledgeFalmer, and in S. J. Ball (ed.) (2004) *The RoutledgeFalmer Reader in Sociology of Education*. London: RoutledgeFalmer, pp. 143–55.

Barber, B. J. (2003), *Jihad versus McWorld*. London: Corgi.

Barber, M. (2001), *Large-Scale Education Reform in England: A Work in Progress*, paper for Managing Education Reform Conference, Moscow, 29–30 October, unpublished.

Barber, M. (2003), *The Framework For Continuous Improvement*, speech delivered at the National College of School Leadership, 11 June http://www.ncsl.org.uk/index.cfm?pageid=ev_auth_barber [Accessed 4 July 2004.]

Barber, M. and Sebba, J. (1999), 'Reflections on progress towards a world class education system', *Cambridge Journal of Education*, 29 (2), 183–93.

Bateson, G., Jackson, D. D. and Weakland, J. (1956), 'Towards a Theory of Schizophrenia', *Behavioural Science*, 1, 251, 123–145.

Bauman, Z. (1989), *Modernity and the Holocaust*. Cambridge: Polity.

Bauman, Z. (1995), *Life in Fragments: Essays in Postmodern Morality*. Oxford: Blackwell.

Bauman, Z. (2006), *Liquid Fear*. Cambridge: Polity.

Bawden, T. and Duncan, G. (2006), 'Top bosses earning 98 times as much as employees', *The Times*, 6 November, 53–4.

Beck, J. (1996), 'Nation, Curriculum and Identity in Conservative Cultural Analysis: a critical commentary', *Cambridge Journal of Education*, 26 (2), 171–98.

Beck, J. (1998), *Morality and Citizenship in Education*. London: Cassell.

Beck, J. (1999a), 'Makeover or Take-over? The strange death of educational autonomy in neo-liberal England', *British Journal of Sociology of Education*, 20 (2), 223–38.

Beck, J. (1999b), 'Should Homosexuality be Taught as an Acceptable Alternative Lifestyle? A Muslim perspective: a response to Halstead and Lewicka', *Cambridge Journal of Education*, 29 (1), 121–30.

Beck, J. (2002), 'The Sacred and the Profane in Recent Struggles to Promote Official Pedagogic Identities', *British Journal of Sociology of Education*, 23 (4), 617–26.

Beck, J. (2003a), 'Citizenship and Citizenship Education in England', in J. Beck and M. Earl (eds) *Key Issues in Secondary Education – 2nd Edition.* London: Continuum, pp. 158–71.

Beck, J. (2003b), 'The School Curriculum, The National Curriculum, and New Labour Reforms', in J. Beck and M. Earl (eds) *Key Issues in Secondary Education – 2nd Edition.* London: Continuum, pp. 14–27.

Beck, J. (2006), 'Directed Time – Identity and Time in New Right and New Labour Policy Discourse', in R. Moore, M. Arnot, J. Beck and H. Daniels (eds) *Knowledge, Power and Educational Reform: Applying the Sociology of Basil Bernstein.* London: Routledge, pp. 181–95.

Beck, J. and Young, M. F. D. (2005) 'The Assault on Professions and the Restructuring of Academic and Professional Identities: A Bernsteinian Analysis'. *British Journal of Sociology of Education*, 20, 2, 187 and Chapter 5 in this volume.

Beck, U. (1992), *Risk Society: Towards a New Modernity.* London: Sage.

Beck, U. (2001), *What Is Globalization?* Cambridge: Polity.

Beck, U. and Beck-Gernsheim, E. (2002), *Individualization.* London: Sage.

Bell, D. (1972), 'On Meritocracy and Equality', *The Public Interest*, 29 (30), 282–97.

Bell, D. (1973), *The Coming of Post-Industrial Society.* New York: Basic Books.

Berger, B. and Berger, P. (1984), *The War Over The Family: Capturing The Middle Ground.* London: Penguin, first published by London: Hutchinson (1983).

Bernstein, B. (1970), 'Education cannot compensate for society', *New Society*, 26 February, 344–7.

Bernstein, B. (1971), 'On the Classification and Framing of Educational Knowledge', in M. F. D. Young (ed.) *Knowledge and Control: New Directions for the Sociology of Education.* London: Collier Macmillan, pp. 47–69, and in B. Bernstein (1975) *Class, Codes and Control Vol. 3: Towards a Theory of Educational Transmissions, 2nd Edition.* London: Routledge and Kegan Paul, pp. 85–115.

Bernstein, B. (1996), *Pedagogy, Symbolic Control and Identity: Theory, research and critique,* London: Taylor and Francis.

Bernstein, B. (1990a), 'Codes, modalities and the process of cultural reproduction: a model', in B. Bernstein *The Structuring of Pedagogic Discourse: Class, Codes and Control Vol. IV.* London: Routledge, pp. 13–62.

Bernstein, B. (1990b), 'Education, Symbolic Control and Social Practices', in B. Bernstein *The Structuring of Pedagogic Discourse: Class, Codes and Control Vol. IV.* London: Routledge, pp. 125–54.

Bernstein, B. (1990c), *The Structuring of Pedagogic Discourse: Class, Codes and Control Vol. IV.* London: Routledge.

Bernstein, B. (1995), 'A Response', in A. Sadovnik (ed.) *Knowledge and Pedagogy: The Sociology of Basil Bernstein.* New Jersey: Ablex, pp. 386–424.

Bernstein, B. (2000), *Pedagogy, Symbolic Control and Identity: Theory, Research and Critique, (Revised Edition)*. Lanham, MD: Rowman and Littlefield.

Best, R. (ed.) (1996), *Education, Spirituality and the Whole Child*. London: Cassell.

Blair, T. (1996), *The Stakeholder Society in New Britain: My Vision for a Young Country*. London: Fourth Estate.

Blair, T. (1998), *The Third Way: New Politics For The New Century*. Fabian Pamphlet 588, London: The Fabian Society.

Blair, T. (2002a), 'My vision for Britain: by Tony Blair', *The Observer*, 10 November, 26.

Blair, T. (2002b), 'Speech to the Labour Party Conference', 1 October 2002, *The Guardian*, 2 October, 9–10.

Blair, T. (2004), *Welfare Reform*. Speech published 11 October. London: The Cabinet Office.
http://www.epolitix.com/EN/News/200410/90eaa670-a2f6-42cd-8c92-a121f4aec1e5.htm [Accessed 22 July 2006.]

Blair, T. (2005), *Speech on Education to City of London Academy*, 12 September, 10 Downing Street website:
http://www.pm.gov.uk/output/Page8181.asp [Accessed 24 March 2007.]

Blair, T. (2006a), *Speech at the Specialist Schools and Academies Trust Conference 2006*, 30 November, 10 Downing Street website:
http://www.pm.gov.uk/output/Page10514.asp [Accessed 8 December 2006.]

Blair, T. (2006b), *Our Nation's Future – multiculturalism and integration*, speech at 10 Downing Street hosted by the Runnymede Trust, 8 December, 10 Downing Street website:
http://www.number10.gov.uk/output/Page10563.asp [Accessed 15 December 2006.]

Blunkett, D. (1998), *Speech To The Labour Party Conference*, London, The Labour Party.

Blunkett, D. (2000), *Radical Changes Will Prepare Higher Education For The 21st Century*. Press notice of speech at University of Greenwich, 15 February, London: Department for Education and Skills.

Blunkett, D. (2001a), *Politics and Progress: Renewing Democracy and Civil Society*. London: Politico's.

Blunkett, D. (2001b), 'We *are* winning', *Guardian Education*, 6 March, 4.

Blunkett, D. (2005), 'For far too long we have left patriotism to the extremists', *The Guardian*, 19 March, 22.

Bolton, E. (1994), 'Divided we fall', *Times Educational Supplement*, 21 January, 7.

Bradley, H. (1996), *Fractured Identities: Changing Patterns of Inequality*. Cambridge: Polity.

Brailsford, H., Hobson, J. A., Creech Jones, A. and Wise, E. F. (1926), *The Living Wage*. London: Independent Labour Party, p. 27. Cited in B. Jackson (2003) 'Equality or nothing? Social Justice on the British Left, c. 1911–31', *Journal of Political Ideologies*, 8 (1), 83–110.

Branigan, T. (2006), 'Call to curb donations from wealthy individuals; need to reconnect with disenchanted voters', *The Guardian*, 27 February, 4.

Brenneis, D. (1994), 'Discourse and Discipline at the National Research Council: a bureacratic *bildungsroman*', *Cultural Anthropology*, 1 (1), 23–36.

BBC (British Broadcasting Corporation) (2007), 'Ministers proposing "Britian Day"', *BBC News UK*, http://news/bbc.co.uk/1/hi/uk/6721239.stm [Accessed 7 June 2007.]

Broadfoot, P. (1998), 'Quality, standards and control in higher education: what price life-long learning?', *International Studies in the Sociology of Education*, 8 (2), 155–81.

Brown, G. (2006), 'We have renewed Britain, now we must champion it', *The Guardian*, 27 February, 15.

Callinicos, A. (2001), *Against the Third Way: An Anti-Capitalist Critique*. Cambridge: Polity.

Carnoy, M. (2000), 'Globalization and educational reform', in M. Stromquist and K. Monkman (eds) *Globalization and Education*. Lanham, MD: Rowman and Littlefield, pp. 43–61.

Cerny, P. G. (1997), 'Paradoxes of the Competition State: the dynamics of political globalisation', *Government and Opposition 1997*, 251–74.

Chadwick, A. and Heffernan, R. (eds) (2003), *The New Labour Reader*. Cambridge: Polity.

Chomsky, N. (2004), *Hegemony or Survival: America's Quest for Global Dominance*. London: Penguin.

Clarke, J., Cochrane, A. and McLaughlin, E. (1994), 'Mission Accomplished or Unfinished Business? The Impact of Managerialization', in J. Clarke, A. Cochrane, and E. McLaughlin (eds) *Managing Social Policy*. London: Sage, pp. 226–42.

Clarke, J. and Newman, J. (1997), *The Managerial State; Power, Politics and Ideology in the Remaking of Social Welfare*. London: Sage.

Clarke, L. (2007), 'New curriculum will make every lesson politically correct', *The Daily Mail*, 26 January, 23.

Commission on the Future of Multi-Ethnic Britain (2000), *The Future of Multi-Ethnic Britain: The Parekh Report* sponsored by The Runnymede Trust. London: Profile Books.

Cox, C. B. and Dyson, A. E. (eds) (1969), *Fight For Education: A Black Paper*. London: The Critical Quarterly Society.

Cox, C. B. and Boyson, R. (1977), *Black Paper 1977*. London: Maurice Temple Smith.

Crick, B. (2002), *Democracy*. Oxford: Oxford University Press.

Crick, B. and Green, D. (2002), 'Should Citizenship be Taught in Schools?', *Prospect*, September, 16–19.

Crick, B. and Porter, A. (eds) (1978), *Political Education and Political Literacy*. London: Longman.

Crouch, C. (2000), *Coping with Post-Democracy*. London: The Fabian Society.

Crouch, C. (2004), *Post-Democracy*. Cambridge: Polity.

Daily Telegraph (2006a), 'Ofsted: Schools failing 3.3m', 24 September, 1.

Daily Telegraph (2006b), 'Has Blair seen the light on multi-culturalism?', 9 December, 25.

Dale, R. (1997), 'The State and the Governance of Education: An Analysis of the Restructuring of the Education–State Relationship', in A. H. Halsey, H. Lauder, P. Brown and A. Stuart Wells (eds) *Education, Culture, Economy and Society*. Oxford: Oxford University Press, pp. 273–82.

Davies, I., Gorard, S. and McGuinn, N. (2005), 'Citizenship Education and Character Education: Similarities and Contrasts', *British Journal of Educational Studies*, 53 (3), 341–58.

Davis, K. and Moore, W. E. (1945), 'Some Principles of Stratification', *American Sociological Review*, 10 (2), 242–49, reprinted in R. Bendix and S. M. Lipset (eds) (1953) *Class, Status and Power – 2nd Edition*. London: Routledge and Kegan Paul, pp. 47–53.

Dearing, Sir Ronald (1993), *The National Curriculum and its Assessment – Final Report*. London: School Curriculum and Assessment Authority.

Delanty, G. (2003), *Community*. London: Routledge.

DES (Department of Education and Science) (1977), *Education in Schools: a Consultative Document*, Cmnd 6869. London: Her Majesty's Stationery Office.

DES (Department of Education and Science) (1987), *The National Curriculum 5–16: A Consultation Document*. London: Department of Education and Science and The Welsh Office.

DfEE (Department for Education and Employment) (1997a), *Excellence in Schools*. London: The Stationery Office.

DfEE (Department for Education and Employment) (1997b), *Excellence for All Children: Meeting Special Educational Needs – a programme of action*. London: The Stationery Office.

DfEE (Department for Education and Employment) (1997c), *Teaching: High Status, High Standards*, Circular Number 10/97. London: Department for Education and Employment.

DFEE (Department for Education and Employment) (1998), *The Learning Age: A Renaissance for a New Britain*. Cmnd 3790. London: Department for Education and Employment.

DfEE (Department for Education and Employment) (1999), *Excellence in Cities*. London: The Stationery Office.

DfEE (Department for Education and Employment) (2001), *Schools: Building on Success*, Cmnd 5060. London: The Stationery Office.

DfES (Department for Education and Skills) (2001), *Schools: achieving success*, Cmnd 5230. London: The Stationery Office.

DfES (Department for Education and Skills) (2002a), *14–19: Extending Opportunities, Raising Standards: A summary*. London: Department for Education and Skills.

DfES (Department for Education and Skills) (2002b), *Time for Standards: Reforming the school workforce*. London: Department for Education and Skills.

DfES (Department for Education and Skills) (2003), *Excellence and enjoyment: a strategy for primary schools*. London: Department for Education and Skills.

DfES (Department for Education and Skills) (2005a), *14–19 Education and Skills*, Cmnd 6476. London: The Stationery Office.

DfES (Department for Education and Skills) (2005b), *Higher Standards, Better Schools for All*. London: The Stationery Office.

DfES (Department for Education and Skills) (2006), *The Standards Site: Academies*,
http//:www.standards.dfes.gov.uk/academies/projects/open academies/?version =1 [Accessed March 2007.]
and
http//:www.standards.dfes.gov.uk/academies/projects/developmentacademies academies/?version =1 [Accessed March 2007.]

DfES (Department for Education and Skills) (2007), *Curriculum Review: Diversity and Citizenship* ('The Ajegbo Report'). London: Department for Education and Skills.

Deuchar, S. (1989), *The New History: A Critique*. York: Campaign For Real Education.

Dixon, W. M. (1938) (first published, 1931), *The Englishman*. London: Hodder and Stoughton.

Dobrowolsky, A. (2002), 'Rhetoric versus reality: the figure of the child and new labour's strategic social investment state', *Studies in Political Economy*, 69, 43–73.

Dobrowolsky, A. (2003), 'Social investment state/civil society interactionism: New forms of governance in Britain'. Online: http://fas.umontreal.ca/pol/cohesionsociale [Accessed 22 February 2006.]

Durkheim, E. (1893/1967), *De la division du travail social: étude sur l'organisation des sociétés supérieurs*. Paris: Alcan. Translated into English by George Simpson, *The Division of Labour in Society* (1933). London: Macmillan; republished (1964) New York: The Free Press.

Durkheim, E. (1977), *The Evolution of Educational Thought: Lectures on the Formation and Development of Secondary Education in France*. London: Routledge. Translation into English by P. Collins of E. Durkehim (1938) *L'Evolution pédagogique en France*. Paris: Alcan.

Eagleton, T. (2005), *Holy Terror*. Oxford: Oxford University Press.

The Economist (2006), 'Specialist Schools: A question of trusts – when charities compete with business', *The Economist*, 5 August, 32.

Elliott, J., Bridges, D., Ebutt, D., Gibson, R. and Niass, J. (1981), *School Accountability*. London: Grant McIntyre.

Elliott, L. (2007), 'Only the rich can end child poverty', *The Guardian*, 2 April, 26.

Esland, G. (1996), 'Knowledge and Nationhood: The New Right, Education and the Global Market', in J. Avis, M. Bloomer, G. Esland, D. Gleeson and P. Hodkinson *Knowledge and Nationhood: Education, Politics and Work*. London: Cassell, pp. 4–26.

Esping-Andersen, G. (2005), 'Social inheritance and equal opportunities policies', in S. Delorenzi, J. Reed and P. Robinson (eds) *Maintaining Momentum: Promoting social mobility and life chances from early years to adulthood*. London: Institute for Public Policy Research, pp. 14–30.

Etzioni, A. (1993), *The Spirit of Community: Rights, Responsibilities and the Communitarian Agenda – British edition with new preface*. London: Fontana.

Evening Standard (2007), 'Ministers call for National British Day', *Evening Standard Lite*.
http://www.thisislondon.co.uk/news/article-23399396-
details/Ministers+call+for+national+British+Day/article.do [Accessed 7 June 2007.]

Fairclough, N. (1992), *Discourse and Social Change*. Cambridge: Polity.

Fairclough, N. (2000), *New Labour, New Language?* London: Routledge.

Faulks, K. (1998), *Citizenship in Modern Britain*. Edinburgh: Edinburgh University Press.

Fitz, J., Davies, B. and Evans, J. (2006), *Educational Policy and Social Reproduction: Class inscription and symbolic control*. London: Routledge.

Frank, R. H. and Cook, P. J. (1996), *The Winner Takes All Society*. New York: Free Press.

Freedland, J. (2007), 'OK, let's have a Britishness test. But it must be for everyone, migrant or not', *The Guardian*, 6 June, 29.

Freedman, M. (1976), *Labour Markets: Segments and Shelter*. Montclair, NJ: Allanheld Osmun.

Freidson, E. (2001), *Professionalism: The Third Logic*. Cambridge: Polity.

Fukuyama, F. (1992), *The End of History and The Last Man*. New York: Free Press.

Galbraith, J. K. (1958) *The Affluent Society*, London: Hamish Hamilton, and also Harmondsworth: Penguin Books (1958).

Gallie, W. B. (1955), 'Essentially Contested Concepts', *Proceedings of the Aristotelian Society*, 56, 167–98.

Gamarnikow, E. and Green, A. (2000), 'Citizenship, Education and Social Capital', in D. Lawton, J. Cairns and R. Gardner (eds) *Education for Citizenship*. London: Continuum, pp. 93–113.

Gamble, A. (1983), 'Thatcherism and Conservative Politics', in S. Hall and M. Jacques (eds) *The Politics of Thatcherism*. London: Lawrence and Wishart, pp. 61–78.

Gamble, A. and Wright, T. (eds) (2004), *Restating the State*. Oxford: Blackwell in association with *The Political Quarterly*.

Garfinkel, H. (1967), *Studies in Ethnomethodology*. Englewood Cliffs, NJ: Prentice Hall.

Garner, R. (2007), 'All-white schools to be forced to find multi-ethnic twins', *The Independent*, 7 May, 1.
http://education.independent.co.uk/new.article2521654.ece [Accessed 8 May 2007.]

Ghouri, N. and Thornton, K. (1998), 'Ministers accused of creeping selection', *Times Educational Supplement*, 30 October, 7.

Gibson, O., Wray, R. and McVeigh, K. (2007), 'Sponsor dumps Big Brother over racism row', *The Guardian*, 19 January, 1.

Giddens, A. (1991), *Modernity and Self-Identity: Self and Society in the Late Modern Age*. Cambridge: Polity.

Giddens, A. (1994), *Beyond Left and Right*. Cambridge: Polity.

Giddens, A. (1998), *The Third Way: The Renewal of Social Democracy*. Cambridge: Polity.

Giddens, A. (2002), *Where Now for New Labour?* London: The Fabian Society and Policy Network in association with Blackwell Publishers Ltd, 2002; republished (2002) by Cambridge: Polity.

Giddens, A. (2007), 'You need greater equality to achieve more social mobility', *The Guardian*, 24 May, 32.

Giddens, A. and Diamond, P. (2005), 'The new egalitarianism: economic inequality in the UK', in A. Giddens and P. Diamond (eds) *The New Egalitarianism*. Cambridge: Polity, pp.101–19.

Gillborn, D. and Youdell, D. (2000), *Rationing Education: Policy, Practice, Reform and Equity*. Buckingham: Open University Press.

Gilroy, P. (1987), *There Ain't No Black in the Union Jack: the cultural politics of race and nation*. London: Hutchinson.

Glennester, H. (1998), 'Does poor training make people poor?', *Times Educational Supplement*, 27 February, 21.

Goldthorpe, J. H. (1996), 'Problems of "Meritocracy"', in R. Erikson and J. O. Jonsson (eds) *Can Education Be Equalized? The Swedish Case in Comparative Perspective*. New York: Westview Press, reprinted in A. H. Halsey, H. Lauder, P. Brown and A. Stuart Wells (eds) (1997) *Education, Culture, Economy and Society*. Oxford: Oxford University Press, pp. 663–82.

Goodson, I. (2007), 'All the lonely people: the struggle for private meaning and public purpose in education', *Critical Studies in Education*, 48 (1), 131–48.

Gopal, P. (2007), 'Anti-racism has to go beyond a facile representation game', *The Guardian*, 25 January, 33.

Gorard, S. and Taylor, C. (2001), 'Specialist schools in England: track-record and future prospects', *School Leadership and Management*, 21 (4), 365–81.

Graham, L. (1995), *On the Line at Subaru-Isuzu*. Ithaca, NY: Cornell University Press.

Gray, J. (1999), *False Dawn: The Delusions of Global Capitalism*. London: Granta.

Gray, J. (2003) *Al Qaeda: and what it means to be modern*. London: Faber and Faber.

Grayling, A. C. (2007), '"I'm right." "You're not"', *The Times Higher Educational Supplement*, 20 April, 17.

Green, C. (2001), 'The railwayman's lament', *The Guardian*, 14 April, 28.

The Guardian, (2007), 'Two churches, one view and a question of conscience', *The Guardian*, 25 January, 6.

Habermas, J. (1991) *The Theory of Communicative Action, Vol. 1: Reason and the Rationalization of Society*. Cambridge: Polity.

Hall, S. (1991) 'The local and the global: glodalization and ethnicity' in A. D. King (ed.) *Culture, Globalization and the World System*, London: Macmillan, pp. 88–114.

Halsey, A. H., Heath, A. F. and Ridge, J. M. (1980), *Origins and Destinations: Family, Class and Education in Modern Britain*. Oxford: Clarendon Press.

Halstead, J. M. and Lewicka, K. (1998), 'Should homosexuality be taught as an acceptable alternative lifestyle? A Muslim perspective', *Cambridge Journal of Education*, 28, (1), 49–64.

Hargreaves, D. H. (1982), *The Challenge for the Comprehensive School: Culture, Curriculum and Community*. London: Routledge and Kegan Paul.

Hari, J. (2007), 'Jaded contempt for the working class', *The Independent*, 22 January, 31.

Hasan, R. (2006), 'Literacy, pedagogy and social change: Directions from Bernstein's sociology', in R. Moore, M. Arnot, J. Beck and H. Daniels (eds) *Knowledge, Power and Educational Reform: Applying the sociology of Basil Bernstein*. London: Routledge, pp. 211–25.

Hatcher, R. (2006), 'Privatization and sponsorship: the re-agenting of the school system in England', *Journal of Educational Policy*, 21, (5), 599–619.

Hattersley, R. (1998a), 'The spaniel rolls over', *The Guardian*, 5 March, 18.

Hattersley, R. (1998b), 'Beware threat of creeping selection', *Times Educational Supplement*, 19 June, 17.

Hattersley, R. (2002), 'Read my lips: there will be selection', *The Guardian*, 1 July, 18.

Hay, C. (1999), *The Political Economy of New Labour: Labouring under False Pretences*. Manchester: Manchester University Press.

Hay, C. (2004), 'Re-Stating Politics, Re-Politicising the State: Neo-liberalism, Economic Imperatives and the Rise of the Competition State', in A. Gamble and T. Wright (eds) *Restating the State?* Oxford: Blackwell Publishing in association with *The Political Quarterly*, pp. 38–50.

Hayek, F. von (1976), *The Constitution of Liberty*. London: Routledge.

Held, D. and McGrew, A. (2002), *Globalization/Anti-Globalization*. Cambridge: Polity.

Her Majesty's Government (2002), *The Education Act*, London: The Stationery Office.

Hesketh, A. (2003), 'Employability in the Knowledge Economy: Living the Fulfilled Life or Policy Chimera?', Lancaster University Management School Working Paper 2003/049. http://www/lums.co.uk/publications [Accessed 24 April 2007.]

HEQC (Higher Education Quality Council) (1994), *Choosing to Change: Extending Access, Choice and Mobility in Higher Education (Robertson Report)*. London: The Stationery Office.

Hickox, M. and Moore, R (1995), 'Liberal-Humanist Education: the vocationalist challenge', *Curriculum Studies*, 3, (3), 45–59.

The Hillgate Group (1986), *Whose Schools? A Radical Manifesto*. London: The Hillgate Group.

Hinsliff, G. (2006), 'Livingstone declares war on race equality watchdog', *The Observer*, 26 November, 2.

Hirst, P. and Thompson, G. (1996), *Globalization in Question*. Cambridge: Polity.

Hirst, P. H. (1974), *Knowledge and the Curriculum: A collection of papers*. London: Routledge and Kegan Paul.

Hirst, P. H. and Peters, R. S. (1970), *The Logic Of Education*. London: Routledge and Kegan Paul.

Hobsbawm, E. (1994), *Age of Extremes: The Short Twentieth Century*. London: Michael Joseph.

Hobson, J. A. (1929), *Wealth and Life*. London: Macmillan.

Hobson, J. A. (1931), *Poverty in Plenty: The Ethics of Income*. London: Allen and Unwin.

Hogan, D. (1997), 'The Logic of Protection: Citizenship, Justice and Political Community', in K. Kennedy (ed.) *Citizenship Education in the Modern State*. London: Falmer.

Hoyle, E. (1974), 'Professionality, Professionalism and Control in Teaching', *London Educational Review*, 32, 19–26.

Huddleston, T. (1956), *Naught For Your Comfort*. London: Collins.

Hugill, B. (1998), 'School shut? God (or Allah) will provide', *The Observer*, 5 July, 10.

Hurd, D. (1988), 'Citizenship in the Tory Democracy', *New Statesman*, 29 April, 15.

Hutton, W. (1997), *The State to Come*. London: Vintage Books.

Hutton, W. (1998a), 'Labour stirs from its slumber on poverty', *The Observer*, 25 January, 26.

Hutton, W. (1998b), 'Even if Gordon Brown never gets the top job, he believes his policies will protect the party from right wing plotters', *The Observer*, 14 June, 26.

Jackson, B. (2003) 'Equality of nothing? Social Justice on the British Left, c. 1911–31', *Journal of Political Ideologies* 8, 1, 83–110.

Jansen, T., Chioncel, N. and Dekkers, H. (2006), 'Social cohesion and integration: learning active citizenship', *British Journal of Sociology of Education*, 27, (2), 189–205.

Jeffries, S. (2007), 'Beauty and beastliness: a tale of declining British values', *The Guardian*, 19 January, 11.

Jenson, J. and Saint-Martin, D. (2003), 'New Routes to social cohesion? Citizenship and the Social Investment State', *Canadian Journal of Sociology*, 28, (1), 77–99.

Jessop, R. (2002), *The Future of the Capitalist State*. Cambridge: Polity.

Jessop, R., Bonnett, K., Bromley, S. and Ling, T. (1984), 'Authoritarian Populism: A Tale of Two Nations and Thatcherism', *New Left Review*, 147, 32–60.

Johnson, P. (2000), 'In Praise of Being British', *Daily Mail*, 11 October, 11–12.

Johnson, R. (1976), 'Notes on the schooling of the English working-class 1780–1850', in R. Dale, G. Esland, and M. MacDonald (eds) *Schooling and Capitalism: A Sociological Reader*. London: Routledge and Kegan Paul in association with The Open University, pp. 44–54.

Johnson, T. J. (1972), *Professions and Power*. London: Macmillan.

Johnston, P. (2006), 'The "what we have done?" moment when Labour faced its multicultural monster', *Daily Telegraph*, 9 December, 10.

Jones, K. (1989), *Right Turn: The Conservative Revolution in Education*. London: Hutchinson Radius.

Jones, K. (2003), *Education in Britain*. Cambridge: Polity.

Jones, L. and Moore, R. (1993), 'Education, Competence and the Control of Expertise', *British Journal of Sociology of Education*, 14, (3), 385–97.

Jones, L. and Moore, R. (1996), Equal opportunities, the curriculum and the subject', in J. Abier, B. Cosin and M. Hales (eds) *Diversity and Change: Education Policy and Selection*, London: Routledge, pp. 111–137.

Jonsson, J. O. (1992), *Towards the Merit-Selective Society?* Stockholm: Swedish Institute for Social Research (University of Stockholm).

Kelly, R. and Byrne, L. (2007), *A Common Place*. London: The Fabian Society.

Kenway, J. (1993), 'Marketing Education in the Postmodern Age', *Journal of Educational Policy*, 8, (1), 105–22.

Kermode, F. (1966), *The Sense of an Ending: Studies in the Theory of Fiction*. Oxford: Oxford University Press.

Kettley, N. (2006), *Educational Attainment and Society*. London: Continuum.

Kirby, T. (2004), 'Violence and vandalism close production', *The Independent*, 21 December, 4–5.

Kunda, G. (1992), *Engineering Culture: Control and Commitment in a High-Tech Corporation*. Philadelphia: Temple University Press.

Ladson-Billings, G. and Gillborn, D. (eds) (2004), *The RoutledgeFalmer Reader in Multicultural Education*. London: RoutledgeFalmer.

Laing, R. D. (1959), *The Divided Self*. London: Tavistock.

Lambert, C. (2007), 'New Labour, new leaders? Gendering transformational leadership', *British Journal of Sociology of Education*, 28, (2), 149–63.

Lansley, S. (2006), *Rich Britain: The rise and rise of the new super-wealthy*. London: Politico's.

Laski, H. (1925/1970), *A Grammar of Politics*. London: Allen and Unwin.

Laski, H. (1927), *Communism*. London: Williams and Northgate.

Lawlor, S. (1994), 'This crazy National Curriculum', *The Observer*, 20 February, 21.

Lawson, M. (2007), 'The monster you can't see', *The Guardian*, 19 January, 32.

Leadbeater, C. (2004), *Personalisation Through Participation*. London: Demos.

Leaton Gray, S. (1994), 'Defining the Future: An interrogation of education and time', *British Journal of Sociology of Education*, 25, (3), 323–40.

Lepkowska, D. (1998) , 'Muslims gain equality of funding: a 15-year battle for state assistance has been won by two Islamic schools', *Times Educational Supplement*, 16 January, 18.

Letwin, O. (1992), *The Anatomy of Thatcherism*. London: Fontana.

Levitas, R. (1996), *The Inclusive Society: Social Exclusion and New Labour*. Basingstoke: Macmillan.

Levitas, R. (2004) 'Lets Hear it for Humpty Dumpty: Social Exclusion, the Third Way and Cultural Capital', *Cultural Trends*, 13, 2, 1–15.

Lister, D. (2006), 'Faith, Fundamentalism and homo-sexuality', *The Times*, 18 November, 6.

Lukes, S. (1973), *Émile Durkheim – His Life and Work: A Historical and Critical Commentary*. London: Allen Lane; London: Peregrine (1975).

Luntley, M. (1995), *Reason, Truth and Self: the postmodern reconditioned*. London: Routledge.

Lyons, A. (2005), *The Every Child Matters Agenda in England and its Impact on Business and Economics Education*, speech at the Association for European Economics Education, London: Ofsted.

MacLeod, D. (2006), 'The quiet revolutionary: interview with Alison Richard', *Guardian Education*, 31 October, 11.

Madely, J. (1999), *Big Business, Poor People*. London: Zed Books.

Malik, K. (2005) 'Born in Bradford', *Prospect*, October, 54–6.

Mann, M. (2005), *The Dark Side of Democracy: Explaining Ethnic Cleansing*. Cambridge: Cambridge University Press.

Marquand, D. (1995), 'Flagging fortunes', *The Guardian*, 3 July, 13.

Marquand, D. (2004a), *Decline of the Public*. Cambridge: Polity.

Marquand, D. (2004b), 'False Friend: the State and the Public Domain', in A. Gamble and T. Wright (eds) *Restating the State?* Oxford: Blackwell in association with *The Political Quarterly*, pp. 51–62

Marr, A. (1998), 'Blair's big secret: he's a Liberal', *The Observer*, 26 July, 21.

Marshall, T. H. (1950), *Citizenship and Social Class*. Cambridge: Cambridge University Press; and published with an essay by T. Bottomore, *Citizenship and Social Class Forty Years On*. London: Pluto Press, (1992).

May, S. (1999a), 'Critical Multiculturalism and Cultural Difference: Avoiding Essentialism', in S. May (ed.) *Critical Multiculturalism: Rethinking Multicultural and Antiracist Education*. London: Falmer Press, pp. 10–41.

May, S. (ed.) (1999b), *Critical Multiculturalism: Rethinking Multicultural and Antiracist Education*. London: Falmer Press.

McKibbin, R. (2005), 'The Destruction of the Public Sphere', *The London Review of Books*, 5 January, 3–6.

McLaughlin, T. H. (1996), 'Education of the whole child?', in R. Best (ed.) *Education, Spirituality and the Whole Child*. London: Cassell, pp. 9–19,

184   *Meritocracy, Citizenship and Education*

McVeigh, K., Wray, R. and Ramesh, R. (2007), 'Channel 4 dodges racism charge as complaints – and ratings soar', *The Guardian*, 19 January, 11.
Midgley, J. and Sherraden, M. (2000), 'The Social Perspective in Social Policy', in J. Midgley, M. Tracy and M. Livermoore (eds) *The Handbook of Social Policy*. Thousand Oaks: Sage Publications, pp. 121–42.
Milburn, A. (2004), *Inequality, mobility and opportunity: the politics of aspiration*.
http://www.ippr.org.uk/articles/index:aasp?id=484. [Accessed 10 August 2006.]
Miliband, D. (2002), *The benefits of diversity: lessons for education from across the border*, speech at the University of Glasgow, 19 September. http//:www.dfes.gov.uk/speeches. [Accessed 21 September 2006.]
Moore, C. and Jones, G. (2000), 'Brown heralds a new age of giving', *Daily Telegraph*, 9 February, 4.
Moore, R. (1987), 'Education and the Ideology of Production', *British Journal of Sociology of Education*, 8 (2), 227–42.
Moore, R. (1990), 'Knowledge, practice and the construction of skill', in D. Gleeson, (ed.) *Training and Its Alternatives*. Milton Keynes: Open University Press, pp. 200–12.
Moore, R. and Jones, L. (2007), 'Appropriating Competence: The Competency Movement, the New Right and the "Culture Change" Project', in R. Moore, *Sociology of Knowledge and Education*. London: Continuum, pp. 130–44.
Moore, R. and Muller, J. (1999), 'The Discourse of "Voice" and the Problem of Identity in the Sociology of Education', *British Journal of Sociology of Education*, 20 (2), 189–206.
Morris, E. (2002), *Professionalism and Trust: The Future of Teachers and Teaching*, speech to the Social Market Foundation, June. London: Department for Education and Skills.
Mortimore, P. (1998), 'A big step backward', *The Guardian Education*, 24 March, 4.
Newman, J. (2005), 'Enter the transformational leader: network governance and the micro-politics of modernisation', *Sociology*, 39 (3), 717–34.
Newman, J. and Clarke, J. (1994), 'Going About Our Business? The Managerialization of Public Services', in J. Clarke, A. Cochrane and E. Mclaughlin (eds) *Managing Social Policy*, London: Sage, pp. 13–31.
Norman, E. R. (1977), 'The threat to religion', in C. B. Cox and R. Boyson (eds) *Black Paper 1977*. London: Temple Smith, pp. 98–104.
Ofsted (Office for Standards in Education) (2005), *Developing Enterprising Young People*, London: Her Majesty's Inspectorate, (2460). http://www.ofsted.gov..uk/publications/index.cfm?fuseaction=pubs. displayfile@id=4093&type=doc [Accessed 2 March 2007.]
O'Neill, O. (2002), *A Question of Trust: The BBC Reith Lectures 2002*. Cambridge: Cambridge University Press.
Peel, Q. (2006), 'A most unhappy union – review of A. Giddens "Europe in a Global Age"' (Cambridge: Polity), *Financial Times magazine*, 21/22 October, 29.

Perkins, D., Nelms, L. and Smyth, P. (2004), *Beyond neo-liberalism: the social investment state? Social Policy Working Paper No 3*. Melbourne: Centre for Public Policy, University of Melbourne with The Brotherhood of St Lawrence.
www.public-policy.unimelb.edu.au [Accessed 14 August 2006.]

Phillips, M. (2006), *Londonistan: How Britain is Creating a Terror State Within*. London: Gibson Square.

Phillips, R. (1998), *History Teaching, Nationhood and the State: A Study in Educational Politics*. London: Cassell.

Phillips, T. (2004), *Deal with difference through integration*, speech at the Multicultural Futures Conference, Tuscany, Italy. London: Commission for Racial Equality.
http//:www.cre.gov.uk/Default.aspx.LocID-Ohgnew00s.RefLocID [Accessed 11 December 2006.]

Phillips, T. (2005), *After 7/7: Sleepwalking to Segregation*, speech given at the Manchester Council for Community Relations, 22 September. London: Commission for Racial Equality.
http//:216.239.cre.gov.uk/Default.aspx.LocID-ohgnew07s [Accessed 19 December 2006.]

The Power Commission (2006), *Power to the People: The Power Report*. London: York Publishing.

Power, M. (1994), *The Audit Explosion*. London: Demos.

Power, S., Edwards, T., Whitty, G. and Wigfall, S. (2003), *Education and the Middle Class*. Buckingham: Open University Press.

Pring, R. (1995), *'Closing the Gap': Liberal Education and Vocational Preparation*. London: Hodder and Stoughton.

Putnam, R. (1995), 'Bowling Alone: America's Declining Social Capital', *Journal of Democracy*, 6 (1), 65–78.

Putnam, R. (2003), *The Forms of Social Capital: Bridging, Bonding and Trusting*, Leverhulme Lectures 2003. Cambridge: Cambridge University Press.

QCA (Qualifications and Curriculum Authority) (2000), *Citizenship at Key Stages 3 and 4: Initial Guidance for Schools*. London: QCA Publications.

QCA (Qualifications and Curriculum Authority (2001), *Citizenship: A Scheme of Work for Key Stage 3*, Circular No. 128/01. London: QCA Publications.

QCA (Qualifications and Curriculum Authority (2005), 'The need for greater personalisation and innovation', London, QCA Futures Project, April.
http://www.org.uk/12933_12938.html [Accessed 11 April 2007.]

QCA (Qualifications and Curriculum Authority) (2007a) 'The Secondary Curriculum Review: reviewing the curriculum', London: QCA, January.
http://www.qca.org.uk/secondarycurriculumreview/ [Accessed: 11 April, 2007]

QCA (Qualifications and Curriculum Authority) (2007b), 'The Secondary Curriculum Review: Programme of Study (non-statutory): PSHEE – Economic well-being key stage 3 and key stage 4', London: QCA, January.

http://www.qca.org.uk/secondarycurriculumreview/ks3/pshee [Accessed 24 April 2007.]

http://www.qca.org.uk/secondarycurriculumreview/ks4/pshee [Accessed 24 April 2007.]

QCA (Qualifications and Curriculum Authority) (2007c), 'The Secondary Curriculum Review: Enterprise', London: QCA, January. http://www.qca.org.uk/secondarycurriculumreview/dimesnions/enterprise [Accessed 24 April 2007]

QCA (Qualifications and Curriculum Authority) (2007d), 'The Secondary Curriculum Review: Citizenship', London: QCA, January. http://www.qca.org.uk/secondarycurriculumreview/ks3/citizenship [Accessed 26 April 2007.]

http://www.qca.org.uk/secondarycurriculumreview/ks4/citizenship [Accessed 26 April 2007.]

Quicke, J. (1988), 'The "New Right" and Education', *British Journal of Educational Studies*, 36 (1), 5–20.

Rafferty, F. and Dean, C. (1997), 'Blair calls in jobs agency', *Times Educational Supplement*, 7 November, 1.

Rawls, J. (2001), *Justice as Fairness: A Restatement*, (ed. Erin Kelly). Cambridge, MA: The Belknap Press of Harvard University Press.

Rayner, J. (2006), 'Frank Field: Still thinking the unthinkable', *The Observer*, 2 July, 33.

Readings, B. (1996), *The University In Ruins*, Cambridge, MA: Harvard University Press.

Reay, D., David, M. and Ball, S. J. (2005), *Degrees of Choice: social class, race and gender in higher education*. Stoke on Trent: Trentham Books.

Reyes, O. (2004), 'New Labour's politics and the hard-working family', in D. Howarth and J. Torfling (eds) *Discourse Theory in European Politics*. Basingstoke: Palgrave, pp. 37–49.

Richard, A. (2006a) *The Well-Educated Undergraduate – Annual Address to the Regent House*. Cambridge: Vice-Chancellor's Office, University of Cambridge.

Richard, A. (2006b), 'In praise of teaching: Interview with Vice-Chancellor Alison Richard', *Cam: Cambridge Alumni Magazine*, 49, Michaelmas, 7.

Richards, C. (1999), 'The primary school curriculum: changes, challenges and questions', in C. Richards and P. Taylor (eds) *How Shall We School Our Children?* London: Falmer, pp. 22–37.

Roberts, A. (2007), 'Britain Day: what a sick joke', *Daily Mail online*, 6 June. http://www.dailymail.co.uk/pages/live/articles/news/newscomment. html?in_page_id=1787 [Accessed 7 June 2007.]

Robson, S. (2001), 'Commentary', *The Guardian*, 10 October, 28.

Rose, J. (2006), *Independent Review of the Teaching of Early Reading*, Nottingham: DfES Publications.

Rose, N. (1993), 'Government, authority and expertise in advanced liberalism', *Economy and Society*, 22 (3), 283–300.

Rose, N. (1999a), 'Inventiveness in Politics – Review article of A. Giddens (1998) "The Third Way: the Renewal of Social Democracy"', *Economy and Society*, 28 (3), 467–93.

Rose, N. (1999b), *Powers of Freedom: Reframing political thought.* Cambridge: Cambridge University Press.

Roth, P. (1996) *Sabbath's Theatre.* London: Vintage Books, and London: Jonathan Cape (1995).

Rowe, M. (1997), 'Blair's guru spreads new social gospel', *The Observer*, 21 September, 13.

Rushdie, S. (1988), *The Satanic Verses.* Harmondsworth: Penguin.

Ruthven, M. (2004), *Fundamentalism: The Search for Meaning.* Oxford: Oxford University Press.

Saunders, P. (2003), *'Fair Go': Do we want to live in a Meritocracy?*, The Bert Kelly Lecture, Australian Institute for Family Studies. www.cis.org.au/Events/bertkelly/bk299text.htm [Accessed 11 August 2006.]

Scruton, R. (1987), 'The myth of cultural relativism', in E. Palmer (ed.) *Anti-racism: The Assault on Education and Value.* London: The Sherwood Press.

Sen, A. (2006), *Identity and Violence: The Illusion of Destiny.* London: Allen Lane.

Sennett, R. (1998), *The Corrosion of Character: The Personal Consequences of Work in the New Capitalism.* New York: W. W. Norton.

Sennett, R. (2003), *Respect: The Formation of Character in an Age of Inequality.* New York: W. W. Norton, and London: Penguin (2005).

Sennett, R. (2006a), *The Culture of the New Capitalism.* New Haven, CT: Yale University Press.

Sennett, R. (2006b), 'Workers will carry on striking until they get a life', *The Guardian*, 25 May, 30.

Simon, B. (1988), *Bending the Rules: The Baker 'Reform' of Education,* London: Lawrence and Wishart.

Sivanandan, A. (2006), 'Attacks on multicultural Britain pave the way for enforced assimilation', *The Guardian*, 13 September, 32.

Strathern, M. (1992), *After Nature: English kinship in the late twentieth century.* Cambridge: Cambridge University Press.

Strathern, M. (ed.) (2000), *Audit Cultures: Anthropological studies in account-ability, ethics and the academy.* London: Routledge.

Straw, J. (1998), *Building social cohesion, order and inclusion in a market economy,* speech to the Nexus conference on Mapping Out the Third Way. http://wwww.netnexus.org/events/july98/talks/straw.htm [Accessed 14 August 2006.]

Sunday Telegraph (1997), 'The Blair Brand' (leading article), *Sunday Telegraph*, 26 October, 34.

Taylor, C. (1992) 'The Politics of Recognition', in A. Gutman (ed.) with S. C. Rockefeller, M. Walzer and S. Wolf, *Multiculturalism and 'The Politics of Recognition.* Princeton, NJ: Princeton University Press, pp. 25–73.

Thatcher, M. (1993), *The Downing Street Years.* London: Harper Collins.

The Times (2007), 'School Britannia: The latest recommendations will not help to establish a national identity', *The Times*, 26 January, 16.

Thompson, J. B. (1990), *Ideology and Modern Cultures*. Cambridge: Polity.

Tomlinson, J. (1993), *The Control of Education*. London: Cassell.

Tooley, J. (2000), *Reclaiming Education*. London: Cassell.

Toynbee, P. (2004), 'Why Trevor is right', *The Guardian*, 7 April, 21.

Turner, B. (1990), 'Outline of a Theory of Citizenship', *Sociology*, 24 (2), 189–2.

UCST (United Church Schools Trust) (2007), *About UCST: United Learning Trust*.
http://www.ucstrust.org.uk/content.asp?id=194&area=1 [Accessed 6 April 2007.]

Weber, M. (1948), 'Science as a Vocation', in H. H. Gerth and C. W. Mills (eds) *From Max Weber: Essays in Sociology*. London: Routledge and Kegan Paul, pp. 129–56.

Webster, P. (2006), 'Blair and Brown unite to face the future', *The Times*, 28 November, 24.

Weeks, J. (1995), *Invented Moralities: Sexual Values in an Age of Uncertainty*. Cambridge: Polity.

Wexler, P. and Grabiner, R. G. (1986), 'America during the Crisis', in R. Sharp (ed.) *Capitalism, Crisis and Schooling*. South Melbourne: Macmillan, pp. 115–28.

Wexler, P. (1995), 'Bernstein: A Jewish Misreading', in A. Sadovnik (ed.) *Knowledge and Pedagogy: The Sociology of Basil Bernstein*. New Jersey: Ablex, pp. 113–23.

White, M. (2006), 'Education briefing: Blair could have done better', *The Guardian*, 1 December, 6.

Whitty, G. (1990), 'The New Right and the National Curriculum: State Control or Market Forces?', in M. Flude and M. Hammer (eds) *The Education Reform Act 1988: its origins and implications*. Basingstoke: The Falmer Press, pp. 21–49.

Whitty, G. (1997), 'Marketization, the State, and the Re-Formation of the Teaching Profession', in A. H. Halsey, H. Lauder, P. Brown and A. Stuart Wells (eds) *Education, Culture, Economy and Society*. Oxford: Oxford University Press, pp. 299–310.

Whitty, G. (2002), *Making Sense of Education Policy*. London: Paul Chapman.

Whitty, G. with Aggleton, P. and Rowe, G. (2002), 'School Knowedge and Social Education', in G. Whitty, *Making Sense of Education Policy*. London: Paul Chapman, pp. 27–45.

Whitty, G. with Power, S. (2002), 'The Overt and Hidden Curricula of Quasi-Markets', in G. Whitty, *Making Sense of Education Policy*. London: Paul Chapman, pp. 94–106.

Williams, H. (2006), *Britain's Power Elites*. London: Constable.

Williams, R. (2006), 'It's not a crime to hold traditional values', *Times Higher Educational Supplement*, 8 December, 16–17.

Wintour, P. (1997), 'The rebranding of Britain', *The Observer*, 9 November, 26.

Woods, P. and Jeffrey, B. (2002), 'The Reconstruction of Primary Teachers' Identities', *British Journal of Sociology of Education*, 23 (1), 89–106.

Wyse, D. and Styles, M. (2007), 'Synthetic phonics and the teaching of reading: the debate surrounding England's "Rose Report"', *Literacy*, 47 (1), 35–42.

Young, M. (1958), *The Rise of the Meritocracy 1870–2033: An Essay on Education and Equality*. London: Thames and Hudson; and (1961) Harmondsworth: Penguin.

Young, M. (2001), 'Renouncing Meritocracy', *The Guardian*, 29 June, 21.

Young, M. F. D. (1998), *The Curriculum of the Future: From the 'new sociology of education' to a critical theory of learning*. London: Falmer Press.

Young, M. F. D. (2000), 'Rescuing the Sociology of Educational Knowledge from the Extremes of Voice Discourse: towards a new theoretical base for the sociology of the curriculum', *British Journal of Sociology of Education*, 21 (4), 523–36.

Young, M. F. D (2005), 'An old problem in a new context: Rethinking the relationship between sociology of education and educational policy', *International Studies in the Sociology of Education*, 14 (1), 3–20.

Young, M. F. D. (2007), *Bringing Knowledge Back In: Theoretical issues and applied studies in the sociology of education*. London: Routledge.

Index

An 'n' after the page number indicates an endnote

increased merit selection (IMS
   hypothesis) 11
innovation overload 153, 154
Islam 15, 63, 93, 129, 132, 138,
   148–9
Islamophobia 135–6

Jackson, Ben 9
Jansen, Th. 148
Jasper, Lee 129
Jeffrey, B. 80
Jeffries, S. 142
Jenson, J. 16
Jerry Springer: The Opera 138
Jessop, Bob 38, 83
Johnson, Paul 145
Johnson, Richard 160–161n.8
Johnson, Terrence 67, 73
Johnston, Philip 131
Jones, George 33
Jones, Ken 54, 83, 112–3
Jones, Lynn 60, 79, 119, 167n.5
Jonsson, J. O. 11
Joseph, Keith (Sir) 100
Joseph Rowntree Foundation
   160n.5
Judaism 15,93

Kelly, Ruth 145
Kennedy, Helena (Dame) 37,
   160n.5
See also Power Commission
Kenway, Jane 60
Kermode, Frank 95
Key Stage 3 Strategy 107
Kirby, T. 139
Kiwan, Dina 152
Knight, Jim 154
knowledge economy 14,
   100–101
Kruks, Sonia 132
Kunda, Gideon 42

labour markets
   and education 76
   and flexibilization 22, 41–3,
      61, 64

Ladson-Billings, Gloria 168n.4
Laing, R.D. 161n.11
Lambert, Cath 19–20
Lambert, Richard 158–9n.11
Lansley, Stewart 23–4, 25,
   158–9n.11, 160n.7
Laski, Harold. 8, 9
Lawlor, Sheila 105
Lawson, Mark 142–3
Leadbeater, Charles 115,
   155n.4
Learning and Skills Council
   166n.3
learning society 77
Leaton Gray, Sandra 82
Lepkowska, D. 63
Letwin, Oliver 54
Levitas, Ruth 29, 155n.2
Lewicka, K. 149
liberal education 89, 97,
   102–4, 123
See also neo-conservativism
Lister, D. 136
Livingston Ken 129, 168n.2
Lukes, Stephen 9
Luntley, Patrick 66
Lyons, Adrian 117

McGrew, Anthony 92
McGuinn, N. 44
McKibbin, Ross 48, 49
McLaughlin, E.
   165n.10,165n.12
McLaughlin, Terence, H. 121
McLean, Neil 116
Macleod, D. 21, 157n.9
McVeigh, K. 142
Madely, J. 50
Major, John (Sir - UK Prime
   Minister 1993–97) 38,
   105
Malik, Kenan 132–3, 141
managerialism/managerializa-
   tion xviii, 18–19, 20, 37,
   46, 48, 57–9, 61–3, 80,
   86, 157–8n.10, 164–5n.9,
   165n.10